PRIVATIZATION: SOCIAL SCIENCE THEMES AND PERSPECTIVES

Privatization: Social Science Themes and Perspectives

Edited by
DEREK BRADDON
and
DEBORAH FOSTER
Centre for Social and Economic Research
Faculty of Economics and Social Science
University of the West of England, Bristol

Dartmouth

Aldershot • Brookfield USA • Singapore • Sydney

Published by
Dartmouth Publishing Company Limited
Gower House
Croft Road
Aldershot
Hants GU11 3HR
England

Dartmouth Publishing Company
Old Post Road
Brookfield
Vermont 05036
USA

British Library Cataloguing in Publication Data
Privatization : social science themes and perspectives
   1. Privatization 2. Economic policy 3. Privatization - Social
aspects
I. Braddon, Derek II. Foster, Deborah
338.9

Library of Congress Cataloging-in-Publication Data
Privatization : social science themes and perspectives / editors,
  Derek Braddon and Deborah Foster.
    ISBN 1-85521-674-4
    1. Privatization–Great Britain. 2. Social service–Contracting
out–Great Britain. 3. Public welfare–Contracting out–Great
Britain. 4. Medical care–Contracting out–Great Britain.
5. Public housing–Management–Contracting out–Great Britain.
6. Privatization–Europe, Eastern. 7. Privatization–Europe,
Southern. I. Braddon, Derek, 1949-   . II. Foster, Deborah, 1962-
HD4148.P735   1996
338.941–dc20
    96-11010
    CIP

ISBN 1 85521 674 4

Printed in Great Britain by the Ipswich Book Company, Suffolk

Contents

Contributors

The Editors

Dr Derek Braddon is Principal Lecturer in Economics and Research Director of the Research Unit in Defence Economics at the University of the West of England (UWE), Bristol. His latest publications include 'The Regional Impact of Defense Expenditure' in Hartley, K. and Sandler, T. *Handbook of Defense Economics*, Elsevier/North-Holland, 1995 and 'Flexible Networks and the Restructuring of the Regional Defence Industrial Base: The Case of South West England' (with Dowdall, P.) in *Defence and Peace Economics*, vol. 7.1, February 1996.

Dr Deborah Foster is Lecturer in Sociology at UWE, Bristol. Publications include 'Industrial Relations in Local Government: The Impact of Privatization', *The Political Quarterly*, vol. 64, no. 1, January - March 1993 and 'Reinventing the Weal? Public Service and Trade Unionism in a Changing State' (with Graham Taylor), forthcoming.

The Authors

Yusuf Ahmad is Senior Lecturer in Social Policy at the University of the West of England (UWE), Bristol. His research interests include the welfare implications of marketization, community development, urban policy and decentralization.

Jonathan Bradley is Senior Lecturer in International Business Economics at UWE, Bristol. He has extensive practical experience of international business and his research interests include economic transformation, privatization and portfolio investment. He has published articles on all of these subjects.

Dr Nicholas Buttle is Senior Lecturer in Politics at UWE, Bristol. Publications include 'Prostitutes, Workers and Kidneys', *Journal of Medical Ethics*, 1991, 'War, Justice and Morality', *Politics*, 1991, and 'Banning Boxing', *Philosophy Today*, January 1995.

Paul Dowdall is Senior Lecturer in Business Economics at UWE, Bristol and a senior researcher in the University's Research Unit in Defence Economics. His latest publications includes 'Puppets or Partners: the Defence Industry Supply Chain in Perspective' (with Derek Braddon) in Latham, A. and Hooper, N. (1995) *The Future of the Defence Firm*, Kluwer Academic Publishers and 'Flexible Networks and the Restructuring of the Regional Defence Industrial Base: The Case of South West England' (with Braddon, P.) in *Defence and Peace Economics*, vol. 7.1, February 1996.

Adrian Kendry is Principal Lecturer in Economics at UWE, Bristol and International Projects Director of the University's Research Unit in Defence Economics. His latest publication is 'The Economic and Industrial Importance of the Airbus Partnership' (with Duffield, P. and Butler, J.), Western Development Partnership, 1995.

Kostas Lavdas is Lecturer in Politics and a Faculty Research Fellow at UWE, Bristol. Publications include 'Crises of Integration', Macmillan/St Martins Press, London / New York, forthcoming; 'Competition Policy and Institutional Politics in the EC' (with Mendrinou, M.), *European Journal of Political Research* vol. 28, 1995 and 'Politics, Subsidies and Competition' Edward Elgar, Cheltenham, forthcoming.

Anthony Plumridge is Lecturer in Economics at UWE, Bristol. He has had papers published on sustainable new settlements and on the environmental impact assessment of development.

Martin Sullivan is Lecturer in Economics at UWE, Bristol. His research interests include the public policy implications of the rise of non-standard employment forms and the impact of changes in regulation policy for the providers of personal and corporate financial services, including private pensions.

Dr Graham Taylor is Lecturer in Sociology at UWE, Bristol. Publications include 'Safe in Their Hands? Public Service and the State Regulation of the Water Industry', Mansell, 1996 forthcoming and 'Risky Business' (with Neary, M.), Macmillan 1996.

Dr Ian Welsh completed his chapter for this book while Senior Lecturer in Sociology at UWE, Bristol. Publications include 'Letting the Research Tail Wag the End User's Dog: the Powell Committee and UK Nuclear Technology', *Science and Public Policy*, February 1994; and 'Nuclear Power: Generating Dissent', Routledge, 1995 forthcoming.

Acknowledgements

The editors wish to acknowledge the particular contribution of the following in the successful publication of this book:

Lesley Gander, whose expertise, enthusiasm, meticulous attention to detail and unending patience were so important in succesfully producing high quality copy for this book; **Peter Scott**, whose outstanding ability to proofread and standardize chapters was matched only by his extraordinary dedication to ensuring the book's successful publication and **Jan Stapley**, for her extremely valuable help in this arduous process; **the Centre for Social and Economic Research** in the Faculty of Economics and Social Science at the University of the West of England, Bristol, for support from the inception of this project; **the authors**, whose hard work, good humour and commitment to accepting and working within our tight editorial schedules made our editorial role less onerous; and **Ann Newell** at Dartmouth, whose enthusiastic support and sound advice throughout the preparation of the book helped to maintain momentum and ensured that the project was brought to a successful completion.

Derek Braddon
Deborah Foster
February 1996

1 Introduction

DEREK BRADDON AND DEBORAH FOSTER

Introduction

In recent years policies of privatization have evoked a great deal of controversy and debate and have served as a catalyst for significant economic, political and social change. In the UK they have been associated with consecutive Conservative administrations pursuing 'Thatcherite' political and ideological objectives, and have played a central role in challenging the post-war welfare settlement and accompanying political consensus, through the re-invigoration of neo-liberal politics reflected in the ideas of the 'New Right'. The importance of privatization policies in other parts of Europe has also been reflected in initiatives pursued by various governments. In Eastern European countries free-market philosophies have been embraced in an attempt to bring about the conditions necessary for their transition to capitalism; and in Southern Europe a commitment to privatization has been intrinsically linked to integration and participation in the European Union (see chapters by Bradley and Lavdas). As a policy tool, privatization has therefore been utilized to fulfil a number of diverse objectives, which in their various contexts have impacted on the social, political and economic life of citizens. The influence of privatization policies and their importance as a topic for contemporary debate is probably best illustrated in the worldwide geographic spread of privatization during the 1990s. For example, in 1988 twenty eight major privatization exercises were conducted in fourteen

1

countries with a total value of $29,230m, whereas in 1991 the number of major privatizations worldwide reached a peak of 161 in twenty three countries, with a total value of $48,482m.

Whilst a large proportion of this book addresses policies of privatization and marketization in the UK, the text does attempt to contrast these experiences with those of other countries, specifically in the regions of Eastern and Southern Europe. The distinctive approach of the book is that it seeks to illustrate the breadth of academic interest in privatization both within and, significantly, between the social science disciplines. Contributions from political scientists, economists, sociologists and from social policy analysts are included and serve to highlight the interdisciplinary character of this subject. Each chapter, although written from a specific social science perspective, is intended stylistically to be inaccessible to all social scientists, so that links between the subject matter of each can be easily drawn. Underlying this objective is our contention that privatization cannot be comprehensively understood within the limitations of disciplinary boundaries because of the variety of social, political and economic outcomes which arise from such policies. Through the exploration of policies in contrasting contexts both the micro and macro effects of marketization receive attention. From the impact on the consumer, on organizations, on employees and managers to the concerns and role of regulatory agencies, governments and countries, this book considers each to be important to the social scientist.

The term 'privatization' requires some further definition. In this book it is applied to a broad range of policies which have in common the aim to transfer publicly owned assets or service functions from the public to the private sector in terms of ownership, management, or control. Privatization is most commonly used to refer to policy initiatives which have, to a greater or lesser extent, served to alter the balance between public and private sectors in favour of the latter. Consequently it has been described as 'rolling back the activities of the state' (see Le Grand, Propper and Robinson, 1992) which, in the UK at least, has also incorporated a commitment to de-politicize areas of the public sector. Nevertheless, the utilization of the term 'privatization' to describe what has essentially constituted a broad range of policies within the public sector has at times been criticized for being politically emotive and ambiguous (see Spencer, 1983). Indeed it is true that the terms privatization and marketization are increasingly being used interchangeably to describe a variety of policies which do not always result in a public service being transferred wholesale to the private sector. In such instances, ultimate responsibility for service provision or regulation remains with a public agency, whilst service delivery is provided by the private sector. However, confusion over the meaning of privatization can to an extent be rectified by reference to specific *aims* which *characterize* all policies which fall under the 'umbrella' term of privatization (see Foster, 1991). Such policies include those which:

1. aim to reduce the role and scope of the public sector, whilst encouraging private sector involvement in the 'gap left';
2. aim to create, by legislative or regulatory means, new opportunities for private sector expansion into traditional areas of the public sector;
3. aim to attract private sector investment and involvement to support government policies;
4. aim to promote competition by increasing market pressures on assets remaining within the public sector.

Heald (1983), Steel and Heald (1984) and Ascher (1987) have identified four forms of privatization which incorporate the aims outlined above. These are as follows:

1. *The sale of public assets*: including the de-nationalization of public corporations and the sale of publicly owned land and buildings (for example, local authority council houses and land).
2. *Charging*: this refers to the privatization of the financial costs of a service which is still provided by the public sector (for example, the greater substitution of user charges for tax finances).
3. *Contracting-out*: this refers to the privatization of the production of a service by means of substituting private contractors for 'in-house' provision, although the service continues to be financed by the public sector. In this instance it is usual for the client organization to retain overall control and responsibility for the service provided. (Contracting-out of services has occurred in the UK health service, local government, central government and other sectors)
4. *Liberalization*: also referred to as deregulation. This involves the

3

relaxation or removal of statutory monopoly provisions, which have prevented private sector firms entering public sector markets (for example, the deregulation of bus services in the UK).

Other commentators, for example Young (1985), have added to these more commonly recognized forms of privatization, drawing attention to policies which do not appear to explicitly fall under the heading of privatization, yet share the characteristic aim to facilitate increased private sector involvement in the public sector domain. Such policies might include the increased use by the public sector of, for example, private sector nursing homes, hospitals and security services, although, more subtly, they may also include the availability of publicly funded government grants and loans to the private sector, or the imposition of private sector practices within the public sector, which in some instances has led to the replacement of public sector employees (particularly at a managerial level) with private sector staff.

Through this brief discussion it is possible to conclude that policies described under the term of privatization, although varied and broad ranging, have in common a number of shared aims and characteristics. To define privatization in such terms, essentially as a policy prescription, is advantageous given that the parameters of the privatization debate are being continually re-drawn with the introduction of new initiatives. The aims of privatization policies are significant for their impact on contemporary social, political and economic thought. In the UK privatization has been ideologically important for the Conservatives, initially serving as a unifying mechanism for a party divided on macroeconomic policy (Steel and Heald, 1984), although later creating an impetus for new radical initiatives in areas of public policy, principally guided by the aim to strengthen the market and reduce the role of the state (see also Bishop, Kay and Mayer, 1994). Whether the latter has been successfully achieved is debateable and features strongly in several chapters by authors in this text. For whilst the role of the state has undoubtedly changed, it may be argued that privatization has created new arenas which necessitate political intervention. The state's role in, for example, regulation (see chapters by Welsh and Taylor) and its role in the creation of new markets has at times left it in a contradictory and ambiguous position. Many of the chapters illustrate the often noted paradox that marketization in the public sector has in itself required intervention on the

4

part of government, and that such political intervention can manifest undesired outcomes. The Conservative government in the UK has discovered this, for whilst aiming to de-politicize parts of the public sector, new political controversies have emerged relating to issues such as directors' pay in the privatized utilities, the role and composition of quangos, the equitable provision of services in the NHS, and the 'invisible hand' of government in industrial relations, to name but a few examples. This has brought to the forefront a whole new debate about what we now mean by 'public service' and what the role of the state is in their provision, a debate which would benefit greatly from further inter-disciplinary investigation.

The opening chapter of the book begins with an examination of three key questions which relate to the ethics of privatization as a concept. First, what are the moral values that provide the foundations for the ethical defence of privatization? Second, how strong are the foundations on which the ethical defence of privatization rest? Third, is it possible to construct a plausible alternative moral conception to oppose that which is articulated by policies of privatization?

Buttle focuses upon ethical issues that are employed to defend the process of privatization which relate to moral objectives in two respects: firstly, privatization is underpinned by the vision of a 'good society' (the 'public' sphere of ethics) and secondly, by the vision of a 'good person' (the 'private' sphere of ethics). The 'good society' is perceived to be a free society in which democratic politics is restricted to a limited range of legitimate concerns. Whilst in the sphere of private ethics the defence of privatization utilizes the vision of a 'good person', the person who possesses the virtues of independence, responsibility and enterprise and is free to employ them in decision-making in daily life.

Buttle also explores criticisms of privatization and its objectives and evaluates these objectives in themselves. Suggestions that privatization has led to a loss of freedom on the part of certain members of society are examined. For example, privatization of former public utilities has often simply transformed public monopolies into private monopolies, creating organizations just as unresponsive to the wishes of consumers as the public enterprises were thought to be. The consequences of other types of privatization, such as opt-outs and competitive tendering in the public sector, are also explored, particularly with respect to housing and welfare policy. Questions are raised as to whether privatization has created a free

5

society of responsible, independent individuals, or whether instead it has empowered those who now own and control the former public enterprises to pursue their own interests.

The author then proceeds by examining the allegation that privatization conflicts with democratic values since it removes important issues from public determination and, therefore, serves to undermine the concept of democracy. A number of issues relating to privatization and equity in resource distribution are considered and attention is drawn to critiques of privatization which argue it has failed on moral grounds, creating a society in which freedom is an illusion, in which decisions are made and implemented by undemocratic institutions and in which the distribution of resources is inherently inequitable. Buttle concludes by proposing an alternative moral vision. Concepts of 'citizenship', 'community', 'republicanism' and 'citizen rights' are explored as the possible basis on which a new emphasis on the public sphere can be built. The chapter concludes that the moral defence of privatization can be challenged once the moral vision on which that process is built is rejected and an alternative vision is put in its place.

Whilst Chapter 2 explores the ethical arguments underlying state policies of privatization, Chapter 3 examines the impact of central government policies on the local state. By utilizing qualitative case study materials, Foster assesses the political, organizational and cultural impact of compulsory competitive tendering (CCT) in local government. The chapter is particularly interested in the ways in which the introduction of competition into local government has affected the attitudes and behaviour of various key groups working within it. This is of interest given that local authorities have been significant in resisting policies of privatization and its underlying ideology, seeking to retain control of their role and autonomy as major providers of public services. Examples drawn from three authorities illustrate the different ways in which Conservative councils have responded to their own party's policy. They also reveal ways in which contracting-out has been contested by councillors, trade unions and employees, who have been unwilling to subscribe to the new 'enterprise culture' in the public sector.

The attitudes of different actors involved in the CCT process are explored and conflicts encountered during the process of change are evaluated. The role of trade unions in opposing the implementation of CCT and the strategies used by them in their campaigns are given particular attention because of the dual function that competition has played in local government: opening up new markets, whilst simultaneously undermining the power and influence of public service trade unions. This serves to illustrate a point raised earlier, that policies of privatization and marketization often embody multiple aims, in this instance weakening trade unions and increasing control over local government.

In the final part of this chapter Foster examines ways in which responses to CCT might be categorized, arguing that in doing so it is important to acknowledge the political, geographical and intra-organizational variations which exist between local authorities. The impact of CCT on organizational and public service culture and the political context of local government are highlighted as factors which may mediate between the vision of new public sector organizations held by government and the actual reality, which has seen local authorities resisting change from within. The chapter concludes by emphasizing the political character of public services, whose so-called 'customers' derive their entitlement to services through citizenship. Moreover, it argues that local authorities are uniquely placed to participate in the reconstruction of the notion of public service, given their democratically elected status and commitment to public service provision.

Chapters 4 and 5 offer different perspectives on privatization within government organizations. In Chapter 4, Ahmad draws together two strands of recent policy-making in the UK National Health Service (NHS): the reorganization of the NHS along 'quasi-market' lines, and the commitment to prioritizing health promotion and disease prevention as outlined in the White Paper *Health of the Nation*. Initially, the chapter explores the reasons why, historically, policies aimed at preventing ill-health, whilst exerting some influence over health policy in Britain, have in practice often been superseded by other policies emphasizing a curative model of health. The reasons for this are explored in some depth and related to central objectives inherent in recent government policy commitments. Ahmad then goes on to examine the rationale underlying the introduction of quasi-markets in health provision and the parameters under which they operate. In the final section of this chapter, the author focuses attention on the relationship between NHS market reforms and the attainment of health care promotion priorities.

Although Ahmad admits that the 'jury is still out' in its evaluation of changes made in the NHS, he argues some conclusions can be drawn. The absence of a 'feel-good' factor as a consequence of market reforms is most notable; this is due in part to the perception that a two-tier system of health care is emerging, creating widening health disparities between regions and population groups in the UK. However, Ahmad does note that in terms of innovation and health promotion the reforms may have brought some positive benefits. The chapter ends by questioning the degree to which a health market in any real sense has been established in the NHS and whether reforms have led to greater fragmentation in health provision. The role of the state in providing a truly *national* health service is also addressed, given that in Ahmad's words the Health Service has 'arguably ended up with the worst of both worlds'.

In Chapter 5, Braddon, Dowdall and Kendry, through an analysis of the UK defence sector, focus upon the issue of what the Public Accounts Committee call the 'inadequate stewardship of public money' and ask the question to what extent privatization, market testing and/or contracting-out have improved, or can improve, such 'stewardship'. As economists, they draw upon the traditional economic theory of privatization and public choice, combining it with more recent discussion in the literature about markets, hierarchies and the boundary of the organization. Against the background of reforms within the defence sector during the 1980s and 1990s, the authors discuss empirical evidence within a theoretical framework.

The chapter concludes that, while emerging markets in the defence sector and its support services are clearly accessible to new entrants, the initial entry costs may well prove to be prohibitive when set against the longer term potential for profits. Such emerging markets are unlikely to remain genuinely 'open' and, in exchange for the granting of a quasi-monopoly position in a new defence market after competitive tendering has been completed, the government is likely to set extremely tight safety, security and other public interest limitations on the winning contractor, seriously constraining its decision-making freedom in this most sensitive of operational areas.

Chapters 6 and 7 examine the privatization process with respect to two other important 'traditional' areas of government social policy: housing and pensions provision. In Chapter 6, Plumridge sets the historical context for the examination of what the author argues to be by far the largest single privatization within the UK, that of social housing. In terms of impact on lifestyles, the privatization of housing is likely to exceed the combined effects of all other privatizations.

The author initially explores the macro-level consequences for the UK economy in general and, specifically, the impact upon housing finance. Next, attention is focused upon the experience of housing privatization at the micro-level, raising issues of the political context, housing tenure and welfare and the role of coercive forces and the 'right to buy'. Plumridge then evaluates the consequences of social housing privatization for the overall supply of housing in the UK in terms of quantity, quality and choice. In the concluding section of the chapter, Plumridge considers the likely evolution of social housing policy, examining housing tenure preferences in a market in which house prices are falling and the potential impact on the supply of dwellings to rent.

In Chapter 7, Sullivan discusses the issue of pension provision and the appropriate role of the state. Recognition of the anachronistic nature of the existing pension arrangements in the UK and the resultant inequitable treatment of different socio-economic groups underpinned the reforms and these aspects form the focus of the initial part of the chapter. The impact of pension arrangements on labour market flexibility and on the public sector borrowing requirement are considered in assessing the origins of the Conservative government's pension reforms. Both the evolution of the state pension scheme from its origins in the Beveridge Report of 1942 and the fiscal burden that developed as a result over the next few decades are explored in detail. Problems encountered during the evolution of pension arrangements towards private pension provision are discussed, particularly the losses suffered by large numbers of individuals leaving occupational pension schemes.

The issue of how to 'pay for the elderly' as demographic forces sharply increase the numbers of pensionable citizens in the decades ahead is addressed and the author concludes that personal pension plans are 'an entirely inappropriate way for a sizeable portion of the workforce to accrue future pension entitlements', which calls into question their potential for reducing long-term government expenditure on the elderly. Any savings that do result will be generated at the expense of certain groups, especially women, the low paid and those with unstable employment patterns. Sullivan suggests that a state-managed personal pension scheme, currently under discussion, may be the answer, setting an industry benchmark against which commercial pensions could be assessed.

Chapters 8 and 9 consider two industrial sectors in the UK, water and electricity supply, and examine the motives underlying the privatization process. In Chapter 8, Taylor explores the privatization of the water industry and the process of regulation through the Office of Water Services (OFWAT). The intention of this chapter is to develop the argument that the restructuring of water services in the UK has necessitated a fundamental redefinition of the notion of what 'public' actually constitutes. The historical and global dimensions of the Conservative government's privatization programme are emphasized, together with the resulting disengagement of the state from direct management of key public services.

The central argument explored in Chapter 8 is essentially that the problems encountered in the provision of water services were attributable to the crisis in Keynesian intervention policies as part of a wider crisis in global capital accumulation. Taylor argues that the emerging 'neo-liberal' structure of the state is an attempt to realign the state and international capital through 'monetarization'. Decisions concerning the allocation of services become de-politicized in this situation and are subordinated to the 'abstract and indifferent' power of money. Taylor examines Fabian socialism and the origins of public service and then considers the problems of maintaining the role of the state as an 'embodiment of the public good' with respect to the water industry. The role of OFWAT in regulating both price and quality dimensions of water supply are assessed. Neo-liberal theory, the notion of citizenship and the crisis of the public service are explored and the catalytic role of monetarism highlighted. The author concludes that the experience of privatization over the last 15 years could rekindle a new and reinvigorated 'politics of the left' as attention is focused on the 'alienating and oppressive forms of the political and economic institutions of capitalist societies'.

In Chapter 9, Welsh examines the implications of the government's recent announcement of its intentions to privatize the nuclear power industry. He argues that all energy privatizations must be considered as an integrated government agenda, which constitute an abdication of responsibility on the part of the state to ensure that British energy interests are represented in an increasingly global market. Moreover, he contends that the role of the state in other areas, for example science and technology policy, have been abandoned to the market. Underpinning this analysis is the belief that such areas of policy are in need of political consideration given their importance to the economy and ramifications in the public domain.

Privatization in the electricity supply sector is viewed as part of an inter-locking state strategy designed to reconstitute market relationships within key sectors of the British economy. In tracing the privatization of the electricity supply from the early days of market incentives to the current policy agenda, Welsh notes the failure of the process to establish effective incentive mechanisms, requiring state intervention to create a market. The role of the Energy Select Committee is singled out for attention in this chapter, noting their view that 'the nuclear tail seems to be wagging the electricity supply industry dog', and the author raises important issues about the uneven treatment given by government to different energy industries during the privatization process. The conclusions drawn from the analysis are that the ideological commitment to privatization appears to outweigh the introduction of 'real' competition and that the process has tended towards a duopolistic (and potentially with nuclear supply, a monopolistic) outcome in which the short-term interests of shareholders will override the long-term requirements of energy policy.

Chapters 10 and 11 focus upon the privatization process in a wider European context and explore various dimensions of that process in Southern and Eastern Europe. In Chapter 10, Lavdas highlights the significant differences in scope, form and goals of privatization policies in Southern Europe. These differences are reflected through political and institutional factors as well as different priorities and objectives between countries in this region. The privatization process in Southern Europe merits consideration as a distinct area in comparative politics since privatization has owed less to ideological debates about neo-liberal policy and state failure, and more to the need to tackle public indebtedness to meet convergence criteria for full participation in economic and monetary union in the European Union.

Lavdas draws on case studies of Italy, Greece, Spain and Portugal to illustrate the range and scope of privatization policies being pursued and their significance in terms of political contestation. The politicization of privatization depends on the exact nature of the enterprises being privatized, the precise process of privatization being pursued, and the timing of its implementation. Lavdas draws attention to the capital sector and the requirements for European convergence that act as a driving force behind the privatization movement. He also draws attention to the need for European-funded rescue packages for important sectors of the Southern European economy (e.g. national airlines), and the important strategic role that privatization plays in this process. Finally, Lavdas points to two important problems that the on-going privatization process will have to address: first, the interactions of different policy patterns and policy responses and, second, the political and social repercussions of privatization for societies in Southern Europe.

In Chapter 11 Bradley carries the analysis of privatization in a European context into the economies in transition (EITs) within the central and eastern European arena. Bradley points to the inextricable association between politics and economics within the EIT nations. Privatization is seen as a critically important process within the overall strategy of creating capitalism from command economies. The particular definitions of privatization appropriate to the EIT nations is discussed and the justifications for privatization considered. The author divides this analysis between justifications offered in the pre-transitional phase and those offered in the post-Communist phase.

The justifications proposed for privatization are examined in detail, focusing upon issues such as the raising of public revenue, the encouragement of competition, property rights and corporate governance, the process of restructuring, reorganization and de-concentration, financial discipline, managerial motivation and entrepreneurial innovation, and 'de novo' business development. Bradley then evaluates various models of privatization, incorporating both historical, non-EIT, models and more specific EIT models. The voucher / mass distribution privatization scheme is considered as a genuinely original model in the EIT context and Bradley offers a comparison between the experience of various countries in central and eastern Europe which have implemented such a privatization measure. Concluding the chapter, the author notes the wide array of meanings ascribed to privatization in general and stresses the need to take account of the unique circumstances that apply in different countries within the EIT group. Market-based models of corporate governance that originate from the UK and the USA, Bradley argues, have been over-emphasized in comparison with models emerging from Japanese or continental European experience.

In the concluding chapter, Foster and Braddon draw on some major themes raised by contributors in this volume to develop a framework for the further analysis of privatization and marketization. Their principal objective is to demonstrate the significance of an interdisciplinary approach that successfully integrates and acknowledges aspects of the political, economic and social characteristcs of both policy and policy outcomes. They contend that although many debates around policy developments within specific contexts have provided useful evidence and analyzes of change, there is a need to go beyond disciplinary boundaries and 'local' approaches to consider the broader picture. This broader perspective is more equipped to address issues about the nature and role of public services in contemporary societies and the positive and negative impact of market-based provision. Key areas around which further discussion can be organized are identified and chosen for their cross-disciplinary relevance within the social sciences.

Foster and Braddon begin by examining the changing role of the state in public service provision, highlighting new problems and dilemmas which have emerged from the introduction of policies of privatization and marketization. They evaluate the contradictory outcomes which have emerged from policies implemented in the UK, whereby political objectives aimed at reducing the role of the state in public service provision have resulted in greater centralization and in some cases further bureaucratization as a consequence of the need to regulate new markets. They then go on to examine whether the economic objectives underlying policies of privatization and marketization have been achieved. In doing so they question the very concept of efficiency and the ways in which it has been interpreted in relation to privatization. Moreover, they cast doubt on whether the principal aim of reducing state expenditure on public services has been realized and whether a purely quantitative approach to efficiency can succeed in an arena that socially and politically must take account of guiding principles of equity and fairness in the distribution of public resources. An examination of the ways in which public services are organized and managed further highlights tensions between efficiency and equity in public service provision whilst also raising issues about the place of quality in calculating value-for-money. The introduction of Citizen's Charters as a means of regulating quality and the reconceptualization of public service users as customers have sought to transform the culture of public services, but have been regarded with a degree of cynicism given the status of service users and the efficacy of quality control mechanisms.

Foster and Braddon acknowledge that radical changes have occurred in the organization of public services and investigate what this means in relation to the concepts of welfare, public service and the public sector. In doing so they evaluate whether it is possible to sustain a distinct set of values or a public service ethos when referring to services provided by a multiplicity of agencies, both public and private. This raises definitional and analytical dilemmas about the very meaning of public service, moreover in doing so it exposes a need to develop new concepts and terminology which can be used to challenge dominant neo-liberal definitions. The authors suggest that the meaning of public service and welfare should embrace a broader range of functions than is traditionally implied and should embrace all areas which have a bearing on citizens' welfare. This concept of welfare is intrinsically bound up with notions of social citizenship and social rights and in recognizing this the authors go on to explore the potential for the development of citizenship rights in the European Union.

In considering changes in public service provision as a consequence of privatization and marketization, Foster and Braddon recognize that this needs to be evaluated in the context of broader social structural change at a national level and in relation to developments which are both post-national, for example the European context, and global. Whilst much of their analysis refers to the UK experience, efforts are made to show the interrelationship of such developments within a wider post-national context. Finally, while sketching out of a framework aimed at widening and developing the privatization debate, they also demonstrate the importance of interdisciplinary cooperation in this area of enquiry and raise questions central to a future research agenda.

References

Bishop, M., Kay, J. and Mayer, C. (1994), *Privatization and economic performance*, Oxford University Press, Oxford.

Foster, D. (1991), *Privatization policy in local government: the response of public sector trade unions*. Unpublished PhD thesis, University of Bath.

Hartley, K. and Parker, D. (1991), 'Privatization: a conceptual framework' in Hartley, K. and Ott, A. F. (eds) *Privatization and economic efficiency*. Edward Elgar, Aldershot.

Heald, D. (1983), *Public expenditure: its defence and reform*, Oxford, Martin Robinson.

Le Grand, J., Propper, C. and Robinson, R. (1992), *The economics of social problems: the market versus the state*, 3rd edition, Macmillan, London.

Spencer, K. M. (1983), *Privatization of urban services*, University of Birmingham (INLOGOV).

Steel, M. and Heald, D. (eds) (1984), *The new agenda in privatizing public enterprises*, London, Royal Institute of Public Administration.

Young, S. (1985), untitled paper on types of privatization, presented at a seminar at the University of Bath, November.

2 Privatization and Ethics

NICHOLAS BUTTLE

Introduction

In this chapter I am concerned with an examination of the ethical issues that are raised by policies directed towards privatization. Privatization, of course, may be regarded as primarily economic, concerned with economic objectives, and to be justified in economic terms. Alternatively, privatization may be regarded as political, concerned with the pursuit of political goals and, consequently, to be justified in political terms. Whilst both the economic and the political interpretations are important neither is exhaustive; privatization should also be regarded in ethical terms concerned with the pursuit of moral objectives and, therefore, appraised in moral, as well as economic and political, terms.[1]

Privatization concerns moral objectives in two respects. First, underpinning privatization is the vision of a good society, a society which is desirable, which ought to be achieved, which has more value than alternative types of society. This concern for the good society I will characterize as a concern for the 'public' sphere of ethics. Second, underpinning privatization is a vision of a good person, of the sort of person who is considered to be morally admirable, whose life is thought to be of value and worth. This vision is primarily concerned with an identification of a range of virtues that a good person should possess if their life is to be morally commendable. This concern for the good person

17

I will characterize as a concern for the 'private' sphere of ethics.

In this chapter I wish to examine three questions concerning the ethics of privatization. First, what are the moral values that provide the foundations for the ethical defence of privatization? Second, how strong are the foundations on which the ethical defence of privatization rest? Finally, is it possible to construct a plausible alternative moral conception with which to oppose that articulated by policies of privatization?

Privatization and moral values

The thrust of privatization policies has been directed towards the limitation and restriction of the extent to which public authorities exercise jurisdiction over the affairs of society. This thrust represents an important shift in emphasis from the policies pursued by governments since the end of the second world war where the emphasis was for more and more areas of society to come under the direction of public institutions; whether through the nationalization and regulation of industry, the extension of the responsibilities of local authorities, or the development of the institutions of the welfare state. Such a change in the nature of the relationship between the public and the private requires a moral justification if there is to be the support from the electorate that the pursuit of privatization requires.[2]

Above, I have suggested that the moral values underpinning the defence of privatization embrace 'public' and 'private' values concerning both an account of the good society and of the good person. Whilst it is not desirable to make a hard distinction between the public and the private in the realm of values, for the sake of interpretative clarity it is useful to disentangle the various strands of thinking that are concerned more with one dimension than the other. In the realm of public ethics the central values that are involved in the moral legitimacy of privatization are those of freedom, democracy, and justice. In the realm of private ethics the important values are those of independence, responsibility, and enterprise. Again, whilst these values cannot and indeed should not be isolated from one another, since each value is implicated with each other, for the purposes of interpretative clarity it is useful to consider each value separately.

18

Freedom

Of the values concerned with the public sphere of ethics, that of freedom is by far the most important.[3] At the heart of the moral vision to which the pursuit of privatization belongs is the vision of a free society. Freedom, however, is a complex value to analyse since controversy exists concerning the very definition of freedom. Some analysts, such as Isaiah Berlin (1969), argue that there are, indeed, two different concepts of freedom, the concepts of negative and positive freedom, and that these concepts come into conflict with each other. Other analysts, however, argue that there is only one concept of freedom, albeit this concept has negative and positive dimensions (MacCallum, 1972). I do not wish to enter this debate here but will take it that there are, at least, two different ways of thinking about the meaning of freedom, or that there are two distinct conceptions of what freedom involves, a negative and a positive conception.

The negative conception of freedom is that persons are free to the extent that they are not prevented from doing what they might wish to do by the deliberate interference in their lives by the actions of other people.[4] The demand for freedom, in this respect, amounts to the demand for such interference to be removed. Berlin suggests that this interpretation of freedom is the interpretation that is typical of liberal political thought. With liberal thinkers, whilst the threats to freedom can come from the interferences in persons' lives from other members of society, the chief threat to freedom was considered to derive from the actions of the public authorities precisely because these authorities possessed the power to enable them to restrict freedom. For the liberal, therefore, the defence of freedom could be interpreted very much as a defence of the freedom of persons from the interference in their lives by public authorities. It is in this context that the libertarian defence of privatization can be appreciated.

A reduction in the extent of the jurisdiction of public authorities is regarded by those thinkers and politicians associated with the neo-liberal ideology of the new right as an essential requirement of 'setting the people free'. The main concern, here, is to free people from the power of administrators, officials, interest groups and politicians to interfere with their wants and preferences. This concern for freedom informs a number of privatization policies. Denationalization, for instance, may be justified in terms of freeing the managers and directors of economic enterprises from the constraints imposed upon them by civil servants and by

19

governments attempting to impose upon enterprises their own agendas. Similarly, selling council houses to their tenants could be justified in terms of freeing the occupants of former council houses from the interference of local government officials insisting on the imposition of various restrictions concerning the terms of occupancy. Similarly, removing regulations on the activities of financial institutions, for example, freed these institutions from state interference in their activities. Finally, policies allowing schools to opt out from local authority control, or to encourage individuals to opt out of state provision of services, could be defended in terms of freeing individuals from public interference in their lives by authorities concerning the type of schooling children will receive, or the type of health care, pension provision, etc.

The other conception of freedom, that of positive liberty, interprets freedom in terms of the ability of persons to direct and control the course of their own lives. Berlin (1969) argues that this is not a liberal interpretation of freedom but an interpretation more at home in socialist, communist, anarchist and even fascist modes of thought. Berlin, however, may be mistaken about this rejection of positive liberty from liberal thinking or, at least, from the thinking of those writers who have influenced the morality of privatization. An important consideration in defence of privatization can be formulated in terms of the positive conception of freedom. Positive liberty is concerned with the extent that individuals exercise control over their own lives; questions of control, however, relate to questions concerning the power that individuals possess to exercise that control. In this respect Mrs Thatcher (1993, p.676) claimed to be empowering the ordinary members of society so that they were free both to make choices for themselves and to fulfil those choices.[5] In the sphere of the consumer, for example, by means of creating a competitive economy the individual was supposed to be given the power to decide what goods and services to purchase and at what price on the basis of their own subjective preferences, rather than having decisions made for them by the administrators of nationalized industries.

Indeed, one of the main criticisms of the nationalized industries was precisely that these industries did not respond to consumer demand and did not provide an adequate range of goods and services for the consumer to choose between. Similarly, a defence of opt-outs and competitive tendering for services could be formulated in terms of empowering individuals so that they can make choices about the services that they prefer rather than having those choices made for them by officials in, for instance, schools, hospitals, local authority chambers. Finally, a justification for the political objective of undermining the power of public sector unions could, again, be formulated in terms of positive liberty since individuals were meant to be provided with the power to decide on whether they wished to join a trade union and the power, through ballots, to decide on industrial action and contributions to political funds (see Pirie, 1988).

The vision of a free society, then, is a vision in which persons are free from public interference in the pursuit of their own objectives, and free to exercise power or choice over the goods and services that correspond with their preferences. But why should freedom be thought to be of value in the first place? Freedom, in both its negative and positive conceptions, is important in two respects. First, freedom is important if the status of persons as rational and responsible agents is to be respected.[6] One of the criticisms of the institutions of the welfare state, for instance, is that these institutions are paternalistic in the way that they treat the members of society, whether this is expressed by teachers knowing what is best for other peoples' children, doctors and health officials knowing what is best for patients' health, or social services officials knowing how people should spend their money. If individuals are to be respected as rational and responsible adults, rather than treated as children, then they need to be free from public interference and able to make choices for themselves concerning the conduct of their own lives. Mrs Thatcher (1993, pp.626-627), for instance, expressed this idea when she condemned what she perceived as the 'nanny state', the state treating the members of society as children for whom the state, like a nanny or parent, has to take responsibility.

The second importance of freedom flows from the positive consequences that are meant to develop from a free society. These positive consequences are both social and personal. On the social side, a free society will be a productive society in which more goods and services will be produced than in an unfree society. A free society is a society in which individuals have an incentive to work hard, to be creative, innovatory, to be productive, efficient, and effective.[7] This defence of freedom would seem, initially, more appropriate to the economic sphere and to justify the privatization of the previously nationalized industries. Contrasts, here, may be made between the inefficient nationalized industries, with little concern for costs and quality, and little incentive to be productive and innovatory, and

21

industries in the private sector where the freedom from state interference and the freedom to control their own affairs result in greater efficiency, consumer responsiveness, and innovation. This defence of freedom, however, may also be extended to spheres other than the strictly economic. A defence of the entry of market forces into health and education is that the removal of public subsidies and regulations and the introduction of competition will result in greater efficiency in the cost and delivery of services and will provide an incentive for those involved in the provision of these services to respond to consumer demand. On the personal level, also, freedom is important since it fosters positive personality traits on the part of individuals. If individuals are free from interference and free to take control of their own lives then they will develop more dynamic personalities, will be more creative, and will be more willing to take responsibility for their own well-being rather than being passive recipients of goods and services from others, especially from public authorities (Pirie, 1988).

Democracy

The relationship between privatization and our second value, that of democracy, is ambiguous; writers whose work provides the theoretical underpinnings for privatization policies, especially those influenced by public choice theory, possess an ambivalent attitude towards democracy (see Gamble, 1988). However, within the context of modern western politics it is not feasible to adopt an explicitly anti-democratic stance, so defenders of privatization need to legitimize their policies by some reference to democracy. Thus, what we find with the relationship between the advocacy of privatization and the value of democracy is an attempt to argue that privatization is compatible with democracy once a proper understanding of the nature of democracy is achieved. A proper understanding of democracy requires thinking clearly about what President Lincoln's definition of democratic government being government 'for the people, by the people, and of the people' might mean in the conditions of modern societies.

A major criticism of modern democratic politics is that this politics has extended the scope of politics beyond its legitimate sphere so that areas of society which should not be the subject for interference by public decision-making have become subject to such interferences (Hayek, 1944; Nozick, 1974). Thus, areas of society which should not be subject to the 'will of the people' have improperly become subject. In these terms a defence of privatization can be formulated on the basis of the claim that the shift from the public to the private is a shift away from an illegitimate extension of democratic politics. Privatization, then, may be justified precisely because it is concerned with re-establishing the legitimate boundaries for democracy and, therefore, is defending democracy from attacks from those who perceive its improper extension, especially in the post-war period.

The critique of the extension of the 'will of the people' into areas that it ought not to be extended embraces a critique of nationalized industries, regulation, and of the extension of power resulting from the development of the welfare state and of local government. Two criticisms can be identified concerning this extension of political power. First, defenders of privatization reject the idea that this extension can be justified in terms of 'government for the people' in the sense that power is exercised in these areas for the public interest. In the public sector, decisions are likely to reflect the interests of trade unions, or of officials and civil servants, or of specialists, such as doctors, teachers and social workers rather than the interests of the general public. Similarly, decisions made in the public sector will reflect the political interests of those parties who seek to manipulate public institutions for their own electoral benefit so that subsidies are provided to nationalized industries, or resources to local authorities and welfare institutions in order to achieve short-term electoral popularity (see Gamble, 1988).

The second criticism of the extension of public power beyond what are perceived to be legitimate areas concerns the irresponsibility of the electorate when confronted with public choices. An argument which goes back at least to Joseph Schumpeter (1976) is that electors are irresponsible in the political sphere because they do not perceive the consequences for themselves of their political decisions. Thus, for instance, voters will support increases in public expenditure in order to provide ever-increasing public services because they do not perceive the consequences for themselves of such support. The more areas of society which are subject to public power, therefore, and the more that power is determined by electoral pressures the more irresponsible decisions will determine society, with a consequent harm to the very public interest that democracy is supposed to serve.

23

Policies of privatization can be defended as a response to the problems of democracy in two ways. First, if the extent to which public authorities are able to interfere in the affairs of society is restricted by transferring public assets to the private sector, by opting out of public control and regulation, and by introducing private and competitive forces into the public sector then this will restrict the extent to which special and sectional interests are able to exert power over society and will limit the extent to which society is subject to the irresponsible wishes of the electorate. Second, if individuals cannot rely on the public sector to provide them with goods and services, especially with goods and services that are free of charge, then this will force individuals to consider the consequences of their decisions. Individuals might not support, for instance, expansions of public provision once they realize that they have to pay for such provision through increased taxes, fees, and charges.

There is, however, a debate amongst thinkers on the new right concerning what the legitimate areas for the exercise of public power might be: some extremists might reject the very legitimacy of the state itself, such as the anarcho-capitalists; others, such as Robert Nozick, wish to see the state limited to the provision of protection; whilst others, such as Hayek, argue that the state should provide a legal framework for the operation of the market and some measure of basic welfare support for the needy.[8] Consensus exists, however, that the state should not be concerned with activities that individuals, groups, and organizations can best provide for themselves, such as with many of the activities which have been associated with social democratic states. Thus, what is best carried out in the private sector should be carried out in the private sector and should not be subject to public jurisdiction or subject to the influence of democratic politics. The democratic will should be restricted, as Schumpeter insisted, to decisions about which political party should exercise the limited powers of the state, not to interfering in areas of society which are not its legitimate concern.

The attitude towards democracy that privatization expresses is not, however, completely negative. Privatization may be defended, as I have already said, in terms of empowerment so that privatization policies may be justified by reference to the idea of 'government by the people'. At this point an important re-interpretation of the meaning of 'government by the people' can be detected. Underlying the models of democracy that have been formulated on the left of the political spectrum, especially since the work of Rousseau, is the idea that self-government must be a collective activity.[9] Thus, 'we the people' exercise political power collectively for our own common good. This interpretation of democracy rests upon the plausibility of the twin notions of a common good and a collective will directed towards that good. The first idea is rejected by the new right to the extent that it expresses some belief that the members of complex, diverse, pluralistic societies possess any shared interests or values over and above some basic support for national defence and internal security. The second idea is rejected since it means that democracy can only be achieved through the exercise of collective institutions, such as parties, unions, public bodies.

The important reformulation of democracy that lies behind privatization policies is the idea that democracy should be concerned with the interests of people as individuals, rather than with some collective interest, and that it is through the actions of individuals, rather than collective action, that the will of individuals is best expressed. In these terms, the empowerment of individuals as a result of reducing the power of public authorities through policies of privatization can be defended as consistent with a proper understanding of democracy. Thus it is as shareholders in private industries, and as consumers in a free and competitive market place, that individuals are able to exercise power over their own lives and over those institutions in the private sector or those remaining in the public sector which affect their lives. It is as individual shareholders and consumers, that is, that the people can exercise power in pursuit of their interests, not as the passive subjects of large state bureaucratic institutions.

If, then, a proper understanding of democracy is formulated, the pursuit of privatization can be seen as consistent with the value of democracy. At one level, privatization involves the restraint of democratic politics to those areas which are the legitimate concern for the exercise of political power. At another level, privatization empowers individuals as consumers and shareholders, thereby enabling them to pursue their interests and exercise power over those institutions which affect those interests.

Justice

The final value that is important for privatization in relation to public ethics is the value of justice. The relationship of privatization to justice is, like that to democracy, ambivalent in that whilst considerations of justice may be appealed to in defence of privatization, they might also be rejected as irrelevant, if not dangerous.

Negatively, thinkers such as Hayek (1979) argue that societies should not be subject to evaluation on the basis of whether the society is just or not. Justice, Hayek argues, is an appropriate value to apply to the legal sphere but is inappropriate to the social sphere. Justice, therefore, cannot be used to justify public institutions, such as the nationalized industries and the welfare state. Hayek's argument, in short, is that, first, there do not exist any objective and independent principles of what social justice might be because values are expressions of the subjective preferences of individuals rather than of some objective reality. In a pluralistic society in which different individuals possess different preferences there will not exist any consensus concerning what a just way of, for instance, distributing resources might be. Consequently, if public institutions are developed to control and regulate the distribution of goods and services, as with the modern social democratic and welfare state, all that will be achieved is a pattern of distribution which will reflect the subjective values of those who have power over those institutions, such as: officials, politicians, vested interests, and trade unions. Second, for Hayek, considerations of justice are irrelevant to an assessment of societies because, at the macro level of the economy, no one is responsible for the distribution of resources. For Hayek resource distribution will be the unintended and spontaneous outcome of the multiplicity of decisions and actions which occur at the micro level and decisions and actions which public authorities cannot hope to control through, for instance, planning institutions. Even the suggestion that markets distribute resources in a just manner because they distribute resources on the basis of merit or desert is rejected by Hayek. Markets respond to the subjective preferences of individuals for goods and services not to the deserts or merits of those offering such goods and services. To take an example of Sir Keith Joseph: if nurses are paid less for their services than the makers of ice-cubes this cannot be condemned as unjust on the basis of a claim about what nurses and ice-cube makers really deserve; the difference in the incomes of nurses and ice-cube makers will reflect the subjective preferences of individuals as reflected in the market (Joseph and Sumpton, 1979).

The negative attitude toward the application of considerations of justice to society and to the distribution of resources between the members of society reflected in the work of Hayek does not, however, represent the only view about distributive questions that underpins privatization. Defenders of privatization claim that, whilst it might not be possible to argue that privatization produces a more just society than that produced by public institutions, at least privatization does not lead to the injustices that are found in the public sector. We have already seen that critics of the public sector argue that public institutions do not distribute resources in terms of some notion of the public interest, but in response to the power of vested interests and groups.

The institutions of the welfare state, for instance, rather than providing resources to individuals who are really in need will provide resources to those who are not in need, such as to the middle classes who benefit from subsidies on health, mortgages, education. Similarly, the nationalized industries do not distribute resources on any basis of need or desert but distribute wages and salaries to employees on the basis of bargaining power, and goods and services to the public on the basis of administrative or political fiat. A shift of resources from the public sector to the private sector, then, could be defended as, at least, not unjust because subject to the competitive market forces of the private sector enterprises will be able to reward employees for their work, creativity, productivity, and to provide the goods and services that the consumer wants. Similarly, to cut back on the services provided to people by the welfare state and to encourage them to opt out and rely on the private sector will release resources to provide for the really needy in society.

Private ethics

Turning now to the realm of private ethics, the ethics concerned with the idea of the good person, the defence of privatization reflects a conception of the virtues which it is thought characterize a good person.[10] First of all, a good person is one who is independent in that they are able to determine the course of their own life rather than being subject to the control of other people. In this respect the defence of privatization will be formulated in terms of destroying what is perceived as the dependency culture. How, for instance, can individuals be independent if the whole culture of society is to foster the idea that the state will look after people from cradle to grave? Similarly, how can the managers of enterprises take independent decisions concerning those enterprises if they are subject to the dictates of officials and politicians?

The defence of the independent individual also connects with the second virtue that privatization is to encourage, that of responsibility. If individuals are able to take independent decisions for themselves this will mean that they will be able to take responsibility for their own lives rather than others being responsible for them. There is an echo here of earlier debate between Catholics and Protestants concerning the issue of who is responsible for the spiritual welfare of persons. Traditionally, Catholic theology held that it is the Church who is responsible for the spiritual (and moral) lives of individuals, whereas Protestant theology, in contrast, insisted that only the individual can take responsibility for finding their way to God.[11]

Similarly, it is argued that individuals should take responsibility for their own material welfare rather than relying on others, namely the state, to provide for them. The more, then, public provision is privatized the more individuals will be encouraged to take responsibility for themselves. This notion of responsibility, for instance, underlies the Conservative interpretation of citizenship, whereby the citizen is seen as a private individual who either individually or in company with other individuals is prepared to take responsibility for the affairs of the community in which they live (Hurd, 1988). The thinking behind neighbourhood watch schemes, for instance, is that people should take responsibility for their own security rather than expecting the police to provide complete security services.

Finally, the virtues of independence and responsibility are, it is hoped, virtues which will encourage the development of the virtue of enterprise whereby if individuals are able to take independent decisions concerning their own lives and to take responsibility for their own well-being, this will release the enterprising qualities of individuals, the qualities that lead to creativity, productivity, innovation, etc.

The defence of the virtues of independence, responsibility, and enterprise is much the same as the defence of freedom that was earlier outlined. Thus, individuals with these virtues can be seen as rational agents of value and importance in their own right and a society of such individuals as a society which benefits by the greater productivity and creativeness that results, in contrast to a society of individuals who are afraid or unwilling to take decisions, to accept responsibility, to show enterprise.

The moral underpinnings for the pursuit of privatization, then, embrace what I have referred to as a public and a private ethics. In the sphere of public ethics the defence of privatization is that which relates to the vision of a good society as a free society, a society in which democratic politics is limited to legitimate concerns and where consumers and shareholders determine their own lives, a society in which resources are distributed on the basis of markets responding to the preferences of people, where merit is rewarded and where the needs of the truly needy are met. In the sphere of private ethics the defence of privatization is that which relates to a vision of a good person, the person who possesses the virtues of independence, responsibility and enterprise.

Critical assessment

Criticisms of the ethics of privatization take two forms: first, critics challenge the success of privatization in achieving its objectives and second, critics challenge the worth of these objectives themselves.[12]

The first problem with privatization is that rather than individuals being freed from external interference in their lives and free to exercise control over their lives, privatization has led to a loss of freedom on the part of the members of society. One reason for this criticism concerns the effects of privatizing the nationalized industries. Rather than former nationalized industries being transferred to the private sector and subject to the competitive forces in that sector, in too many cases, especially with the former public utilities, public monopolies have simply become private monopolies as unresponsive to the wishes of consumers as the public enterprises were thought to be. Similarly, the idea that individuals as shareholders in private enterprises could exercise influence over those enterprises is rejected in the light of the fact that many individuals who initially bought shares in the former nationalized industries soon sold those shares in order to make a short-term profit and that the bulk of the shares and hence of the influence in the privatized industries lie with large institutions, such as insurance and investment companies, rather than with individuals.[13]

Similar criticisms can be made concerning the consequences of other types of privatization, such as with opt-outs and competitive tendering in the public sector. Many individuals who have opted out of public housing, for instance by purchasing their own former council house, have not had an increase in freedom but, because of problems with mortgage payments and the costs of maintenance, former council tenants have found themselves at the mercy of banks, building societies and loan companies rather than free from external interference. With welfare state institutions similar criticisms of the consequences of privatization can be made. Whilst the freedom of some individuals might indeed result from greater private provision, from opt-outs and from market forces, the result for other individuals is a loss of freedom. The loss of freedom with respect to the welfare state may arise in two respects. Firstly, if a result of privatization of welfare provision or of restrictions in provisions aimed at breaking state dependency is a reduction in the resources that are available to those individuals who require these resources then their freedom to exercise control over their own lives will be constrained rather than expanded. Similarly, if a result of people opting out of public provision by opting for private schooling, health care, housing, pensions, etc., is to reduce the resources available for those provisions that remain in the public sector then, again, the freedom of those individuals who remain reliant on public provision will be curtailed as the quality and variety of public provision declines.

Thus privatization has not resulted in a free society of independent and responsible individuals but, rather, has resulted in a society where important decisions are made by those who own and control the former public enterprises and where the freedom of those who require public provision is curtailed. These points also have significance with respect to the relationship of privatization to democracy. Criticisms of privatization concerning the consequences of privatization for democracy are, first, that privatization does go against democratic values precisely because it does remove important issues from public determination and, therefore, undermines the notion of democracy as self-government. If, for instance, schools opt out of local education authority control this means that local communities cannot participate in decisions concerning local education. Similarly, the extent that services in the public sector are privatized or contracted out removes decisions concerning those services from democratic participation. Second, the shift of enterprises from the public to the private sector does not result in individuals as consumers or shareholders being able to exercise more control over the institutions that influence their lives than was the case when these enterprises were part of the public sector. Decisions in former public enterprises will not reflect the wishes of individual shareholders, the 'Sids', but will reflect decisions made by the directors and managers of these enterprises as well as responding to the influence of the large institutional shareholders. Whilst in the public sphere, at least, economic enterprises were subject to some measure of democratic control through the political process, once in the private sector such control is largely lost. Privatization, then, results in an impoverishment of democracy and leaves large areas of society's affairs beyond democratic influence.

With respect to the consequences that privatization has on the distribution of resources between the members of society, a number of criticisms can be made concerning the fairness of privatization. First, the privatization of public enterprises results in a loss of revenue for the public purse so that instead of profits being used by the state for the public interest, such as to finance welfare institutions, these profits go to private individuals, institutions, banks, etc., with no commitment to the interests of society as a whole.

Second, rather than resources being distributed to employees in the former public enterprises on any basis of merit, income, for instance, would seem to reflect positions of power within organizations. Whilst the managers and directors of the former public utilities, for example, would seem to have used their position to vastly increase their own incomes, the incomes of the ordinary employees have been held static or cut back, as well as the number of people employed in these industries being reduced.

Third, the benefits and the costs produced by the former nationalized industries are distributed unfairly. Whilst some people may find that the costs of services have been reduced others find that costs have been increased and, even, services withdrawn. With bus services, for instance, whilst deregulation, privatization and competition may have resulted in lower fares on profitable city routes, on unprofitable routes in inner city areas or rural areas, costs have increased and services been withdrawn. With services in the public sector, at least, cross subsidization could try to provide uniform services at uniform costs so that some members of society were not disadvantaged.

Critics of privatization, then, argue that the pursuit of privatization has been a moral failure. Rather than a society of free individuals, a society where individuals can control their lives as consumers and shareholders, and where resources are distributed on the basis of preferences and merit, privatization has led to a society in which for many individuals freedom is an illusion, in which decisions are not in the hands of individuals but exercised by undemocratic institutions, and in which the distribution of resources is grossly unfair. These points, of course, impact on the private sphere of ethics underpinning privatization since in an unfree, undemocratic, and unfair society, whilst some privileged individuals may be independent, responsible, and enterprising, for many the opportunity to develop and exercise these virtues does not exist. For those locked into cycles of poverty and deprivation the removal of public provision does not foster positive virtues but leads only to greater misery and hopelessness. Similarly, for those who require decent health, education, housing, and employment to become independent, etc., the erosion of these has negated any opportunity for the development of the positive virtues that underpin privatization.

These criticisms, however, may not be taken as criticisms of privatization as such but of the way that privatization has been carried out. If, for instance, measures are taken to ensure proper competition in the private sector, and if proper targeting of resources to the needy was followed, then many of the problems with privatization could be resolved. However, there are deeper criticisms of the ethics of privatization: namely, that the pursuit of privatization itself is morally objectionable. The chief criticism, here, is that the commitment to privatization involves a commitment to placing a value on the private and to rejecting the value of the public (Marquand, 1986; Plant, 1992). It is best, defenders of privatization claim, for activities to be carried out in private rather than in public. This erosion of the value of the public, however, has resulted in a society where any sense of community, any sense of shared interests, any sense of shared responsibilities has been undermined.

What privatization has achieved is a sort of Hobbesian world where isolated individuals confront other isolated individuals with opposing and hostile interests. What privatization has achieved is a society in which individuals are concerned only with the pursuit of their own interests, a society in which individuals retreat into themselves, a society of metaphysical stockades behind which we crouch and view others nervously and suspiciously. The moral vision underpinning privatization, then, is a poor and impoverished vision, a vision which results in a state of nature characterized by the war of all against all in which, for many, life is nasty, brutish and short.[14]

32

An alternative ethics

If privatization rests upon a failed and impoverished moral vision then the question that should be asked is whether there exists an alternative moral vision. The main objective of an alternative moral vision is to provide some ethical perspective in terms of which the public domain can be reclaimed and provided with moral legitimacy. Those on the old left of the political spectrum may think that an appeal to traditional socialism can provide the moral vision that can underpin a commitment to the public. The problem with this is that many of the criticisms of Morrisonian nationalization, of the paternalistic welfare state, of the inefficiencies of local authorities made by defenders of privatization have considerable force. Nationalized industries, for instance, showed little concern for the 'public interest' and were responsive to the demands of vested interests. Local authorities and the institutions of the welfare state were often dictatorial and unresponsive to the wants and preferences of people. Traditional socialism, then, I think does not provide an alternative moral vision which can be persuasively placed in opposition to that of privatization.[15]

Will Hutton has suggested that the reason why the Conservatives were, in part, able to launch an attack on the public sector is because of the lack of a strong tradition of citizenship in Britain and that what needs to be developed in opposition to privatization is the notion of republicanism. It is in terms of the ideas of citizenship and republicanism (Hutton, 1995, chs.1,11,12) that an alternative ethics may be constructed to provide a defence of the moral importance of the public sector.

If we begin with the idea of citizenship, we can analyse the notion of the citizen in terms of someone who is a member of a community. What is important here is precisely that the citizen is a member of a community rather than an isolated and self-contained individual. However, as a member of a community, citizenship should be interpreted in terms of the citizen possessing a status in that community and able to play a role. The status of the citizen is that status of someone who counts in the community, someone who is of value and of standing.[16] The role of the citizen is that of the person able to participate in and exert influence over the affairs of the community. However, in what way might citizenship be best secured in a modern society? Whilst there might be controversy concerning the requirements of citizenship, commentators such as T.D. Marshall (1950) argue that citizenship is best interpreted in terms of the possession of rights and that since the 17th century the struggle for citizenship has been a struggle for the extension of rights to more and more groups in society. The rights which Marshall thinks are important to citizenship are civil, political, social and economic rights. These rights are important because they present a public statement of the status of persons as citizens and provide persons with the opportunity and the means to perform the role of citizen.

A concern for citizenship, if this concern is to be made secure, might well require constitutional change in Britain so that citizenship rights are enshrined in a basic Bill of Rights and therefore protected from the erosion that has occurred since 1979. Also, if citizenship is interpreted in terms of social and economic rights then the institutions of the welfare state may be defended not on the basis of meeting the deficiencies of individuals but on the basis of recognizing the position of persons as citizens, as valued members of the community with a role to play in that community.[17]

The idea of persons as citizens rather than as private individuals, then, does provide a moral conception which can provide legitimacy for the public sphere since it is in the public sphere that citizenship is expressed and fulfilled. The other important idea establishing the legitimacy of the public sphere is that of republicanism. The republican tradition has a long and controversial history, stretching back to Aristotle and, later, to Machiavelli (Pocock, 1975).

Whilst there may be debate over the precise content of republicanism, I will take republicanism to be that tradition of political thought which places an emphasis on the importance of balance within a political system. Balance should exist between the state and the citizen, between the central and the local, and between the executive, legislative and judicial branches of government. From the republican tradition power, in other words, should not be concentrated in society but should be diversified as far as possible. The reason why republican thinkers, such as Machiavelli, argued for the importance of balance was to avoid the dangers of the republic becoming corrupted in terms of power coming to be exercised by special interests rather than being exercised for the benefit of the people as a whole.

The republican tradition has a number of important implications for the ethics of privatization. First, republicanism reasserts the importance of the person as a citizen rather than as a private individual. In the republican tradition, indeed, persons as citizens have a duty to participate in public affairs and need to develop civic virtue, that is the virtue of recognizing this duty. The duty of participation is important both because the citizen has a duty to defend the republic from corruption by, for instance, resisting the influence of vested and special interests, but also because it is only by being concerned with public affairs that the individual can resist the corruption of their own interest. Thus, the sphere of the public in which the citizen can participate is of value as a means of avoiding the sorts of corruption that results if special interests are not resisted (Skinner, 1990).

The second importance of republicanism is the idea that there should exist a balance between the various powers in the state, both at the central level and at the local level. Thus an independent sphere of local government is important to challenge the dangers of power being concentrated, and hence corrupted, at the centre. But also other institutions in civil society are important as a means of preventing power being concentrated and, hence, abused. In these terms, it is important to defend the various institutions of the welfare state as institutions independent from central government and as institutions in which citizens can exercise influence.

The former nationalized industries similarly are important. It might not, of course, be either desirable or feasible for all the former nationalized industries to be returned to the public sector. Some activities, such as making cars, airplanes, etc., might best be carried out in the private sector. With these industries the relevant issue concerns whether their profits are used to benefit society as a whole or to benefit only a small minority. Here we are confronted with the general issue of taxation which applies to all industries. The task is to devise a system of taxation which will raise revenue to finance the public sector, but a system which will not kill the golden goose by undermining profitable activity, such as by weakening incentives. Nevertheless, the important point is that any taxation of industry that is devised can be justified by reference to its importance in financing the public sector, and legitimized precisely in terms of the value of the public sector for citizens.

With other industries, however, there might be a case to be made out for their return to the public sector, especially with the utilities such as water, gas, and electricity, together with important public services such as transport. What is important with these industries, though, is not so much whether they are publicly or privately owned, but whether they operate in the interest of the members of society in general or whether they operate to the benefit of a few. One of the problems with privatization in this respect is that it has not produced the sort of competition that was supposed to achieve public responsiveness. The solution to this has been with the setting up of various regulatory agencies to try to ape competitive forces and to consider the public interest. The existing regulatory agencies, however, would seem inadequate: on the one hand, they do not allow for the participation of citizens in their (often secret) deliberations, unlike, for instance, organizations such as Community Health Councils; on the other hand, they are not subject to the sorts of parliamentary scrutiny that republicanism insists to be necessary if they are not to be captured by special interests (such as the very industries they are supposed to regulate) (see Graham and Prosser, 1991). What is required with the utilities, then, is a system of regulatory agencies in which citizens can participate to defend their interests, and a system of parliamentary scrutiny to ensure that these agencies do, indeed, act in the interests of the public.[18]

The moral defence of privatization can be challenged, then, once the moral vision underpinning that defence is rejected and once an alternative vision is constructed which places an emphasis on the value of the public sphere. Such an alternative vision can be built, I believe, on the basis of ideas concerning citizenship and republicanism.

Notes

1. For discussions of the economic and political aspects of privatization see Marsh (1990), Wolfe (1991), and Dobek (1993).
2. On the need for a moral underpinning for economic policies see Plant (1992).
3. For general discussions of the ideology of the new right see Bosanquet (1983), King (1987), Green (1987), and Barry (1987).
4. One of the most influential advocates of negative liberty is Hayek (1960).
5. See Thatcher (1993, pp. 676-687) for her views on privatizations.
6. This justification of freedom may be found in the work of thinkers such as Locke and Kant.
7. The 'classic' expression of this is in Mill (1972).
8. For a useful discussion of theories of the state see Dunleavy and O'Leary (1987).
9. For a discussion of democracy see Held (1987).

10. For a review of these values see Heelas and Morris (1992) and a defence see Young (1992).
11. The 'classic' discussion of this is Weber (1930).
12. For a critical account of the consequences of the policies of the Conservative government in Britain since 1979 see Hutton (1995).
13. For the figures see Lee (1994).
14. These criticisms are echoed by those writers characterized as 'communitarians'. For debates on this see Avineri and de-Shalit (1992).
15. For discussion of the problems with socialism in general and nationalization in particular see Marquand (1986) and Prosser (1986).
16. For one of the most powerful accounts of this see Rawls (1993).
17. For a defence of social and economic rights see Plant (1988).
18. For a more detailed discussion of the institutional implications see Hutton (1995), chs.11,12.

References

Avineri, S. and de-Shalit, A. (eds) (1992), *Communitarianism and Individualism*, Oxford University Press, Oxford.

Barry, N. (1987), *The New Right*, Croom Helm, London.

Berlin, I. (1969), 'Two Concepts of Liberty' in Berlin, I. *Four Essays on Liberty*, Oxford University Press, Oxford.

Bosanquet, A. (1983), *After the New Right*, Heineman, London.

Dobek, M. (1993), 'Privatization as a Political Priority: The British Experience', *Political Studies*, vol. 41.

Dunleavy, P. and O'Leary, B. (1987), *Theories of the State: The Politics of Liberal Democracy*, Macmillan, London.

Gamble, A. (1988) *The Free Economy and the Strong State*, Macmillan, London.

Graham, C. and Prosser, T. (1991), *Privatizing Public Enterprise*, Oxford University Press, Oxford.

Green, D. (1987), *The New Right*, Wheatsheaf, Brighton.

Hayek, F. (1944) *The Road to Serfdom*, Routledge, London.

Hayek, F. (1960), *The Constitution of Liberty*, Routledge, London.

Hayek, F.(1979), *Law, Legislation and Liberty*, vol.3, Routledge, London.

Heelas, P. and Morris, P. (1992), 'Enterprise Culture: its values and value', in Heelas, P. and Morris, P. (eds) *The Value of the Enterprise Culture*, Routledge, London.

Held, D. (1987), *Models of Democracy*, Polity Press, Oxford.

Hurd, D. (1988), 'Citizenship in the Tory Democracy', *New Statesman and Society*, 29 April.

Hutton, W. (1995), *The State We're In*, Cape, London.

Joseph, K. and Sumpton, J. (1979), *Equality*, Murray, London.

King, D. (1987), *The New Right: Politics, Markets and Citizenship*, Macmillan, London.

Lee, G. (1994), 'Privatization', in Jones, B. (ed.) *Political Issues in Britain Today*, Manchester University Press, Manchester.

MacCullum, G. (1972), 'Negative and Positive Liberty' in Laslett, P. et al (eds) *Philosophy, Politics and Society*, Blackwell, Oxford.

Marquand, D. (1986), *The Unprincipled Society*, Cape, London.

Marsh, D. (1990), *Privatization in Britain: An Idea in Search of a Policy*, Essex University Papers in Politics and Government, no. 72.

Marshall, T.D. (1950), *Citizenship and Social Class and other Essays*, Cambridge University Press, Cambridge.

Mill, J.S. (1972), *On Liberty*, Dent, London.

Nozick, R. (1974), *Anarchy, State and Utopia*, Blackwell, Oxford.

Pirie, M. (1988), *Privatization: Theory, Practice and Choice*, Wildwood House, Aldershot.

Plant, R. (1988), *Citizenship, Rights and Socialism*, Fabian Tract, no. 531.

Plant, R. (1992), 'Enterprise in its Place: the Moral Limits of Markets', in Heelas, P. and Morris, P. (eds), *The Values of the Enterprise Culture*, Routledge, London.

Pocock, J. (1975), *The Machiavellian Moment: Florentine Political Thought and the Atlantic Tradition*, Princeton University Press, Princeton, N.J.

Prosser, T. (1986), *Nationalised Industries and Public Control*, Blackwell, Oxford.

Rawls, J. (1993), *Political Liberalism*, Columbia University Press, New York.

Schumpter, J. (1976), *Capitalism, Socilism and Democracy*, Allen and Unwin, London.

Skinner, Q. (1990), 'The Republican Ideal of Political Liberty', in Bock, G., Skinner, Q. and Viroli, M. *Machiavelli and Republicanism*,

Cambridge University Press, Cambridge.

Thatcher, M. (1993), *The Downing Street Years*, Harper-Collins, London.

Weber, M. (1930), *The Protestant Ethic and the Spirit of Capitalism*, Allen and Unwin, London.

Wolfe, J. (1991), 'State Power and Ideology in Britain: Mrs Thatcher's Privatization Programme' *Political Studies*, vol.39.

Young, D. (1992), 'Enterprise Regained', in Heelas, P. and Morris, P. (eds) *The Value of the Enterprise Culture*, Routledge, London.

3 Competitive Tendering in Local Government: Trade Unions and Organizational Change

DEBORAH FOSTER

Introduction

This chapter will examine the policy of compulsory competitive tendering (CCT) within the local government context. It will focus upon the introduction of CCT and its subsequent impact on public service trade unionism and organizational change within local authorities. The objective is to provide an insight into the actual consequences of CCT at an organizational level, rather than a general overview of debates that have resulted from its implementation. For this purpose qualitative case study material is presented, documenting the experiences of CCT in three local authorities in South West England. Based on interviews with local councillors, managers, trade union officials and rank and file members, it illustrates attitudes and responses to policy at all levels within an organization. CCT has aroused much interest amongst policy analysts and political scientists, who have largely interpreted its introduction into local government as consistent with broader Conservative Party objectives to open up public sector markets to competition. The approach underlying this discussion is, however, equally influenced by a concern for the industrial relations objectives of CCT and its consequences for trade unions. At a sociological level this focus provides an insight into trade unions and the ways in which they interpret and manage change but, in doing so, is also concerned with the more general impact of policy on different groups within organizations and, ultimately, how change impacts on the organization itself in particular its *culture*. The introduction of market principles into the public sector is an issue of great controversy in itself and is explored comprehensively in other chapters, whereas a focus on the impact of policies of 'marketization' on the culture of public service *organizations* is an area that has elicited less attention. The second half of this chapter will therefore pursue a theoretical exploration of the impact of CCT on the organizational culture of local authorities.

Privatization of municipal services first emerged with the 1980 Local Government Planning and Land Act, introducing CCT into some aspects of housing maintenance and highways work. This sometimes resulted in work previously done by local authority workforces being contracted out to the private sector. From hereon, CCT, as a policy, became an issue of both political and ideological significance, supported in particular by 'New Right' local authorities and opposed by Labour-controlled councils.[1] Between 1980 and 1988 competitive tendering was extended in some Conservative authorities to include services not covered by legislation. Authorities involved in such 'experimental tendering' were keen to promote policies of privatization or marketization and, significantly, also viewed competitive tendering as an opportunity to weaken the influence of public service trade unions, by exposing hitherto 'sheltered' workforces to the mechanisms of competition. This forced 'in-house' council workforces to bid for their own jobs against private contractors. Competition in what were highly labour-intensive services usually resulted in cuts in wages and conditions of employment. Trade unions therefore found themselves in a 'no win' situation: accepting cuts in employment to retain services 'in-house', or risking wholesale privatization and almost inevitable de-recognition. These piecemeal attempts to promote competitive tendering were extended through the 1988 Local Government Act, which stipulated that six[2] major manual services in local government, previously provided by in-house workforces, must be regularly subjected to *compulsory* competitive tendering. This extension of CCT was consistent with other strands of Conservative policy during the 1980s that aimed at reducing the size and scope of the public sector. However, because of the character of local government, as a democratically elected and locally accountable tier of government, tensions arose in other political and policy areas. Most notably, the new legislation raised issues concerning municipal autonomy and the role of local authorities in provision and management of services to their communities.

42

The introduction of CCT must be seen in the context of broader changes in the structure and functions of local government. In recent years the introduction of major pieces of legislation has engendered a fundamental shift in its role. The 1988 Education Reform Act brought about the local management of schools; this and other legislation has enabled the transfer of schools and further education colleges from direct local authority control, whilst creating demand for contracted-out services from newly autonomous bodies. In many respects, local authorities are losing their role as direct service providers and are instead becoming *enabling* authorities. Escott and Whitfield (1995, p. 5) describe the *enabling authority* as featuring 'widespread contracting out of services; a rigid client-contractor split across the organization; adoption of internal markets, business units and business planning; and privatization of services. It is based on the belief that the authority should not directly provide services but rather 'enable' others to do so'. This changing role (not universally embraced by all local authorities) has led many in local government to question the motives of consecutive Conservative administrations which, through CCT and other 'marketization'policies, have undermined its purpose and autonomy. Suspicion of central government motives and fears of loss of control of services is evident in the case studies to be presented. In particular, case study two demonstrates the lengths to which even a Conservative local authority will go to fight perceived Government encroachments on local government autonomy. The future of central / local government relations may be further strained by the expansion of CCT into local government white-collar functions via the 1992 Local Government Act, which Escott and Whitfield (1995) estimate will affect over 270,000 staff. This may lead to further privatization, or to the 'externalization' of services (sale of white-collar services to private 'host' companies (Escott and Whitfield, 1995, p. 6) as a strategy to 'avoid' further CCT).

Throughout this chapter emphasis is placed on the need to acknowledge the ways in which the distinctive character of local government, its political nature and geography, is significant in explaining how local circumstances mediate between policy objectives and outcomes (see also Foster, 1993; Painter, 1991). It is therefore crucial to avoid generalizing about local government, and to acknowledge that organizational and cultural differences exist between authorities and are analytically important in evaluating the impact of CCT. These differences are best explored through case study materials highlighting the *cultural aspects* of an authority by reference to the attitudes and opinions of different key constituent groups. Too often the study of organizations assumes that a general label can describe the internal culture of a given organization, whereas in reality organizational culture is not static but ever-changing, as people within it experience change and respond to new circumstances. This point is particularly relevant to local government which, because of legislative change and policies of 'marketization', has experienced considerable upheaval. This has led to a re-evaluation of its philosophy, functions, internal organization, management approach, employment relationships and, most importantly, its role in the provision of public services. The case material therefore helps to provide a picture of events in three authorities during this period of change: spanning events prior to the introduction of the 1988 Local Government Act, the crucial implementation stage of CCT, and subsequent events following the first round of CCT.[3]

The three case studies of local authorities will be presented, followed by an exploration of the attitudes of key actors towards CCT. Views of local politicians and trade unionists are given particular emphasis to highlight, first, significant political and ideological variations between the authorities - all of whom, it should be noted, were Conservative-controlled - and, second, the important impact of CCT on trade unions. Case studies are numbered rather than named, for confidentiality. Case study 1 is a marginal Conservative-controlled urban authority with a history of ideological support for the process of CCT, demonstrated in its willingness to submit some services to voluntary 'experimental' tendering before the 1988 Local Government Act. Case study 2 is a Conservative-controlled district council which enjoyed a substantial majority but, significantly, never embraced 'Thatcherite' ideology. This authority displayed no historical support for voluntary competitive tendering and, importantly, was wholly opposed to the introduction of compulsory competitive tendering. Case study 3 is another urban council where political control has oscillated between Conservative and Labour groups. It had a history of 'experimental' non-compulsory competitive tendering whilst in Conservative control prior to the 1988 Act, which sparked off a period of industrial unrest followed by a well-orchestrated union campaign opposing privatization. This council is now Labour-controlled, and enjoys the support of the Conservative group in opposing white-collar CCT. After the case studies, a broader debate drawing on contemporary literature seeks to address how policies such as CCT have impacted on the culture of local authorities as organizations and how policies of 'marketization' more generally have changed perceptions of what is meant by 'public service'.

Case study 1 - 'The Free Marketeers'

In many respects this council provides a useful history of CCT in local government. In particular, it highlights the organizational impact of government legislation in this area for, as early as 1980, an ideological commitment to testing the market for manual services was established. This was accompanied by a management reorganization programme in 1981, whereby incumbent managers were largely replaced with more 'commercially-minded' private sector ones, and separate 'client' and 'contractor' departments were established for work to be subjected to competitive tendering.

Enthusiasm for competitive tendering and a commitment to make the Direct Service Organization (DSO) more efficient was seen by managers and councillors to be obstructed by municipal employment practices that were not mirrored in the private sector. Following the loss of several contracts to the private sector, staff reductions in the building section produced, as one manager commented, 'a leaner workforce, reduced from 116 to 27 full-time employees over twelve months'. Loss of staff was viewed as an opportunity to innovate in new ways of organizing and managing the DSO. As a consequence, a 'Contractor Service Group' (CSG) was set up, which became organizationally separate from the Council, managing its own budget and taking control of day-to-day decisions. The rationale behind the establishment of the CSG was to liberate the council from constraints, particularly relating to employment and industrial relations issues. The CSG had the power to hire and fire employees without reference to the authority's Personnel Department and established its own Joint Consultative Committee, independent from the Council's Personnel Committee, for industrial relations purposes. Nonetheless, CSG's 'separateness' was essentially artificial, as it was subject to the scrutiny of a council sub-committee.

The fact that the CSG was set up in 1981, seven years prior to the 1988 Local Government Act, demonstrates the degree of enthusiasm and commitment to competitive tendering by this council. From the outset staffing levels, working practices and organizational culture were challenged. Political interference in management was perceived as bad practice; a strategy of replacing a large full-time labour force with a small core of staff with specialized skills and a larger peripheral, temporary workforce consisting of ex-local authority employees or sub-contracted labour to create a flexible work-force (cf. Atkinson, 1985) was pursued, to increase the competitiveness of the CSG. However, despite these measures CSG managers believed they were still competitively disadvantaged, legally constrained to compete for contracts in the private sector and burdened by the labour costs of core staff employed on nationally agreed local authority terms and conditions. The crux of the problem, as one senior manager commented, was this:

> we're met with the politician's dichotomy, wanting to be seen as good employers but wanting value for money. The CSG is their compromise. It's a way of keeping their hands clean.

Despite these constraints the CSG operated successfully during the period 1980-1988 prior to the extension of CCT in the Local Government Act. During this period the council had experimented in extending competitive tendering. The first service to be subjected to non-compulsory competitive tendering was catering in 1981, following attempts by trade unions and the Labour Group on the council to draw up an 'efficiency blueprint' demonstrating possible savings in the competitive tendering process, which resulted in a private sector win. This was followed by 'efficiency reviews' in other service areas, principally refuse collection where savings were proposed through sixteen redundancies and changes in working practices. Despite union recommendations that this proposal be accepted to avert privatization, the workforce began a campaign of industrial action culminating in the service being awarded to an external contractor in December 1982. As late as January 1988 a tender in the Parks Department was awarded to a private contractor in what one Conservative councillor commented as 'an attempt to test the water for forthcoming legislation'. This preparation for new legislation had been on-going since 1980 and actively lobbied for, underpinned by a strong political commitment to both the principles of CCT and an unrestricted public sector market.

As is evident from this case study, CCT was politically and ideologically embraced by the dominant Conservative group. Councillors interviewed expressed enthusiasm for CCT as a means of increasing the efficiency of services and as a way of reforming labour and employment practices. Inefficiency was equated with over-staffing, a high wage bill, and trade union power. The concept of the customer and delivering cheaper yet more responsive services to the public was not a considered argument in support of CCT. A strong ideological commitment to the market and an equally powerful hostility towards trade unions were the prime motivations for privatizing services.

Managers' support for CCT was also unequivocal, although this was not a consequence of ideological conviction but a commitment to private sector business practice. Formerly managers of private sector firms operating at 'arm's length' from the council in the CSG, they felt no loyalty to either the council or workforce, for as one senior manager commented:

> We realize we are no longer in the business for (the Free Marketeers). Our jobs depend on whether we succeed. If the tide turns and competition lapses, we'll make a killing from the Council, no qualms.

This attitude was accompanied by contempt for past local authority management, which in the opinion of one CSG manager had been a 'sham', leading to 'sloppiness and laziness'. It was also believed that trade unions had got 'what they deserved' by privatization; managers, in essence, had regained the 'right to manage' and unions were on the defensive. Nonetheless, managers expressed the belief that an 'interdependent' relationship existed between managers and unions: both sides needed to cooperate with each other, the unions were desperate to retain their membership in the public sector and managers needed compliant but loyal employees. Nevertheless, it might be a more appropriate way to describe the relationship as 'instrumental', since the unions were organizationally weak and possessed little bargaining power.

The conflicts inherent in the situation of the CSG were eventually resolved by a management buy-out of the DSO in 1989 and, although two thirds of the company's work remained with the council, as a private concern the organization was free to tender for contracts externally. The newly established company employed 250 former council employees, who sadly by 1990 faced redundancy when the company met with bankruptcy after losing a number of lucrative contracts through both competition and poor quality of service delivery. Ironically, the management buy-out had been held up as a model for the future of service delivery in local government by pro-privatization lobby groups and politicians and became somewhat of an embarrassment. The situation for local trade union branches was more serious, though not wholly unexpected. Attempts by unions, principally the National Union of Public Employees (NUPE) and the General, Municipal and Boilermakers' Union (GMB), to open up debate about the long-term implications of privatization with members in branches had largely failed. Apart from the industrial action in refuse, which had occurred against union advice, little activity or discussion had been provoked on the subject of CCT amongst rank-and-file union members, who had gone along with the actions of the CSG without expressing opposition. Given the historical background of this council's stance on CCT this might seem surprising. However, interviews with employees revealed a general mood of fatalism that was in part political but also related to a feeling of powerlessness associated with a perception of declining union power.

Trade union officials interviewed expressed dismay at their membership's attitude. They argued that they had 'tried to educate their members' about CCT, but were unable to overcome fatalistic attitudes. Anticipated inter-union solidarity over the issue had not materialized as each union had members located in different service areas and dealt with threats of privatization on a service by service basis. A blue / white-collar divide was also evident in the authority. Manual employees refused to discuss competitive tendering with National and Local Government Officers' Association (NALGO) branch members because they were 'the bosses' union' whilst, on the whole, NALGO members saw competitive tendering as a blue-collar rather than a white-collar problem. Employees in services that had been contracted out by the council early in its 'experimental' period seemed confused and expressed a sense of betrayal yet, rather than blame their union or even their local authority, they directly blamed central government. This recognition of the political nature of privatization, however, simply led to acceptance and fatalism rather than calls for resistance.

Case study 2 - 'Consensualism'

Case study 2 provides an interesting contrast to case study 1. This safe Conservative-controlled District Council was the most fervent opposer of CCT. Unlike the previous case, this council lent no ideological support to contracting-out and did not undertake any pre-emptive tendering exercises. CCT was interpreted at all levels within the authority as an attempt by central government to interfere with and erode the autonomy of local government. Organizational attempts to circumvent legislation led to an uncharacteristic alliance between councillors, managers and trade unions more common in Labour authorities.

This case study illustrates that support for CCT is not always clearly defined along party political lines and demonstrates that political variations with regard to policy can occur within a party as a consequence of the interplay of central/local government relations. Hostility towards CCT in this council did not centre around a rejection of the concepts of competition and efficiency. Indeed, the council had a history of pursuing commercial practices, evident in the setting up of its own holding company and business park. Opposition to CCT was political in character and framed within the perception that it would undermine local representative democracy. This, it was believed, would occur in two central ways. First, if services were delivered by private contractors the quality of provision would be affected and control of services would be lost. Second, councillors in particular viewed the council's role as an employer in the locality as highly influential and saw council employment as significant in affecting factors in the local economy. These two issues were seen to be inseparable. Quality services could only be delivered by dedicated, experienced in-house staff and these people lived and worked in the locality and contributed to its economy. The workforce was therefore seen as in need of 'protecting'. One Conservative councillor thus declared: 'I know these attitudes are paternalistic, but I unashamedly voice them.'

Many councillors interviewed were 'insulted' by Government assumptions that all councils were inefficient and rejected this criteria as a justification for implementing CCT. The Government's 'version' of efficiency did not encapsulate quality, but threatened to increase bureaucracy whereby savings in manual wages would be simply cancelled out by increases in white-collar employment required to manage and monitor procedures arising from the tendering and implementation process. [4] One Conservative councillor attempted to redefine a central tenet of CCT, that of 'value for money', arguing that for years local government had carried too many overheads and that CCT added to this problem by increasing what he referred to as white-collar 'pen pushers' whilst reducing the numbers of 'real service providers' - manual employees.

The impact of CCT on manual employment was significant in this council's opposition to legislation. The consequences of tendering were recognized to include labour intensification, casualization and a loss to the council of dedicated staff, which would undermine good employment practices and industrial relations. A leading councillor with many years' negotiating experience at a national level defended Whitleyism as a system of bargaining and expressed the view that 'mutual respect' between employers and unions would be undermined by localized bargaining resulting from CCT. Because of the strong 'paternalistic' attitude of councillors towards their DSO workforce an alliance was formed between councillors, managers and the three most prominent trade unions: NUPE, NALGO and the GMB. This alliance sought to develop a joint strategy aimed at retaining the present DSO workforce.

The authority's initial response to CCT was to commission a management consultancy report into the viability of setting up an 'arm's length' company which would operate under the Companies Act. Managing directors would be drawn from the council itself and the consequent report advised that the council hold a 25 per cent equity in the company and a share option scheme would be instituted for employees. DSO employment, it was suggested, would be transferred to the company, although voluntary redundancy would be available for older staff. No compulsory redundancies were proposed. The most contentious aspect of this plan was the idea that the private company would be guaranteed contracts lasting from three to five years from the Council. This was enough to elicit substantial financial backing from a major bank. It was believed that, by awarding contracts to the private firm just one month before the 1988 Act came into effect, services would not have to be re-tendered.

These plans illustrate how far both councillors and managers went to ensure that the DSO and council services were retained in their control, albeit at arm's length. Their belief, however, that they had circumvented the legislation was thwarted when the Secretary of State intervened and declared their practices 'anti-competitive'. The key problem was the intention that the council retain a 25 per cent equity in the company. A working party was then constituted to investigate alternatives and, through a council circular in February 1988, 'approved in principle the proposals to retain a unified workforce'. This would be achieved through the setting up of a private limited company with which the council would negotiate for all contract work. The council itself would hold no direct stake in the company, although its director would be a member of the existing management team. Ironically, one Conservative councillor described this as 'going down the socialist line to preserve jobs' and was undisturbed by questions of legality or anti-competitive behaviour.

Attitudes of different actors

Councillors, though Conservative, held directly opposing views to their colleagues in central government. By exploring strategies that involved going beyond the confines of the council their central objective was to avoid the restrictions of legislation and retain a workforce intact. Both councillors and senior managers were united in this objective, the eventual outcome of which was that all services remained with the former DSO workforce following the first round of CCT.

Trade unions had a complex and confused role. Initially, suspicions were aroused at what in effect was a proposal for wholesale privatization of the DSO. NUPE in particular were uncomfortable with the plans, which would have removed their members from the public sector. NALGO and the GMB were more willing to embrace the idea, given that at all stages they had been consulted and invited to participate, though they voiced worries about the legality of some proposals and the motives of councillors. One union official spoke of 'the realities versus the ideology of the situation'. By this, he meant that national union policy stressed there should be no involvement with privatization initiatives, yet it also stressed the union's role in fighting to retain jobs and employment conditions. The council's proposals guaranteed the latter and the unions who participated in persuading members to accept them were promised full recognition and bargaining rights.

The degree of trust between two of the consenting unions, councillors and managers was unusual. Full consultation and access to information amongst all parties involved meant that trust overcame an ideological commitment to keeping services within the public sector. Inter-union cooperation in this case study was exceptionally good and the unions were a united bargaining

51

unit. Nonetheless, NUPE, bound by national policy, did not ultimately recommend the proposals to its members. The workforce as a whole were well informed about issues arising from CCT and council proposals. Their support was seen as vital to all parties involved: it was won after a series of detailed mass meetings arranged jointly by senior managers and regional trade union officials.

The conclusion to events was complicated by the council's abandonment of the already constituted private company, reportedly because of direct central government interference. Nonetheless, despite extremely tight timetables for submitting services to CCT, all services remained in-house at the end of the first round of tendering and no compulsory redundancies were incurred amongst permanent staff. To date, this council still provides all its services through its DSO.

Case study 3 - 'Conflict'

The implementation of competitive tendering was highly contested in this case study, which highlights particularly the role of trade unions in challenging change and the political context of CCT generally. This council's first experience of competitive tendering occurred in November 1982 when a cleaning contract was awarded to a private company. Despite eleven job losses, employees affected were un-unionized, thus no visible trade union opposition materialized. Following this, the ruling Conservative group enthusiastically pursued their ideological commitment to market principles, drawing up a list of at least five other services to be submitted to competitive tender. Their intentions were declared in a press release to the local newspaper, which enraged local unions, who read that in a Conservative councillor's opinion: 'the risk to conflict with the work-force is small'.

The local newspaper became a vehicle for a counter-attack launched by four unions: NUPE, NALGO, the Transport and General Workers' Union (TGWU), and the GMB, who also joined forces in establishing a 'Public Services Defence Committee'(PSDC), consisting of full-time regional officials. PSDC formulated campaign strategies opposing privatization and elicited the support of other local trade unions and Labour Party branches. NUPE and the TGWU were the strongest manual unions in terms of membership and organization, and NUPE sent in an experienced campaign manager to coordinate action. This action began with demonstrations, rallies, petitions and press articles aimed at attracting public support.

In reply the council set up a 'Privatization Sub-Committee' composed entirely of Conservative councillors. The Committee aimed to undertake 'efficiency reviews' with the objective of privatizing services. Promises of consultation with unions did not materialize, heightening tensions. Demands by Labour councillors for representation were eventually met, though their status was of mere observers. This led to a bizarre scene of Conservative councillors conducting discussions on one side of the room whilst insisting opposition councillors sat out of earshot at the other end!

Contracting-out became a highly politicized issue, and the unions' skilful use of advertisements in the local press ensured wider public debate. This debate was reflected in the high priority the local Labour Party accorded privatization in the 1983 council elections, the outcome of which cut a comfortable Conservative majority to just one. Trade union members played a supportive role throughout by distributing Labour Party leaflets during bin rounds and pledging their support which, according to one union official, 'rubbed off on the membership, who began to see (privatization) in broader political terms'.

Behind the scenes, however, the union offensive was in crisis. Rank-and-file trade unionists, disappointed that Labour had not won, became apathetic and defeatist. Attempts to mobilize members through an idea to 'work like a contractor for a week', by reducing the workforce and paying those not working strike pay, were rejected through a ballot. On the surface, the failure of unions to gain membership support was a blow, though underlying this was a split between the two key unions, NUPE and the TGWU. Both had officially backed the idea, but secretly the TGWU was urging its members to oppose action because it could not afford strike pay and did not want to be humiliated into accepting money offered by NUPE to fund the venture.

Correspondence between the two main unions during this period revealed both tensions in their relationship and dismay at membership fatalism. A crucial flaw in the PSDC's strategy was an inability to involve members in its work. The campaign run by full-time paid union officials had succeeded in alienating ordinary members. Resentment was also present against the NUPE official who had been brought in from outside the area to coordinate the anti-privatization campaign. To fill an emerging 'credibility gap', the Committee coopted a handful of enthusiastic shop stewards. One union official described events from here on as 'a big bluff that amazingly at the end won'.

The 'bluff' took the form of persuading the council that the unions would call their members out on strike if they were not fully involved in efficiency reviews. Once involved, the unions pursued a strategy of influencing tender specifications in contract documents. They pushed for stringent clauses in all contracts and insisted that council equipment, vehicles and workshops must be used by contractors. They also negotiated pay and conditions to reflect local authority rates. Trade unions were helped throughout by hostile press coverage of the Conservative group.

Union officials working alongside managers who were NALGO members claimed this worked to their advantage. One union official revealed: 'we were allowed to make amendments in specifications being set. The tender documents were altered in the union's favour.' In many respects this was portrayed as a 'victory' for union cooperation, although the unions risked losing through competitive tendering itself.

The eventual outcome of competitive tendering was resolved in favour of the DSO, despite a number of lower bids dismissed as 'unrealistic'. The local newspaper carried a report entitled 'Workers Beat Private Deal', lending support to the unions' 'victory' analysis - though behind the headlines lay fifteen job losses, the true price paid. Later, the unions admitted that newspaper coverage had largely been a propaganda exercise, though it succeeded in persuading the council to abandon further 'experimental' competitive tendering.

Subsequent events have seen a shift in political control from Conservative to Labour, accompanied by a strong attachment to the in-house team. Since the introduction of CCT only one service has been privatized, an event so important that it prompted an internal enquiry to investigate the loss. The Labour Party, with the support of the Conservatives, has attempted to manage change to the benefit of the DSO, and is presently undertaking a thorough reorganization to 'blunt' the impact of white-collar CCT.

Attitudes of different actors

Case study 3 demonstrates the importance of acknowledging social struggle in the process of political and organizational change. The highly political nature of the privatization issue had a direct impact on industrial relations and conflict. Lack of consultation resulted in confrontation with trade unions, who fought an external campaign of 'keeping services public' aimed at eliciting broad-based public support whilst struggling internally against inter-union rivalries, sectionalism, and rank-and-file apathy to maintain the appearance of a united front. Because struggles around privatization were pursued outside the confines of the organization and within the locality, all actors involved were subject to external political pressures.

The 'political contingency' evident here consequently influenced the outcome and future course of events surrounding CCT. Councillors on the ruling Conservative group pursued non-compulsory tendering for ideological reasons. These surpassed any consideration of industrial relations implications or organizational disruption, factors which proved significant in the formation of a unified opposition. The opposition, moreover, had the advantages of an experienced NUPE campaigner, an accessible media, and the support of Labour councillors who identified with trade union concerns. Importantly, however, disputes between unions over tactics dominated the anti-privatization campaign: NUPE strongly believed in the efficacy of industrial action alongside campaigning; NALGO pursued an unsustainable national policy of non-cooperation; whilst the TGWU leant towards some form of negotiation with the council.

The role of managers was somewhat ambiguous in this case. Many managers in principle agreed with the trade union response opposing tendering, though felt unable to support the NALGO stance of non-cooperation. Their role was most important in the specification stage of tendering, where they supported the unions by weighting specifications in the DSO's favour. However, evidence since the 1988 Act's implementation suggests that managers rather than (now) opposition Conservative councillors are the main protagonists in favour of change and CCT, even though such a stance is opposed by the present ruling Labour group. To date, this council still holds to an agreement with the unions of no compulsory redundancies.

Categorizing responses to CCT

The most significant factors to emerge from the case studies are the variable responses of the three local authorities to CCT and the different strategies employed by trade unions to oppose the policy. The fact that all authorities were Conservative-controlled, a possible weakness in such a sample, emerged as a strength. It illustrates ideological differences both between Conservative politicians in central and local government and, significantly, highlights variations in Conservative policy around CCT within local government itself. It also illustrates how variations can occur within one region, the South West. These findings contrast with larger but less detailed analyzes from samples in other parts of the country. For example, Shaw *et al.*, (1994) examined the responses of local authorities in the North of England. They then sought to categorize authorities and their responses to CCT under four headings; 'enthusiastic', 'pragmatic', 'neutral' and 'hostile'. They found that although predictably few authorities displayed 'enthusiasm' for CCT given the dominance of the Labour Party in this region, more surprisingly almost three quarters of their sample's responses 'were located between the 'pragmatic' and 'neutrality' categories' (Shaw *et al.*, 1994, p. 204). However, categorizations can result in over-determinism, because the absence of detailed evidence can serve to over-generalize support for, or opposition towards, a policy within an organization. The qualitative, actor-based approach here enables differentiation between groups and their role in influencing policy implementation. It also avoids making 'crude' universal statements which may only reflect limited opinion. For example, a council labelled as 'enthusiastic' may only be so politically; support for CCT might not be reflected throughout the organization. This distinction between groups in an organization may be crucial if political support is undermined, either directly by trade union opposition, as in the 'Conflict' case, or by more subtle forms of resistance, e.g. sabotage of the tendering process by senior officers, or weighting of contract specifications in favour of the DSO (again a feature of case study 3).

This debate raises the question of how to determine such categories and whether they are in any sense meaningful? Whose opinions within an authority should we seek to measure support for, or opposition to, CCT? The student of organizational behaviour might draw on the work of writers such as Child (1972), and conclude that decision-making in organizations is a complex process which involves the mediation of different interest groups. In the 'Free Marketeers' case, a typical 'enthusiastic' council by Shaw *et al*'s categories, political support for CCT was unequivocal; managerial support was also, although it was mediated by a different set of values and assumptions. Private sector managers did not embrace a political view of CCT, but a commercial one and, although it might be argued that the political view embraced commercial principles, this did not occur conversely. Amongst the workforce 'fear' and 'fatalism' were prevalent and, moreover, 'hostility' at one point emerged in the form of strike action. Was this council therefore uniformly 'enthusiastic' and, if so, was this founded upon a political agenda? The 'Conflict' council illustrates this point further. Competitive tendering became a highly contested issue and 'enthusiasm' amongst councillors was reflected neither among officers nor trade unions; instead, hostility manifested itself in outright opposition and sustained campaigning by trade unions and their members. In this case study, struggles precipitated by competitive tendering were ideological in terms of public versus private provision; political, both in respect of party politics and visions of public provision and employment; and sectional, in respect of differences arising between the interests of various groups, principally trade unions.

The 'Consensual' case study exemplifies a rebellious Conservative District Council, which broader evidence suggested was not wholly alone in its hostile and paternalistic response. This council saw CCT as a political attack on local government, particularly its role in the democratic provision of services and as a significant local employer. This case was interesting for the degree of unanimity between key groups in the organization and a high degree of trust. Moreover, interviews with Conservative councillors revealed a determined opposition to CCT, constructed around arguments mirroring trade union objections in anti-privatization campaigning literature. However, even within this 'consensual' model it is apparent that different interest groups pursued their opposition to CCT for different reasons. The politicians wanted to retain control over public service decision-making in the local community and therefore fought against possibilities of increased centralism and assaults on local government autonomy; managers had some interests tied into the proposed new 'arm's length' company as well as holding some identification with their union, NALGO; the unions generally wanted to protect jobs and services. Two features of this council which might go some way towards explaining its political stance were, first, a strong belief in local representative democracy and, second, a majority of traditionalist Conservative councillors hostile to Thatcherite values.

The picture that emerges, therefore, is characterized by diversity: significant, because all three councils were Conservative-controlled.

Interestingly, trade union responses were not uniform, but also shaped by local contextual events and did not necessarily conform with broader union policy. In the case of trade unions their need to respond to local circumstances may become more important, for underlying government policies of 'marketization' are industrial relations objectives which seek to deregulate the labour market and promote localized bargaining.[5] Above all, these factors serve to emphasize the need to consider locality and avoid broad-based categorizations. Moreover, it is also argued that an examination of the impact of CCT on organizational culture is appropriate, for it is at the level of organizational analysis that useful insights into reasons why a single policy can create numerous reactions can be gained.

Organizational culture

The remainder of this chapter addresses some broader issues of sociological significance relating to the way in which CCT as a policy has influenced the organizational culture of local authorities. Already it has been shown that CCT has had a variable impact on relationships between key groups in three local authorities. It is further argued that this will be applicable to all authorities, given that variables of a political, geographical and organizational nature will apply between authorities across the country. However, despite such evidence, analyzes of changes in organizational culture within the public sector and local government too often create the impression that a new 'enterprise culture' is emerging which has identifiable characteristics and is applicable across the public sector. The work of Painter (1992) is exceptional in its rejection of such a view, for he questions the very use of the word 'culture' and ways in which it is unproblematically employed, most notably in business management literature (see Peters and Waterman, 1982), to present a view of homogenous, unitary organizations in both public and private sectors. He goes on to develop a way of analysing the 'cultural aspects' of an organization or local authority by examining the behaviour of groups and individuals within the organization and their specific responses to change. In this sense, Painter (1992, p. 60) argues, culture is 'an activity or process... constituted and reconstituted through the practices of groups and individuals', and therefore necessarily differs from one organization to another'.

58

Changes in material practices, such as the introduction of competition through CCT and institutional procedures accompanying that policy, bring about changes in the 'discursive practices' of groups within the organization (Painter, 1992). New organizational values and cultures may emerge as a consequence of change, as illustrated to some extent by other studies on the impact of CCT on local government (Shaw *et al.*, 1994; Walsh and Davis, 1993). However, it should be recognized that change may be uneven between and within organizations, since attempts to displace old value systems and methods may be defended by some groups or individuals (Colling, 1993). Trades unions have been at the forefront of defending established value systems, although analyzes of their attempts to do so (Foster and Taylor, 1994) suggest that problems arise when the neo-liberal project they seek to attack is sustained by their very lack of alternative visions of 'public service'. Trade unions, whilst contesting the discourses constructed around CCT, have done so through a defensive strategy of largely arguing for the preservation of a system that neo-liberal policies have sought to discredit. Their most successful strategy has been to appeal to a notion of 'public service' largely Fabian in origin (although this itself requires re-definition or refinement as a credible alternative) and to build alliances where possible with other groups contesting change.

It is significant that CCT as a policy was largely imposed on local government, for immediately the potential for resistance and struggle was created. Research prior to the implementation of the 1988 Local Government Act (Ascher, 1987; Foster, 1991; Institute of Personnel Management/Incomes Data Services Public Sector Unit, 1986) demonstrates strong opposition from councillors to CCT among both Labour and Conservative authorities. Where 'experimental' tendering occurred prior to legislation, in case study 1 for example, organizational opposition was often resolved before compulsion and legislation merely reinforced change. However, in most other authorities CCT *forced* changes in organizational structure and accompanying culture. In many authorities new roles, such as the establishment of DSO managers, and the separation of 'client' and 'contractor' roles, meant new cultures incorporating competitive and commercial values. However, the extent to which these new values were adopted voluntarily or out of necessity is significant, since the adoption of roles and values instrumentally does not necessarily preclude the existence of countervailing values that may re-emerge in a more favourable political climate.

To understand the further impact of CCT on organizational culture it must be put into a political context. CCT represented central government intervention into local government, which was largely interpreted as part of an on-going strategy to curb the power and spending of councils. In addition, the policy contained industrial relations objectives aimed at curbing the power of public sector trade unions and deregulating the labour market; this in itself was also viewed as political from both a trade union and local government perspective. At an organizational level CCT introduced commercial values which sought to override the traditional public service 'ethos', precipitating a variety of responses, most notably management reorganization and the introduction of new modes of control into the labour process through the separation of service provision and delivery. The widespread use of contract specifications is one example of how work tasks have become more defined and formalized in an attempt to reassert control, although how comfortably such 'neo-Taylorist' (Pollitt, 1993) measures rest with post-Taylorist emphases on consumerism and quality is questionable. Paradoxically, trade unions have often supported the stringent specification of working methods and standards as a tactic to discourage private contractors from competing. This strategy could however be counter-productive because the tacit skills possessed by DSOs in terms of knowledge and experience are real advantages when competing for a contract and contesting control mechanisms.

These material practices of control alongside the compulsory practice of competition impact on the behaviour of actors in local authorities. Nonetheless, the extent to which practices are carried out by staff who only hold a symbolic commitment to competition of which they are highly cynical may mediate between policy and outcome. Du Gay and Salaman (1992, p. 630) assert: 'it is useful to note that in order for an ideology / discourse to be considered hegemonic it is not necessary for it to be loved'. To some extent this is true, though the way in which an ideology is applied and the consequent outcomes may be mediated by those who seek to undermine it: in short, the role of social struggle requires some acknowledgement. Case studies 2 and 3 show resistance to policy through opposition and hostility, which has consequently led to the contracting-out of only one service, an event worthy of an internal enquiry. It is therefore argued that the way in which a dominant discourse or ideology is mediated by the agency/organization involved is significant in determining the outcome of CCT. As Colling (1993, p. 15) concludes from an analysis of managing CCT in two contrasting councils, 'tendering should be viewed as a dynamic process and local authorities as active agents within it'.

Du Gay and Salaman (1992, p. 616) refer to a 're-imagination of the organization' which, within the public sector market, has often entailed the elevation of market principles above all other considerations. In local government resistance has often meant that 're-imagined' organizations have not always conformed to the idealized model envisaged by central government. The role of bureaucracy is still important in providing mechanisms for the equal and impartial distribution of services to the 'customer' because ultimately the market does not respect democracy and citizenship. Similarly, the reversal of a trend which once saw 'good practice' as emanating from the public sector, but now elevates aspects of private sector practice (see Farnham and Horton, 1992) for dealing with employment policy, has had some influence. However, municipal support for 'fair employment' policies remains, becuase of authorities' role in the local economy. At the level of consumption of services it might be argued that, however much 'best practice' appears to follow market principles (Farnham and Horton, 1992, p. 54), the very market served is often monopolistic, captive and, in the case of local authorities, the provider is largely self-regulatory and must consider factors outside the market, namely politics; therefore, the 're-imagined' organization is to some extent illusory.

What must be remembered in any organizational analysis of local government is that it operates within a political environment. Attempts to make direct comparisons with the private sector often obscure this. With regard to CCT, it was political legislation and subsequent regulatory and bureaucratic mechanisms that ensured the sustainability of markets, which on a voluntary basis were unpopular. The discourse of enterprise in local government in this context is, therefore, more a product of *force* than appeal. Originating from an ideological commitment to subject hitherto sheltered sections of the public sector to the market, it also assumed that the private sector would be willing to compete. This has occurred, although it has been patchy in places and profits have been marginalized as multi-national firms have pushed out smaller competitors. Furthermore, the private sector itself will only participate in new markets created by CCT while they are profitable; their labour-intensive nature may create limits on that profitability. Threats to this market have also come from trade union action, which is currently contesting CCT through legal recourse in the European courts. Debate around the Transfer of Undertakings (TUPE) legislation may adversely affect private contractors, as it protects the jobs, pay and conditions of DSO staff transferred into the private sector.[6]

The discourse of enterprise is thus sustained by (imposed) material practices whilst the discursive practices of certain groups, including councillors, some managers, and - most obviously - trade unions seek to undermine its dominance. These are rivals to the discourse of enterprise and obstacles to a new 'cultural cohesion'. The degree to which opposition groups represent a threat to the discourse of enterprise within the public sector may, however, hinge on their ability to offer a sustainable alternative vision of 'public service' itself. Unions have begun to recognize the poor image of public services prior to CCT and the new need to address consumption interests (Foster, 1991). Gyford (1987, p. 152) argues that 'the final battle for the future of local government will be fought out between the decentralizers and the privatizers', Labour left authorities in this context representing the decentralizers. Yet the 'enabling' emphasis still present in this vision of local government (see Stoker, 1988; Stewart, 1989) continues to threaten the employment interests of union members. Moreover, where decentralization has occurred in Labour authorities there is evidence of union resistance (see Heery's (1988) study of the London Borough of Islington and the GLC). Thus, whilst social struggle and contestation continues in local government, often covertly, the seriousness of its threat must be measured against the ability of opposing groups to present a coherent, unified alternative. Such an alternative may have to incorporate consumer and producer interests, together with employment concerns and a clear vision of what local government should be providing in the community. Whether an alternative which succeeds in addressing all vested interests is possible is one problem; another related concern, however, is the need to establish a clear concept of what 'public service' actually is.

Alternative visions of public service in local government cannot be divorced from debate about the role of the local state and, in particular, its need to be empowered to act in the local community. However, whilst continued attachments to the welfare state and notions of public service that embrace principles of equality over commercialism persist, these need to be effectively developed. Public services are essentially political in character, arising from the distinct relationship between service providers and users. Unlike the private sector, so-called 'customers' derive their entitlement for services from citizenship and therefore values of equality necessarily play a more central role. A profound ambiguity arises between the values of public service and private sector practices. These ambiguities may be the contested space between traditional and neo-liberal visions of public service that create confusion. In a recent review of literature on 'New Public Management', Prior (1993, p. 458) concludes that problems relating to analyzes of parts of the public sector 'are a reflection of the fact that the concept of the public sector has itself become confused', though he contends that local government management is distinctive: 'local government retains an independence of purpose which, given sufficient will, can provide the basis for a genuine reconstruction of the ideal of public service' (Prior 1993, p. 459). It may be further argued that the distinctiveness of local government as a provider of public services lies in its proximity to democratic and accountable procedures. Whilst policies of privatization and marketization in other parts of the public sector have largely increased the distance between the providers and users of these services, in the context of local government a direct political relationship still exists between a local authority and its electorate. In this sense the political character of public services is more obvious and, for this reason, a reconstitution of the ideal of public service which incorporates more traditional values of welfarism may be possible. Resistance within local authorities to policies of marketization and tensions in relationships between local and central government around issues of autonomy, ideology and politics may continue to mediate the policy outcomes of CCT and the future character of local services.

Notes

1. The introduction of CCT into local government was initially perceived as a 'New Right' initiative and support or opposition for the policy was often portrayed in terms of party political differences. However, as the case studies here show, and further evidence (e.g. Shaw *et al.*, 1994) demonstrates, party politics is not always a reliable indicator in assessing reaction to the policy in local government. The interplay of central / local government relations is also significant.

2.   The six services were: building cleaning; refuse collection; other cleaning (street cleansing); catering (school, welfare and civic); grounds maintenance; vehicle maintenance. Sports and leisure management was added with effect from January 1991.

3.   Much of the fieldwork is drawn from research into the introduction of CCT into local government, charting events between 1985 and the implementation of the 1988 Local Government Act. Research following policy implementation was continued in depth until 1991, but contacts were sustained with key case study respondents in years following.

4.   See discussion in Escott and Whitfield (1995, p. 9), which cites studies showing that CCT savings have been exaggerated in practice, as the Department of the Environment (1994) now accepts.

5.   Evidence of the extent to which this is happening in local government is patchy. Whilst a number of councils have withdrawn from national bargaining arrangements, this has ironically often been for the purpose of improving white-collar staffs' wages and conditions. Nonetheless, as DSOs attempt to undercut local contractors, national bargaining is threatened. See also the NHS.

6.   Much unresolved confusion surrounds the application of TUPE. For a useful discussion, however, see Escott and Whitfield (1995).

References

Ascher, K. (1987), *The Politics of Privatization: Contracting Out Public Services*, Macmillan, London.

Atkinson, J. (1985), 'Flexibility: Planning for an Uncertain Future', *The IMS Review*, vol. 1, Summer.

Child, J. (1972), 'Organizational Structure, Environment and Performance: the Role of Strategic Choice', *Sociology*, vol. 6, no. 1, pp. 1-22.

Colling, T. (1993), 'Contracting Public Services: The Management of Compulsory Competitive Tendering in two County Councils', *Human Resource Management Journal*, vol. 3, no. 4, pp. 1-15.

Department of the Environment (1994), *CCT and Local Government in*

England: Annual Report for 1993, Department of the Environment, London.

Du Gay, S. and Salaman, G. (1992), 'The Cult(ure) of the Customer', *Journal of Management Studies*, vol. 29, no. 5, pp. 615-633.

Escott, K. and Whitfield, D. (1995), *The Gender Impact of CCT in Local Government*, Discussion Series, Equal Opportunities Commission, Manchester.

Evans, S. (1990), 'Ensuring Efficient Services', in Adam Smith Institute (ed.), *The Tender Traps*, ASI, London, pp. 17-24.

Farnham, D. and Horton, S. (1992), 'Human Resources Management in the New Public Sector: Leading or Following Private Sector Practice?' *Public Policy and Administration*, vol. 7, no. 3, Winter, pp. 42-55.

Foster, D. (1991), 'Privatization Policy in Local Government: The response of Public Sector Trade Unions', unpublished PhD thesis, University of Bath.

Foster, D. (1993), 'Industrial Relations in Local Government: The Impact of Privatization', *Political Quarterly*, vol. 64, no. 1, pp. 49-59.

Foster, D. and Taylor, G. (1994), 'Re-inventing the Weal: Privatization and the Crisis of Public Service Trade Unionism', paper presented at the Employment Research Unit Annual Conference, *The Contract State?* Cardiff Business School, 27-28 September.

Gyford, J. (1987), 'Decentralisation within Authorities', in Parkinson, M. (ed.), *Reshaping Local Government*, Policy Journals, Oxford.

Heery, E. (1988), 'A Common Labour Movement? Left Labour Councils and the Trade Unions', in Hoggett, P. and Hambleton, R. (eds), *Decentralisation and Democracy: Localising Public Services*, Occasional Paper no. 28, School of Advanced Urban Studies, University of Bristol, Bristol, pp. 194-214.

Institute of Personnel Management / Incomes Data Services Public Sector Unit (1986), *Competitive Tendering in the Public Sector*, Incomes Data Services, London.

Painter, J. (1991), 'The Culture of Competition', *Public Policy and Administration*, vol. 7, no. 1, Spring, pp. 58-68.

Painter, J. (1992), 'The Geography of Trade Union Responses to Local Government Privatization', *Transactions of the Institute of British Geographers*, New Series, vol. 16, no. 2, pp. 214-226.

Peters, T. and Waterman, R. (1982), *In Search of Excellence*, Harper and Row, New York.

Pollitt, C. (1993), *Managerialism and the Public Services*, second edition, Blackwell, Oxford.

Prior, D. (1993), 'In Search of the New Public Management', Review Article, *Local Government Studies*, vol. 19, no. 3, pp. 447-460.

Shaw, K., Fenwick, J. and Foreman, A. (1994), 'Compulsory Competitive Tendering for Local Government Services: The Experiences of Local Authorities in the North of England 1988-1992', *Public Administration*, vol. 72, no. 2, Summer, pp. 201-217.

Stewart, J. (1989), 'A Future for Local Authorities as Community Government', in Stewart, J. and Stoker, G. (eds), *The Future of Local Government*, Macmillan, Basingstoke, pp. 236-254.

Stoker, G. (1988), *The Politics of Local Government*, Macmillan, London.

Thatcher, M. (1994), 'Has the Government finally been Defeated over TUPE?', *Personnel Management*, vol. 26, no. 7, July.

Walsh, K. and Davis, H. (1993), *Competition and Service: The Impact of the Local Government Act 1988*, HMSO, London.

4 Health Promotion, Quasi-Markets and the NHS

YUSUF AHMED

Introduction

Two separate but not mutually exclusive strategies appear to structure contemporary health policy in Britain. First, and the one that has received the most public attention, is the attempt to reorganize the National Health Service (NHS) along 'quasi-market' lines in an effort to ostensibly improve the efficiency/effectiveness of health-care delivery. This is contained in the 1990 NHS and Community Care Act. The second strategy is one which advocates the introduction of policies and programmes which, in stressing health promotion and disease prevention, aim to make people less dependent on the health services. This is most clearly articulated in the White Paper *The Health of the Nation* (Dept. of Health 1992). It has been the government's contention that the health promotion objectives contained in the White Paper can be best delivered as a consequence of reforms contained in the 1990 Act. The purpose of this chapter is to discuss how and the extent to which the market reforms in the NHS are likely to deliver health policy objectives of the kind contained in *The Health of the Nation*.

The chapter begins with a brief historical overview of the relationship between health policy based on public health interventions and health policy based on medical interventions. The section examines some of the reasons why health promotion and disease-prevention issues have resurfaced on the health policy agenda, which in the first quarter of a century after the second world war was dominated by concerns arising out

67

of a medical model of health. The next section looks at how these concerns manifest themselves in *The Health of the Nation*. This is followed by looking at the background to and the implications of the changes introduced by the 1990 NHS and Community Care Act. Finally, the third section is concerned with exploring the relationship between market reforms and the achievement of health promotion objectives.

The chapter illustrates the complex nature of the contemporary health policy process. It shows that there are a multiplicity of interest groups vying with different degrees of success to insert their agenda into the policy process. It analyzes the trends emerging in health policy that stem both from cost-containment and ideological pressures as well as from an increased scepticism of the efficacy of medical services in ensuring good health. The chapter also explores the tension between policy intentions as articulated in legislation, White Papers and other official documents and the outcomes that emerge in the process of implementation.

Health promotion, disease prevention and the NHS

It is now a part of conventional wisdom that the eradication of a variety of infectious diseases that were common in nineteenth century Britain was a consequence of factors other than medical intervention. Various writers (e.g. McKeown, 1976) have demonstrated that the improvements in health at the end of the nineteenth century and the beginning of this one were a consequence of public health measures (improvements in nutrition, sanitation, housing). Ashton and Seymour (1994) argue that it was the public health movement led by health professionals and backed by legislation such as the National Public Health Acts of 1848 and 1875 which resulted in these environmental improvements. Thus in Victorian times the emphasis was very much on a public health approach to health policy with a focus on tackling health issues through collective interventions at the community level. Underlying this was a recognition that health was a 'public good'.

The beginning of the twentieth century witnessed a move away from public health to the provision of health care, particularly hospital services. With the development of the germ theory of disease and the potential offered by immunization and vaccination there was also a shift of emphasis onto a more individualistic approach. This period is also marked by an increasing involvement by the state in the provision of medical services. Nevertheless there is research evidence (Winter, 1982) which suggests improvements in health, particularly the falling rate of infant and maternal mortality, cannot be attributed to levels of medical intervention. The overall emphasis on prevention is superseded completely in the 1930s by what is termed as the 'therapeutic era' and associated with the discovery of insulin and the sulphonamide group of drugs. The impact of this was to shift health priorities away from preventive strategies to cure-based ones. Organizationally this marked the weakening of departments of public health and a shift of power and resources to hospital-based services. Professionally it marked the consolidation of the power of the medical profession in all matters related to health.

By the end of the second world war there was immense public support for a comprehensive and free health service. However, stiff resistance from the medical profession to the idea of a state-provided universal health service existed. Aneurin Bevan, the Minister of Health in the first post-war Labour government, charged with the task of setting up the NHS, was forced in the face of this opposition to arrive at a compromise. Doctors would provide a health service free at the point of delivery and funded by central government and in return the medical profession was granted both clinical autonomy and a high degree of representation in the administration of the new structure. As a result the medical profession achieved the ability to veto policy change by defining the limits of the acceptable and by determining the policy agenda (Day and Klein, 1992, p. 468). Thus, post-war health policy was dominated by concerns to do with the NHS, which in turn was dominated by the interests of the medical profession. A major consequence of the adoption of a 'medical model of health' has been that the NHS has been more concerned with curing diseases than with preventing them and promoting health. This has meant that the NHS has historically operated on the basis of the assumption that high standards of health depend on high standards of medical care. Medicine had become synonymous with health.

National health policy became centrally concerned with the development of medical services. This was notwithstanding the fact that both the 1942 Beveridge Report and the 1944 White Paper, *A National Health Service*, explicitly acknowledged the need for a strategy which encompassed both preventive and cure-based approaches as well as recognizing the wider social and political dimensions to health. The Ministry of Health lost many of its public health responsibilities, including housing and water, to local government. The status of public health professionals too became subordinated to hospital-based medical doctors. The consequence of these developments was that, in Klein's (1980) words, 'Britain had a health service but no policy for health' (cited in Baggot, 1995, p. 239).

In the decades since the inception of the NHS there has been an increasing scepticism amongst policy makers and professionals, both nationally and internationally, about the effectiveness of health-care systems built on the medical model of 'after the event cure' in dealing with the health problems of contemporary societies. Continuing problems include increasing levels of chronic illness, growth in infectious diseases and degenerative diseases such as heart disease and cancer, and health problems arising out of pollution, deprivation and increasing levels of stress. There has also been a recognition that much ill-health is preventable, and that in the interests of both efficiency and effectiveness what was required was an overall long-term strategy to promote health gain. Preventive health care, it is now acknowledged, has less to do with medical practice than with measures aimed at what constitutes health risks in a modern society. These include diet, working conditions, lifestyle and behaviour; in general, the social and physical environment. But this recognition of the social and environmental routes of much ill-health required that health be defined in a much wider sense than simply signifying the absence of disease.

This move to redefine health was accompanied by a growing body of sociological work which was increasingly critical of health-care delivery, particularly the power of the medical profession. There was also a greater articulation of lay concerns around this and more generally patient/consumer rights.

Many commentators (cf. Stacey, 1991; Scott-Samuel, 1992) point to the 1978 WHO (World Health Organization) declaration in Alma Ata, which called for policies to reorientate health services towards prevention and primary care strategies rather than concentrating on disease treatment and high-tech medicine, as being a turning point in discussions on the organization of health care. The WHO declaration defined health as:

> a state of complete physical, mental and social wellbeing and not merely the absence of disease or infirmity. The enjoyment of the highest attainable standard of health is one of the fundamental

human rights of every human being without distinction of race, religion, political belief, economic or social condition. (WHO 1978, p. 2)

At the same conference, the WHO (of which Britain is a member) laid out the basis for a strategy of health promotion by both identifying the prerequisites for such a strategy as well as establishing key principles. The prerequisites were identified as being conditions where the basic needs of populations were being met, that there be an absence of war, and that there be the political will to carry out such a strategy. The key principles underlying the strategy were:

* building public policy on health: action at a national level to enable people to lead healthy lives through the creation of a positive social, economic and physical environment, and to ensure that health considerations inform all spheres and levels of government policy;
* provision of a supportive, healthy environment: protection of the environment through state intervention at a national and international level;
* development of personal skills;
* strengthening community action;
* influencing priorities within the health service: to act in ways that will alter the balance of services from curative to primary health care, that will achieve equality of access to health services and develop services to meet the varied needs of communities.

While the WHO and other bodies have drawn attention to the social and environmental roots of much ill-health, perhaps the key element in the renewed emphasis on health promotion and disease prevention (i.e. on public health within health policy) has to do with the perception that in the long run there is an immense potential for the reduction of health service costs (Research Unit in Health and Behavioral Change, 1989). The economic recession in the mid 1970s coincided with the publication by the Labour government of a consultative document, 'Prevention and Health: Everybody's Business'. This was followed in 1977 by a White Paper (DHSS, 1977) and the setting up of the Health Education Council, now transformed into the Health Education Authority (HEA), a quango which until the early 1980s focused on changing individual behaviour through publicity campaigns in the media. The period also saw the development of pressure groups, such as ASH (Action on Smoking and Health), who were involved in public campaigning, lobbying Parliament and providing education. In terms of all the different national and international developments there was a recognition of the importance of incorporating health promotion issues into national economic planning processes and of the centrality of political will to implement such a strategy.

However, in the UK the implementation of a health promotion strategy was piecemeal and there was an evident lack of political enthusiasm. The issue was treated as an international matter of little relevance to domestic policy (Scott-Samuel, 1992). This can be explained in terms of the unwillingness of both Labour and Conservative governments to take on board the issues of social inequality and deprivation that were central to the strategy. Also, such a strategy would involve a shift in priorities and resources away from purely medical services and the medical establishment as reluctant to engage with it.

The publication in 1980 of the DHSS report, *'Inequalities in Health: Report of a Research Working Group'* (more commonly known as the Black Report), further underlined and emphasized the social determinants of health. However, this government-commissioned report (albeit by the outgoing Labour government) was also by and large ignored, though aspects of health promotion, particularly those elements that stressed individuals taking responsibility for their own health, were accepted by all the major political parties. The following statement by an under-secretary of Health in the incoming Conservative Government in 1979 illustrates how the 'health for all' message was seamlessly incorporated with ideological individualism:

> This government is committed to the goal of better health for everyone. We believe that in a free society this can only be achieved by the informed exercise of personal responsibility. (Finsburg, 1982, p. 8, quoted in U205 Course Team 1985).

While this approach has been described as 'victim blaming' and seen as an attempt by the government to distract attention from the real causes of health problems (Graham, 1983; St. George, 1981) it nevertheless ensured that health education was placed on the health policy agenda. The combination of a greater understanding of the nature of contemporary health problems, cost considerations, pressure groups, international developments, research evidence and the gradual acceptance that medical interventions were not necessarily the most effective strategy led to the publication of the *The Health of the Nation* in 1992.

The health of the nation

The Health of the Nation (Dept. of Health, 1992) was published as a government White Paper in 1992, based on a green paper (Dept. of Health, 1991) of the same title published the previous year. It was generally welcomed, being described by some commentators as the most significant policy development in influencing the health of the population since the inception of the NHS in 1948 (South East Institute of Public Health, 1991, p. 2). However, it was also seen as a politically astute diversion from increasing public dissatisfaction with hospital services (Ben-Shlomo, 1992, p. 7). This comment has to be understood in the context of the market-based reforms introduced in the NHS with the passing of the 1990 NHS and Community Care Act (see below). Essentially the latter represented the most wide-ranging set of organizational reforms, which is arguably having the impact of changing the very essence of the NHS.

The Health of the Nation (Dept. of Health 1992) sets out a strategy for health in England. It does so by selecting five 'Key Areas' for action and sets national objectives and targets in these key areas. It indicates some initiatives through which the strategy is to be implemented as well as setting a framework for monitoring and reviewing it. The document:

> emphasizes disease prevention and health promotion as ways in which even greater improvements in health can be secured, while acknowledging that further improvement of treatment, care and rehabilitation remain essential. (Dept. of Health, 1992, p. 4).

The 'Key Areas' selected are:

*   coronary heart disease and stroke
*   cancers
*   mental illness

73

*   HIV/AIDS and sexual health
*   accidents

Virginia Bottomley, the then Secretary of State for Health, in her introduction to the White Paper makes the point that the strategy is dependent not only on the NHS, but also on other branches of government, as well as on individuals and families. Nevertheless, it posits that the role of the NHS as the main provider of health-care is vital to the success of the strategy. In fact, critics of the strategy have made the point that, in spite of statements to the contrary:

> The strategy is highly limited by a Health Service perspective... major thinking about implementation is solely applied to the NHS (Rayner, 1992, p. 3).

In other words a strategy for health is confused with a strategy for the health service.

That the nature of health policy has shifted towards (in essence if not in detail) a greater emphasis on health promotion with the publication of *The Health of the Nation*, is a view shared across most commentators. However, the sincerity of the government's intentions is called to question over both the omissions in the document as well as other policy measures it is also implementing. The document has most seriously been criticized for failing to sufficiently take account of the WHO strategy mentioned above. In particular it overlooks key social, economic and environmental issues which underlie the achievement of good health. There is, it is argued, little real commitment to increasing community participation, in spite of statements in the document that talk about involving people at all strategic and operational levels. Other criticisms of the document are that it continues to make 'curative and medical intervention its main focus at the expense of genuinely preventive and health promoting measures' (HVA, 1991, p. 1). Coupled with this, the document continues to be more concerned with early identification and treatment of ill-health rather than with prevention. However, the shortcomings of this document notwithstanding, it represents an important shift in the direction of health policy away from a cure-based strategy to one which is much more prevention based.

A major claim within the White Paper is that the reforms of the NHS make the strategic approach to health promotion possible:

> The government's reforms of the NHS mean that health authorities can now respond strategically to the health needs of the populations they serve. Above all, they have improved systems of accountability and introduced the concepts of targets so that each part of the NHS can be actively managed, monitored and improved.... Increasingly, NHS authorities' performance will be measured against the efficient use of resources, and working with others, to achieve improvements in the health of local people (Dept. of Health, 1992, pp. 33-34).

Indeed, this message was reinforced in recent advice issued jointly by the Department of Health (DH) and the Department of the Environment (DoE):

> the prime responsibility of the NHS is to maintain and improve the health of the population; the public health function underpins all NHS purchaser and provider activity...Proper discharge of the public health function requires an assessment of the state of health, and the health needs, of any given population to inform decision making on aims and priorities so as to achieve appropriate and effective services leading to improved health and value for money (DH/DOE, 1994, pp. 1-2).

Whitehead (1994) identifies three aspects to the strategy outlined in the White Paper:

* assessment of health of the population and the needs they have in relation to improving their health,
* assessment of the effectiveness of different policy measures and associated service for meeting those needs,
* devising ways of allocating resources efficiently to meet identified needs.

The government expects the Regional Health Authorities (RHAs) in conjunction with the District Health Authorities (DHAs) to play a vital role, particularly in the development of multi-agency approaches to the priorities set out in the White Paper. Specifically, the role envisaged for RHAs is to develop and agree local health targets with purchasers (i.e DHAs and Family Health Service Authorities (FHSAs)) and to ensure that these purchasing organizations build target specifications into their purchasing plans. These are then a part of the contractual relationship with provider organizations. It is assumed that the targets will then be delivered by the providing bodies. At this level the White Paper does not spell out in any detail how this will be monitored, other than to say that Community Health Councils will have the opportunity to monitor performance against set targets, nor does it detail how success will be measured, or what penalties will be incurred if targets are not met.

The success of the strategy is clearly linked to the 'market' reforms introduced by the 1990 NHS and Community Care Act and, in particular, the separation of the 'purchasing' function from the 'providing' function and the set of contractual arrangements that link the two.

The NHS and quasi-markets

The next section examines aspects of the reforms as well as exploring the policy context within which the reforms were set. We examine the context and implications of the introduction of market-based reforms in the NHS. The 1990 NHS and Community Care Act has been described as representing the most radical change in the delivery and organization of health care since the 1948 NHS Act resulted in the setting up of the NHS (Robinson, 1994, p. 2). Here we are centrally concerned with that part of the Act that relates to the creation of a competitive market within the NHS, and between the NHS and the private sector. The strategy contained in the Act is based upon a 1989 White Paper, *Working for Patients* (Secretary of State, 1989). This has been described as being:

> a compromise solution in which a variety of market-oriented initiatives (were) superimposed upon the existing top-down administrative structure (Butler, 1992).

The sense in which the reforms have introduced markets, in any conventionally understood use of the word, is a matter of intense debate. One side argues that NHS internal markets are a complete sham and are in fact achieving the opposite of what the reforms were meant of achieve. The other side, while concurring that the reforms are a failure, argues that this is precisely because market values and mechanisms have been introduced inappropriately into an enterprise which by its very nature is not amenable to being delivered by the market.

The context of the reforms

There are various factors which can be seen as influential in underpinning the reforms. While the underlying rationale behind these can be explained to a certain extent by the emergence and dominance of the 'New Right' in British politics, many commentators point to the fact that health services in most developed countries have come under critical scrutiny. The rising cost of health services at a time when governments have been under severe fiscal pressure, along with a perception that health care systems were both ineffective and inefficient has led to a call for the re-evaluation of health-care systems.

The pressure on costs and performance can be seen as arising out of a number of factors. First, many writers point to the potentially unlimited nature of the demand for health care. Demographic changes, particularly the increase of the ageing population and the decline in the proportion of the population of working age, both increase the demand for health care and at the same time restrict the resources available through taxation to meet demand (Robinson and Judge, 1987; Ham, 1992).

Demand for health care is also connected with advances in medical science and technology. These have amplified public expectations of health-care services, as well as strengthening the demographic pressure as it increases longevity and therefore the pressure on a higher proportion of resources now generally acknowledged as being associated with an ageing population. The technology itself has tended to be expensive, thus further adding to the cost of health care (Davis, 1990).

It is now generally accepted that the distribution of health and illness are unevenly spread across the population (Blackburn, 1991; Blaxter, 1990). Social class and particularly the condition of poverty has a major effect on the level of mortality and morbidity, leading to higher levels of need in lower social classes. The extent to which social inequality has increased over the last decade and a half would also put an upward pressure on demand for health-care.

Some commentators (Manning, 1994) also point to the historic ability of health professionals, particularly consultants, to make clinical decisions without reference to costs as another factor in the rise of demand for health-care resources. This lack of financial accountability was also seen as a key factor in the perceived inefficiency of the system. The labour intensive nature of the system and the accompanying above inflation wage costs also play a significant part in the high-cost pressure in the system.

This concern with cost has to be viewed in tandem with the political and ideological agenda of the incoming Conservative government in 1979. It is now commonly agreed amongst most social policy commentators that the election of Mrs. Thatcher marked a period of radical restructuring of the ideology, values, organization and practices of the welfare state. Key aspects of the government's strategy included an overtly anti-welfare rhetoric, along with the objective of cutting public expenditure. This was underpinned by a determination to reduce the role of the state, based on the belief that individuals are the best judges of their own welfare and should be allowed the maximum possible choice, and that centrally planned, state provided services were of necessity inefficient and bureaucratic. With respect to welfare, it was felt that services were organized around the needs and interests of welfare professionals rather than those of the users of services. Thus, these changes, which were justified on the basis of efficiency and effectiveness, placed a great deal of rhetorical emphasis on the satisfaction of consumer/user needs. A key element in how these were to be effectively met was to break the professional monopoly that welfare occupations ostensibly have had.

The Government placed a great deal of reliance on the introduction of market forces to rectify what was seen as wrong with the British welfare state. The state's role was ideally perceived as minimalist. State intervention was seen as having undermined a natural moral order which was based on both individual responsibility and individual choice. Also the state as a provider and distributor of services was technically inadequate in that it could never possess the intelligence to coordinate supply and demand. Furthermore, state providers are inevitably concerned with the achievement of their own vested interests to the detriment of users of services.

Markets, it was believed, were better at ensuring a more efficient production and distribution of goods and services. It was agreed that the invisible hand of the market, the price system, can be relied upon to reflect changes in demand, technology and resources faster and more effectively than the state ever could. The market argument with respect to the NHS can be found in this critique of the service by Arthur Seldon, a leading theorist of the New Right:

> The NHS has done the health of the people a 'dis-service' because it has prevented the development of more spontaneous, organic, local, voluntary and sensitive medical services that would have grown up as incomes rose and medical science and technology advanced. If it were not for the *politically* controlled NHS we should have seen new forms of medical organization and financing that better reflected *consumer* preferences, requirements and circumstances (Seldon, 1980, p. 5).

In response to the problem of the emergence of producer monopolies in the delivery of health care (in particular the ability of the medical profession to limit access to the profession and to use their power to maximize incomes) the purist market answer is one which would create an open market for medical services through the abolition of medical licensure. Thus Friedman (1962, p. 158) argues that anyone should be:

> free to practise medicine without restriction except for legal and financial responsibility for harm done to others through fraud and negligence.

He rejects quality assurance arguments for medical licensing thus:

> the great argument for the market is its tolerance of diversity; its ability to use a wide range of special knowledge and capacity. It renders special groups impotent to prevent experimentation and permits the customer not the producer to decide what will serve the customers best (ibid., p. 160).

For opponents of the market-based approach, the problem lies in the view that the very nature of the supply and demand for health makes the market an inappropriate mechanism through which to organize the delivery of health-care. First, the impact of price in health-care is disguised in that the consumer (patient) of health-care very seldom pays directly for services used. This is true not only in public systems of health-care like the NHS, but also in the private sector where a substantial share of the expenditure is covered by insurance. Therefore, the ability of the price mechanism to adjust demand is blunted. Further, the nature of the demand for health-care provision is determined not directly by the wishes and needs of the patient so much as by the medical practitioner, who operates both in the role of principal supplier as well as the creator of demand. Thus the demand for health-care is very heavily influenced by the supply. In the case of health promotion, the role of professionals has been very much to create demand through, for example, public campaigns. Moreover, as stated earlier, the nature of technological advances has meant that there is no point at which the demand for health-care stabilizes. What all this adds up to is that there is no straight-forward interplay between the forces of supply and demand, making it difficult for any kind of market equilibrium to be reached.

Implementing the reforms

Political and pragmatic considerations have prevented successive Conservative governments from being able to create the kinds of markets envisaged by the arguments presented above in all policy areas. In some areas (such as state-owned industries, public utilities, council housing) the market was introduced directly through wholesale privatization. In other areas such as education and health, where political considerations prevented outright privatization, bureaucratic mechanisms of service delivery were replaced by competitive systems based on what Le Grand (1991) has termed 'quasi-markets'. These are distinguished from 'normal' markets in that the provision of services remains free at the point of delivery, the state continues to be the funder and regulator of welfare services, but the:

> task of providing services has been transferred from a set of state owned and managed enterprises to a variety of independent provider organizations including not-for-profit organizations, private companies and state owned units under devolved managements (Propper *et al.*, 1994, pp. 1-2).

These provider units are meant to be in competition with each other for the receipt of state funds held by purchaser organizations. Thus the essence of the internal markets created is one where the responsibility for purchasing and commissioning services has been separated from the responsibility of providing them. Structurally, the rules of the game have been changed: efficiency overriding need as the prime criteria for making decisions. Needless to say, the implementation of these changes has been patchy, with many unintended consequences along the way.

This introduction of quasi-markets resulted in significant organizational changes within health and welfare agencies. These have been in terms of both values and structure. Organizational values derived from the world of corporate capital have been imposed on the 'public service' ethos that formed a part of the culture of health and welfare agencies. Managerialism was a key strategy through which this was achieved (Clarke, Cochrane, and McLaughlin, 1994).

In order to see how these changes affected the NHS it may be useful to remind readers about how it used to be organized. It was the largest single component of the welfare state, locally administered through District Health Authorities, accountable directly to the Secretary of State, funded up to 90 per cent by the Treasury. Resources were allocated to the districts through Regional Authorities, who in turn received funds according to an agreed formula from the centre. DHAs were responsible for both the overall planning of services and the running of hospitals and other units. Primary health care was the responsibility of Family Practitioner Committees, who employed General Practitioners (GPs).

In practice, there was little integration between primary health care and secondary health care and it is argued little attention was focused on achieving the right balance of prevention and treatment. NHS employees were employed on national terms and conditions of service. While in theory pre-reform NHS appeared to be a textbook example of a hierarchically organized bureaucracy, in practice it was far from being so. This was because of the high degree of autonomy enjoyed by the medical profession (Challis *et al.*, 1994). Hospital-based senior clinicians in the service were by far the most powerful group of employees. GPs were very much in a subordinate position, treated like 'supplicants, seeking treatment on the consultants waiting lists' (Glennester *et al.*, 1994, p. 74). Because of its size and expense, Butler (1992, p. 43) suggests that the NHS was bound to be the target of the reforming zeal of a government bent on

81

rolling back the frontiers of the state. However, because of its symbolic place in the structure of the post-war welfare state, the presentation of the reforms to the public at large was one which insisted that they were nothing more than a 'reformist reform' which would preserve the central ethos of the NHS.

Ham (1994) identifies five key elements contained in the NHS reforms:

* the move from an integrated system to the separation of purchaser and provider roles,
* the creation of self-governing NHS trusts to take responsibility for service provision,
* the transformation of district health authorities into purchasers of services on behalf of local people,
* the establishment of general practitioner fundholding (GPFH),
* the use of contracts or service agreements to provide the link between purchasers and providers.

The idea was to create a pluralistic system of both purchasers and providers. This was because 'competition' was central to the argument behind the reforms. The claims were that old style bureaucratic regulation would give way to market incentives and that competitive pressures would force 'inefficient' units to improve standards or go out of business; the increased efficiency thus created would improve quality and control rising aggregate costs. But for competition to exist there had to be a multiplicity of players, hence the desegregation of NHS units into smaller operational entities as well as the encouragement of greater private sector involvement.

A greater organizational pluralism within the NHS was rejected at its inception, because it was argued that it would undermine the coordination of a national service and cause problems of accountability. Pluralism was more acceptable - indeed desirable - in the context of the 1990 Act because issues of service coordination and accountability were seen as less important to arguments about efficiency and consumer choice. However, supporters of the reforms argued that any problems arising out of the independence of the providers could be dealt with through the regulation of the market.

Despite this regulation in the first year of the reforms, the government insisted that a 'steady state' be maintained. The purpose behind this was to ensure the 'smooth take-off' of the changes. In practice, what this meant was that the DHAs as purchasers were instructed to maintain a flow of funds to providers on the basis of historical patterns of service delivery. They were also prohibited from introducing new contracts with private providers for the first year. The newly created Trusts that, at the beginning of the reform process, were to be the key to the decentralizing trends contained in the legislation, had their room to manoeuvre significantly curbed. Initial Department of Health guidance stressed the significant managerial freedoms they were to possess: to acquire and dispose of resources; borrow; retain an operating surplus; determine their own management structures and levels of pay, etc. However, as Hughes (1994) shows, the actual legislation was more about operating constraints. The Secretary of State for Health determined membership of Trust Boards, set financial objectives, determined the limits of borrowing and had the power to dissolve Boards and transfer their assets to another body.

While there has been a gradual relaxation of government controls over the last couple of years (Ham, 1994), many commentators are now agreed that what has occurred is an increasing regulatory role for the centre through the Regional Health Authorities (RHAs). The detailed financial control being exercised by the National Health Service Management Executive (NHSME) has led, it is argued, to the micro-management of both purchasing and providing behaviour.

Thus, in terms of competition, it appears that little exists in the conventional sense of the word. The way in which it does operate is tightly regulated; for instance, the prices charged by providers have to be based on cost of delivery rather than reflecting levels of demand. Research suggests that one year block contracts continue to be the preferred form of contract, though with the increase of General Practitioner Fundholders (GPFHs) there has been a greater plurality of purchasers (Harrison and Wistow, 1992).

In the new NHS, in addition to the District Health Authorities, those general practices that held their own budgets (GPFHs) are the 'purchasers' of health-care. DHAs are responsible for assessing the health needs of their resident population and for purchasing services that best meet these needs. However, GPFHs receive budgets subtracted from overall district allocations with which they can buy a range of diagnostic procedures and secondary care for patients registered with them.

GP fundholders are thus an important part of the demand side in the new internal market. Given their ability to make independent purchasing decisions, they have the potential to disrupt any overall strategy the DHA may have arrived at with respect to the health needs of the population it serves.

The necessity to identify needs and priorities, it has been argued, represents a shift toward explicit rationing. Harrison and Wistow (1992) identify two difficulties faced by purchasers in carrying out their assessment functions. First, cognitive difficulties, i.e. knowing how to determine either needs or priorities as distinct from responding to existing demands for current services, arise from the fact that DHAs are subject to directives from the RHAs and central government about priorities. They have inaccurate information about the referral intentions of GPFHs, whose expenditures are deducted from DHA budgets, leading to uncertainty about levels of needs. Second, political difficulties arise from having to make explicit rationing, in the context of DHAs being appointed rather than elected bodies, raising questions about their legitimacy to make these kinds of decisions.

The theory behind the internal market is that the relationship between providers of health care and purchasers is regulated through the contract. In addition to being the prime way in which competition has been introduced into the NHS, it also represents the new management model where the relationship between purchasers and providers is based on an explicit articulation of levels of service, standards and costs. As such, it replaces the traditional command and control approach, where planning and service delivery were part of the same management and organizational structure. However, Ferlie (1994) makes the point that the nature of the market is one where in addition to there being only a limited number of purchasers and providers in each area, there is a close relationship between them. They are colleagues who share the same value system, which may have the effect of trying to keep things 'in the family'. As Ferlie states:

> One might expect well established local cliques and networks to continue to dominate decision making. Within the quasi-market there will be continuing barriers to market entry and exit; inherited contracting patterns may be rolled forward and there may be little reletting of contracts (Ferlie, 1994, p. 214).

Thus, there continues to be a high degree of continuity in the upper reaches of both purchasing and providing organizations. This has to a certain extent ensured a degree of stability in the system. However, there is some evidence, particularly within provider organizations, of influential non-NHS outsiders bought in at the non-executive levels. While this may have considerable impact internally on the dynamics, it has so far not intruded too much on the contractual relationships between purchasers and providers.

Contracting is meant to ensure a greater degree of control over what services are provided and at what cost. In terms of public health the construction of purchasing plans, based on an evaluation of needs and assessment of outcomes, is the responsibility of district directors of public health, supported by public health doctors and researchers. The potential gain from this separation of purchasers from providers is that they can make objective decisions about the health needs of the population without necessarily having to worry about the organizational implications of meeting these needs. It is also argued that the contract may shift power away from those with a vested interest in the maintenance of clinical domains towards those with a more global outlook. It should therefore be less easy for clinicians in the prestigious and powerful specialities to appropriate for themselves an unreasonable share of the districts' resources. Simultaneously, it could enable more funding to be directed towards areas such as prevention and health promotion, which have suffered in the past because of a lack of political leverage. However, this has to be set against the patterns of purchaser/provider relationships outlined above.

The above scenario assumes that not only do purchasers have the competence to carry out the needs assessment role, but also that in any given district it is possible to coordinate and create strategic purchasing plans. But one of the key problems with respect to this has been that the purchasing function in any given district is shared with fundholding GPs, who are able to enter into contracts independently of the DHAs. This has the potential to undermine district-wide strategic plans. Also, the extent to which the contracts will be purchaser driven has been questioned. Dobson (1993) argues that if health promotion expertise lies with the providers then the likelihood is that the contract will be provider driven.

Thus providers are faced with a range of different purchasers (DHAs, FHSAs, GPFHs and non-fundholding GPs) and may have to enter into contracts that pull in contradictory directions, compromising the coherence and strategic intent required by *The Health of the Nation* strategy.

Moreover, the competitive situation between providers will militate against the sharing of information and resources, which could further hamper coordinated response. Providers might also choose not to offer services that the purchaser seeks. The inbuilt imperatives of costing required by the reforms could lead to a supply of health-care dominated by:

> finite, measurable treatments, such as surgical operations, rather than broader less quantifiable, prevention targets, and the businessmen appointed to the new health authorities, used to reading company profit and loss accounts, may encourage this (McCarthy, 1992, p. 57).

Trusts must break even on income and expenditure year on year and earn a financial return of 6 per cent on net assets. They must also submit an annual business plan, annual report and annual accounts to the NHSME. In addition to requiring a regulatory machinery for monitoring and evaluation, all this encourages 'short termism', which is at odds with a health gain strategy, the fruits of which can only emerge in the medium to long term. This is reflected in managerial behaviour, as Catford (1995, p. 42) states: long term benefits are not attractive to those whose own personal performance (and pay) is assessed on an annual basis.

In practice the setting up of NHS Trusts has incurred implementation costs in terms of staff and the setting up of new administrative and managerial roles, which in the past would have occurred only once at the DHA level. The introduction of private sector managerial and organizational structures; a greater emphasis on costs; lessening of clinical decision making; has been replaced with a greater emphasis on financial rather than clinical priorities.

Thus the kind of 'markets' that emerged from the reforms have been described variously as 'planned markets' (Saltman and von Otter, 1992), 'managed markets' (Ham, 1994) or 'quasi-markets' (Le Grand, 1991). What all these terms imply is the creation of new markets through the use of state power, that are consciously designed to achieve state policy objectives through the limited and selective use of market mechanisms. It is explicitly political criteria which structure the context within which these markets operate. It is the state which sets the objectives to be attained by the new system, the degree of competition to be permitted and the incentives to be used. Therefore, in addition to the purchasers and providers, there are national policy players (central government) who play an important part in shaping the market. Emerging evidence (Challis *et al.*, 1994) suggests the health market is still very much regulated by higher bureaucratic tiers (the region, the management executive outposts) who set the rules concerning prices, rates of financial return and productivity targets and, crucially, set the global cash limits within which the whole service operates. The rhetoric of the free market is in actual fact rooted by the heavy weight of continuing regulatory apparatus. It is this very characteristic of the reformed NHS that would allow the shift of priorities envisaged in *The Health of the Nation* to take place.

Paradoxically, it is this very strengthening of central control of the operational objectives of the health service that has been the source of criticisms of the reforms from the right of the political spectrum. It is argued that this has created a situation where providers who are supposed to behave like private sector firms are not actually being allowed to make decisions based on commercial criteria. Similarly, on the purchasing side neither GPFHs nor DHAs are being permitted to use their funds as they see fit.

Evaluation

It is important to state at the outset that the jury is still out as far as making any conclusive statements about the changes. For the free marketeers the market has not been given a chance, being undermined by excessive state intervention and regulation. While for the anti-market lobby their argument is that the situation is characterized by market failure, excessive transaction costs, and inequity in an emergent two tier system.

Ham (1994, p. 295) suggests, in evaluating the reforms, that while for the first few years there was little evidence of competition between providers, more recently the market has come into play to a greater extent, particularly in places like London where there is a concentration of providers. This has often resulted in hospital closures, mergers and service rationalizations.

At a general level it is suggested that the most important effect of the reforms has been to change the balance of power within the NHS away from the providers, who in the old system were the most influential stake holders, to purchasers (although this is mediated by the social embeddedness of the reforms discussed above). The extent to which this shift of power is reflected in purchasing contracts which prioritize health promotion and disease prevention will be a key issue in determining whether the reforms enable the achievement of *The Health of the Nation* targets. Equally, the nature of the contract itself is going to play an important part in determining provider behaviour. If the contracts are couched simply in the quantitative language of throughputs, without regard to more qualitative issues, then the possibility of real health gains will necessarily be limited.

The role of GPs has also significantly increased. DHAs are having to work more closely with them in deciding which service to buy and where to place contracts. However, the danger is that if the coordination is not successful the coherence of any health gain strategy will be jeopardized.

The purchaser/provider system is proving to be more expensive to administer than an integrated system. This is particularly so with management and transaction costs. The increase in transaction costs is compounded by the fragmentation of purchasing between the growing number of GPFHs and DHAs. According to Ham (1994, p. 296):

> Management in the NHS has come to resemble a paper chase as NHS trusts seek to secure their income by negotiating with different purchasers and as all players in the market invest in information systems to monitor contract compliance.

This adds considerably to what has historically been a relatively low level of administration costs. Given the cash limited nature of the system, coupled with the still dominant power of medical interests, this would make any shift of resources toward health promotion activities difficult to achieve.

The reforms have posed a challenge to equity in that GPFHs patients in many parts of the country have been able to secure quicker access to hospitals than other patients. Given the concentration of GPFHs in more affluent parts of the country, this has served to accentuate Tudor-Hart's law of inverse care which states that access to good medical care is most available where it is least needed. This has had the effect generally of enhancing negative public perception about what is happening to the NHS, and as such it contributes to a 'feel-bad' factor. While this aspect is very difficult to definitively measure, it is an important aspect of our analysis.

The implication of a 'feel-good' factor was clearly recognized by Bevan at the inception of the NHS, with respect to the health of the nation:

> Society becomes wholesome, more serene and spiritually healthier, if it knows that its citizens have at the back of their consciousness the knowledge that not only themselves but all their fellows have access, when ill to the best that medical skill can provide (Bevan, in Foot, 1975, p.105).

In so far as the 'market' reforms have resulted in a perception of an emerging two-tier system, then it would be fair to say that it is likely to have a negative impact on overall health.

The principal reason for the reforms was efficiency and in theory money was meant to follow patients, which has not occurred. This is because most contracts are block contracts where providers receive a sum of money to deliver a range of services to the community every year. This is a reflection both of the underdeveloped state of information systems within the NHS as well as the concerns of the purchasers to keep within budgets. These contracts, it is argued, are not sensitive to changes in productivity during the year and they represent little improvement from the providers' perspective on the old system of global budgets. Further, it has been argued (Whitehead, 1994) that providers have an inbuilt incentive to concentrate on serving more prosperous and healthy populations at the expense of those patients with chronic conditions, who are more expensive to treat.

On a more positive note, Butler (1992) has suggested that the reforms - by opening up the system to much needed change - have resulted in a climate that has encouraged innovation and change. They have ensured that debates about priorities and rationing have become more open, as have debates about quality. This has been important in placing public health and health promotion issues much more centrally on the agenda than would otherwise have been the case. In practice, the development of concepts such as 'purchasing for health gain' have led to the setting up of departments of public health in each purchasing authority, and the NHS has centrally funded various research initiatives in the area. However, as Whitehead (1994) points out, compared to expenditure involved in developing financial information systems, the funds allocated to assessing health needs and outcomes have been modest.

Conclusion

This chapter has drawn together two separate but inter-linked elements of contemporary health policy and assessed the extent to which the organizational reforms within the NHS were likely to achieve health policy objectives that were concerned with disease prevention and health promotion. While conclusive evidence concerning these issues is not available, trends would suggest that the reforms are leading to a situation where health disparities between regions and between population groups are widening, mirroring more general social and economic disparities. The reforms have created an incentive structure which favours the better off at the expense of those in greatest need. The strategy contained in *The Health of the Nation* is both incomplete and contradictory. Incomplete because in spite of overwhelming evidence stressing the importance of tackling social inequalities in order to ensure the overall health of a population, the White Paper effectively ignores this dimension. Thus, the role the NHS could play in ameliorating social inequalities is not a serious consideration in local and national policy making.

These policies are contradictory because while they implicitly recognize the centrality of the role of the state, of the NHS and of the central planning and coordination, they expect the strategy to be delivered by a system which is composed of a network of semi-autonomous purchasers and providers essentially motivated by organizational self-interest. The assumption that the aggregate of such self-interests is the manifestation of national/societal interest is fallacious in both a philosophical and empirical sense. Indeed, fragmentation has been a major charge against the market reforms, coming from sources such as the government's own former Chief Medical Officer (Beck *et al.*, 1992).

While this chapter has shown how the reforms have not really introduced a market in any conventional sense of the word, there is evidence of a shift in the organizational culture of the NHS towards values and an ethos derived from the private sector. Thus the health service has arguably ended up with the worst of both worlds.

References

Ashton, J. and Seymour, H. (1988), *The New Public Health*, Open University Press, Milton Keynes.

Baggot, R. (1995), *Health and Health Care in Britain*, Macmillan Press Ltd., Basingstoke.

Ben-Shlomo, Y. (1992) 'Introduction', in Public Health Alliance and Radical Statistics Health Group, *The Health of the Nation: Challenges for a new government,* PHA, London.

Beveridge, W. (1942), *Social Insurance and Allied Services (The Beveridge Report)*, Cmnd 6404, HMSO, London.

Blackburn, C. (1991), *Poverty and Health, Working with Families*, Open University Press, Buckingham.

Blackman, T. (1995), 'Recent Developments in British National Health Policy: an emerging role for local government?', *Policy and Politics*, vol. 23, no. 1.

Blaxter, M. (1990), *Health and Lifestyles,* Tavistock/Routledge, London.

Butler, J. (1992), *Patients, Policies and Politics: Before and After 'Working for Patients'*, Open University Press, Buckingham.

Catford, J. (1995), 'Health promotion in the market place, constraints and opportunities', *Health Promotion International*, vol. 10, no. 1.

Challis, L., Day, P., Klein, R. and Scrivens, E. (1994), 'Managing quasi-markets: institutions of regulation', in Barlett, W., Propper, C., Wilson, D., and Le Grand, J.(eds), *Quasi-Markets in the Welfare State*, SAUS Publications, Bristol.

Clarke, J., Cochrane, A. and McLaughlin, E. (eds), (1994), *Managing Social Policy*, Sage, London.

Davis, C.M. (1990), 'National Health Services, Resources, Constraints and Shortages', in Manning, N. and Ungerson, C. (eds), *Social Policy Review 1989-90*, Longman, London.

Day, P. and Klein, R. (1992), 'Constitutional and Distributional Conflict in British Medical Politics: The Case of General Practice 1911-1991', *Political Studies*, vol. 50, pp. 462-78.

Dept. of Health (1988), *Public Health in England,* Report of the Acheson Committee of Inquiry into the Future Development of the Public Health Function, Cmnd 289, HMSO, London.

Dept. of Health (1991), *The Health of the Nation: A Consultative*

Document for Health in England, Cmnd. 1523, HMSO, London.

Dept. of Health (1992), *The Health of the Nation: A Strategy of Health for England,* Cmnd. 1986, HMSO, London.

Dept. of Health and Department of the Environment (1994), *Public Health: responsibilities of the NHS and the roles of others,* London.

Dept. of Health and Social Security (1977), *Prevention and Health,* Cmnd 7047, HMSO, London.

Dept. of Health and Social Security (1980), *Inequalities in Health,* report of a Research Working Group, HMSO, London.

Dobson, J. (1993), 'Promotion or Regulation', *Health Service Journal,* vol. 103.

Ferlie, E.(1994), 'The Evolution of quasi-markets in the NHS: early evidence' in Bartlett, W. *et al.*, (eds), *Quasi-Markets in the Welfare State,* SAUS Publications, Bristol.

Finsberg, G. (1982), *Prevention and Health Education,* Speech to Environmental Health Institution Congress, DHSS, London.

Foot, M. (1975), *Aneurin Bevan,* vol.2, 1945-1960, Davis-Poynter, London.

Friedman, M. (1962), *Capitalism and Freedom,* University of Chicago Press, Chicago.

Glennerster, H., Matsaganis, M., Owens, P. and Hancock, S., (1994), 'GP fundholding: wild card or winning hand?', in Robinson, R and Le Grand, J. (eds), *Evaluating the NHS Reforms,* Kings Fund Institute, Hermitage.

Graham, H. (1983), 'Health Education', in McPherson, A. and Anderson, A. (eds) *Women's Problems in General Practice,* Oxford University Press, Oxford.

Ham, C. J. (1994), 'Reforming Health Services: Learning from the UK Experience', *Social Policy and Administration.* vol. 28, no. 4.

Harrison, S. (1991), 'Working the Markets: Purchaser/Provider Separation in English Health Care', *International Journal of Health Services,* vol. 21, no. 4.

Harrison, S. and Wiostow, G. (1992), 'The Purchaser/Provider Split in English Health Care: Toward Explicit Rationing', *Policy and Politics,* vol. 20, no. 2.

Health Visitors' Association (1991), *Building a Healthy Britain: An HVA Response to the Health of the Nation,* Health Visitors' Association, London.

Hughes, D. (1993), 'Health policy: letting the market work?', in Page, R. and Baldock, J. (eds), *Social Policy Review 5*, Social Policy Association, Canterbury.

Klein, R. (1980), *Between Nationalism and Utopia in Health Care*, Lecture, Yale University, New Haven (unpublished).

Le Grand, J. (1991), 'Quasi-markets and social policy', *Economic Journal*, vol. 101, no. 408, pp. 1256-1268.

Manning, N. (1994), 'Health Service: Pressure, Growth and Conflict', in George, V. and Miller, S. (eds), *Social Policy Towards 2000, Squaring the Welfare Circle,* Routledge, London.

McKeown, T. (1976), *The Modern Rise of Population*, Edward Arnold, London.

McCarthy, M. (1992) 'Preventive medicine and health promotion' in Beck, E., Lonsdale, S., Newman, S. and Patterson, D., (eds), *In the Best of Health? The status and future of healthcare in the UK*, Chapman and Hall, London.

Ministry of Health (1944), *The National Health Service*, Cmnd. 6502, HMSO, London.

Propper, C., Bartlett, W. and Wilson, D. (1994) 'Introduction', in Bartlett, W. *et al.*, (eds), *Quasi-Markets in the Welfare State*, SAUS Publications, Bristol.

Rayner, G. (1992), 'The Health of the Nation: What's in it and what's not', in Public Health Alliance and Radical Statistics Group, *The Health of the Nation: Challenges for a new government*, PHA, London.

Research Unit in Health and Behavioral Change (1989), *Changing the Public Health,* John Wiley and Sons, Chichester.

Robinson, R. (1994), 'Introduction', in Robinson, R. and Le Grand, J. (eds), *Evaluating the NHS Reforms*, Kings Fund Institute, Hermitage.

Robinson, R. and Judge, K.(1987), *Public Expenditure and the NHS: Trends and Prospects*, Kings Fund Institute, London.

Saltman, R.B. and von Otter, C. (1992), *Planned Markets and Public Competition*, Open University Press, Buckingham.

Scott-Samuel, A. (1992), 'Still got a long way to go: An International Perspective', in Public Health Alliance and Radical Statistics Group, *The Health of the Nation: Challenges for a new government*, PHA, London.

Secretary of State (1989), *Working for Patients,* Cmnd. 555, HMSO,

London.

Seldon, A. (1980), 'The NHS - Success? Still on Trial? or Failure?', in Seldon, A. (ed.), *The Litmus Papers: A National Health Disservice*, Centre for Policy Studies, London.

Smith, M.J. (1993), *Pressure Power and Politics,* Harvester Wheatsheaf, London.

South East Institute of Public Health (1991), *Report on the Conference on the Health of the Nation,* South East Institute of Public Health, London.

Stacey, M. (1991), 'Medical Sociology and Health Policy: an historical overview', in Gabe, J., Calnan, M. and Bury, M. (eds), *The Sociology of the Health Service,* Routledge, London.

St. George, D. (1981), 'Who pulls the strings at the HEC?', *World Medicine,* 28 November.

U205 Course Team (1985), *Caring for Health: Dilemmas and Prospects,* Open University Press, Milton Keynes.

Whitehead, M. (1994), Is it Fair?: Evaluating the equity implications of the NHS reforms', in Robinson, R and Le Grand, J. (eds), *Evaluating the NHS Reforms*, Kings Fund Institute, Hermitage.

Winter, J. (1982), 'Aspects of the Impact of the First World War on Infant Mortality in Britain', *Journal of European Economic History,* vol. 11.

World Health Organization (1978), Alma Ata 1978: Primary Health Care (Health for All series, no. 1), WHO, Geneva.

5 Organizational Reform, Market Testing and Defence

DEREK BRADDON, PAUL DOWDALL AND ADRIAN KENDRY

Introduction

The eighth report of the Public Accounts Committee in 1994 questioned the financial control mechanisms of the Ministry of Defence (MoD) and commented, in general, upon the 'inadequate stewardship of public money'. Such allegations are a frequent part of the landscape of public scrutiny of defence spending and refer to a wide range of activities and programmes. In this chapter we explore and contrast the theory and practice of privatization, deregulation, contracting-out and market testing in the defence sector, with particular reference to what would constitute adequate stewardship in such activities and programmes.

Parameters such as national security, 'life-critical' quality in defence equipment, and the lack of a competitive culture in much of the defence sector complicate the issues and blur the boundaries of public/private sector provision. Questions and controversies surrounding the degree of publicness (Sandler and Cauley, 1975; Sandler and Murdoch, 1990) of defence as a good (embodying the characteristics of non-excludability and non-rivalry) further position the real world of defence some way from the pages of traditional privatization texts. Moreover, as suggested in this chapter, it is the combination of specialized demand conditions and unique structural change, both exogenous and endogenous, defence-specific and non-specific, long-term and short-term, that calls into question the efficacy and appropriateness of the privatization practices currently being applied to the UK defence sector. Adequate stewardship in the management and allocation of defence finances can only be achieved, *inter alia*, through privatization if such a process recognizes the unique structural forces that have been at work.

The evidence and analysis provided below calls upon primary research conducted over the period 1990-94 and supports the 1994 Report of the Public Accounts Committee in its concern for the stewardship of defence expenditure. Furthermore, it suggests that, at present, after various measures to introduce privatization, deregulation, contracting-out and market testing into the defence sector, 'stewardship' has not improved. However, the responsibility for this state of affairs is inevitably multicausal, given the complexities underpinning the behaviour of buyers and sellers in public procurement.

The scale of defence spending

The Statement on the Defence Estimates, 1995, gives the estimated annual outturn UK defence budget for 1994-95 as £22,320 million. This represents 3.3 per cent of GDP, down from 4.2 per cent in 1991-92 (MoD 1995). Tables 5.1 and 5.2 below provide evidence of the size of UK defence expenditure relative to other NATO countries. The procurement budget alone takes up 40 per cent of this and as such the Ministry of Defence is UK business's largest single customer.

MoD employment plans for 1996 stand at 231,000 service personnel and 128,700 civilian personnel (113,000 UK and 15,700 locally entered overseas) (Ministry of Defence, 1995). Worldwide, it is estimated that expenditure on defence rose to a peak of $1000 billion in 1987, generating jobs for over 30 million service personnel and an estimated 15 million jobs in the supplying arms industry (Wulf, 1993). Notwithstanding the contractions in defence spending in the 1990s, defence remains one of the most significant areas of public sector activity and expenditure. It is not surprising then to find, as detailed below, that the general thrust to privatize and deregulate has targeted many activities in the defence sector with, potentially, substantial impact upon industrial and commercial sectors and employment throughout the economy. However, the determinants and processes of defence privatization include many considerations that deviate some way from those common to all public sector activities.

Table 5.1

Trends in defence spending as a percentage of gross domestic product (GDP) for western allies

Country	1987 d	1990 d	1992 e	1995 e	% Change 90-95a
USA	6.5	5.6	5.2	4.1b	-27
Germany	3.1	2.8	2.1	1.5	-46c
N Zealand	1.8	1.9	1.8	1.4	-26
Belgium	3.0	2.4	2.1	1.8	-26
Denmark	2.1	2.0	1.9	1.5	-26
Netherlands	3.1	2.7	2.4	2.0	-25
UK	4.6	4.0	4.0	3.4	-14
France	3.9	3.6	3.3	3.1	-14
Japan	1.0	1.0	1.0	0.9	-8
Canada	2.1	2.0	2.1	1.9	-5
Australia	2.6	2.2	2.4	2.2	-2
Spain	2.4	1.8	1.8	2.0	6
Turkey	4.2	4.9	5.3	5.3	8

Notes: a) Reported percentages have been rounded.
b) Based on February 1993 budget estimates.
c) This large figure is due in part to the unification of Germany which has increased GDP by more than defence expenditures.
d) Actual.
e) Estimated.
Source: Sandler, T. and Hartley, K. (1995).

Table 5.2

**Trends in real defence expenditures for western allies
(in billions of constant 1992 US dollars)**

Country	1990d	1992e	1995e	% Change 90-95a
USA	330.5	305.2b	258.6b	-22
Germany	46.1c	38.2	31.2	-32
N Zealand	0.8	0.7	0.6	-19
Belgium	4.9	4.5	4.1	-18
Denmark	2.6	2.6	2.3	-13
Netherlands	7.9	7.2	6.6	-17
UK	43.8	42.9	39.7	-9
France	45.6	44.0	43.6	-4
Japan	33.4	35.2	37.0	11
Canada	11.7	12.0	12.2	4
Australia	6.6	7.1	7.2	10
Spain	10.4	10.5	12.8	22
Turkey	5.4	5.7	7.2	34

Notes: a) Reported percentages have been rounded.
   b) Based on February 1993 budget estimates.
   c) Includes only West German expenditures for 1990.
   d) Actual.
   e) Estimated.

Source: Sandler, T. and Hartley, K. (1995).

These peculiarities of defence privatization are examined in the following section.

Forces driving change and paradigmatic shifts

In common with other parts of the public sector, as detailed elsewhere in this book, the MoD has been under intense scrutiny from those who would preach the gospel of privatization. The reader is likely to be well aware of the standard arguments for privatization and deregulation, namely: a Public Sector Borrowing Requirement that stubbornly resists efforts at reduction; the welfare losses accompanying public ownership; x-inefficiency; abuse of monopoly power; and low incentives to innovate in product and process design. This chapter is, therefore, more concerned with travelling the less well-trodden path of analysing those factors that are specific to defence privatization.

The dramatic changes that the world has witnessed in the changing geo-political environment since the 1980s have led governments to reassess the function and size of national defence forces. Clearly, as the role and capability is reviewed so the attendant budget comes under scrutiny. In the UK, pressure mounted in the late 1980s and early 1990s for government to deliver a 'peace dividend'. The juxtaposition of political, economic and socio-cultural demands for reduced military spending, together with the apparent reduction in perceived threat in the strategic environment, placed irresistible pressure upon the defence budget. Consequently, the 'frontiers of the state' were being rolled back in the defence sector, independent of the economic and political rationale for privatization. Defence spending in the UK is targeted to fall by around 14.5 per cent in real terms between 1992-93 and 1997-98 (MoD, 1995). Tables 5.1 and 5.2 above and 5.3 and 5.4 below quantify the decline.

However, not all demands and pressure worked in the same direction, recognizing that the changes in the geo-political/strategic environment did not necessarily mean a reduction in perceived threat, merely a change in the nature of that threat. Indeed, it has been contested that the shift from the predictable bipolar world of the Cold War to a new uncertain and unpredictable international environment has resulted in a widening as opposed to deepening of threat.

Table 5.3

Trends in UK defence spending

	91/92	92/93	93/94	94/95	95/96	96/97	97/98
Budget (£m)	24438	22910	22757	22323	21723	21924	22317
% of GDP	4.2	3.8	3.6	3.3	3.0	2.9	2.8
Budget (£m) Real Terms	26188	23611	22757	21885	20627	20310	20219
Real Change (%, yearly)		-9.8	-3.6	-3.8	-5.7	-1.5	-0.4

(*Statement on the Defence Estimates, 1995*)

Table 5.4

Ministry of Defence manpower ('000s)

	91/92	92/93	93/94	94/95	95/96	96/97	97/98
Civilians	168	159	146	139	132	125	121
Service	305	293	419	257	236	221	216
Total	474	452	419	396	367	346	336

(Adapted from *Statement on the Defence Estimates* 1995)

The countervailing pressure resulting from this viewpoint clearly contributes an additional parameter affecting the scale and scope of privatization in the defence sector. The 'Options For Change' doctrine presented to the House of Commons, 25 July, 1990, targeted 'smaller forces, better equipped, properly trained and housed and well motivated'. This statement from Tom King, then Secretary of State for Defence, was in essence a tri-service rearguard action with Parliament being offered a plan for savings in the defence budget. 'Options For Change' could be construed as an attempt to minimize inter-service disputes in the face of demands for a 'peace dividend' and a shrinking budget. The 1994 Defence Costs Study, *'Front-Line First'*, continued this thinking with the MoD seeking to achieve and manage a compromise between pressure on the budget and the maintenance of operational capability:

> every recommendation for change was examined against one major criterion: would it directly or indirectly reduce the operational capability of the armed forces.....If the judgement was made that a proposal would damage the operational capability of the armed forces, it was rejected (MoD, 1994a, pp. 5-6).

It is against this background of countervailing pressure that the practice of privatization, deregulation and contracting-out in the defence sector must be viewed. It is clear that 'adequate stewardship of public money' in defence must embrace the question of operational capability. This, however, raises further issues: what is the operational role of the defence services? what is the perception of threat? what timescale should be considered, and, if capability includes quality, what constitutes 'quality' in defence provision?

Market-testing in the defence sector

Privatization may be a manifestation of 'the political creed of the 1990s' (Jackson, 1994) but the transformation of public into private ownership in many areas of economic activity (notably the regulated utilities) remains a deeply controversial policy in the United Kingdom and elsewhere. Much of the controversy, and the accompanying unpopularity of privatization, is located in the failure of government to transform public monopolies into anything other than private monopolies. In many instances, the guarantee of a monopolized market increases the price of sale, and revenue generated, for a government preoccupied with controlling the budget deficit. Under these circumstances, the efficiency gains from a privatized competitive industrial structure are no longer quite so compelling.

In the case of the defence sector, an example of the complete transfer of a government undertaking to the private sector was the privatization of the Royal Ordnance factories. Even in this case, the government remains the primary purchaser of ammunition in a tightly regulated market. The more common practice, as shown in the example of the Naval Support Command (NSC) below, is the lowering of entry barriers to private contractors and the creation of a 'market' that is contestable at the periphery of the activities of the NSC.

Contractorization in the Naval Support Command

Within the MoD, NSC is responsible for the support of the in-service fleet of submarines and surface ships. The particular group cited here is the Director Auxiliary's and Systems (ADXA) Group. ADXA supplies engineering expertise to support the running of the Fleet in the areas of hydraulics and compressed air systems. The group is regarded as the expert in this field and is the focal point for technical investigations. Clearly, as an in-house function, the barriers to entry are extremely high and even with an invitation to tender entry is extremely difficult. Recently, ADXA has lowered these entry barriers and allowed external contractors to bid for discrete tasks. The total hours contracted out to consultants in the financial year 1994/1995 was 2,690 out of a total of 8,090 hours. As detailed below (Figure 5.1), the consultancies to whom this work has been contracted-out now take one-third of the total 'market'.

The economics of public provision and private production

The NSC example illustrates the sub-contracting of hitherto publicly provided goods to private producers. This widening of the scope of privatization embraces both the application of market testing mechanisms and philosophies, with the inculcation and incorporation of best practice

102

techniques from the private sector. The traditional arguments for government providing goods and services associated with the defence and security of the realm have emphasized:

1) the market failure that comes from private markets generating a less than optimal quantity of goods in cases where the goods concerned possess a significant degree of non-excludability.

2) the duty of the state to ensure the defence and security of the country through public ownership and control of the armed forces and their equipment.

3) the importance of ensuring quality, and safeguarding security, in cases where defence services and goods are to be considered for market testing and, potentially, private production and provision.

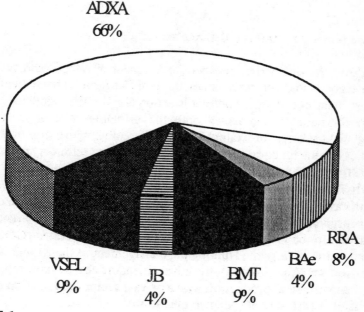

ADXA
66%

VSEL
9%

JB
4%

BMT
9%

BAe
4%

RRA 8%

Figure 5.1

The contemporary debate recognizes that the distinction between non-excludable and excludable benefits from defence goods and services is a complex one, particularly in an international environment of declining

103

national defence budgets and increasing international interdependency in defence production. Additionally, the standard arguments concerning excludable and non-excludable public goods revolve around the extent to which the preferences of consumers are fully known to the providers of the public goods.

In the case of the defence sector, the proximate consumers are the armed forces (Air Force, Army and Navy), operating under budgetary constraints established by the MoD, itself constrained by the budget allocated from central government. In these circumstances, the arguments surrounding the optimal provision of public goods, privately provided, are of little relevance; what is critical is the perception and reality of greater efficiency, and reduced costs, that emanate from the MoD pursuing a policy of market testing and competitive tendering in particular segments of procurement.

Contractorization and the defence sector

Therefore, the distinction between government-provided, and privatized, defence goods and services, is not the point at issue. The critical area of debate focuses upon contractorization and the defence sector. Contractorization encompasses both the principle of contracting-in, an arrangement where, for example, the MoD retains ownership of a site and facilities but the function is performed by a private sector organization, and contracting-out, an arrangement where the MoD would buy services directly from a private sector organization's own facilities (MoD, 1994b). In both cases, the contractual relationship between government and private sector organizations may underpin the development of market testing initiatives. In the Government-Owned, Contractor-Operated [GOCO] case of contracting-in (e.g. the Hunting plc management of the Atomic Weapons Establishment, Aldermaston), the government office may have replaced 'in-house' departmental production with a private sector organization imported to manage a Ministry of Defence operation.

In the Contractor Owned, Contractor Operated case [COCO], the government office may well replace the 'in-house' team by contracting directly with a private sector organization. Market testing, however, involves not only the reality of substituting 'in-house' production with outside agencies or firms but, significantly, the threat of substitution. Such

104

a threat is intended to 'test' and to galvanize the government department, requiring it to demonstrate attainable strategies for increasing productive efficiency.

The experience of contractorization

Following on from the 1991 White Paper, *Competing for Quality*, the Ministry of Defence introduced a market testing programme in 1992 designed to build upon previous contractorization experience. During the period April 1992 to September 1993, 36 support activities were tested, originally costing £346m per year. Of these programmes, 18 were directly contractorized and 18 exposed to competition, with eight of the latter contracts being awarded to in-house teams.

Prima facie, these figures suggest a greater degree of competitive entry into government contracts than was apparent across the government's market-testing programme as a whole. Overall, 'in-house' teams won 57 per cent of the bids by value, and 91 of the 150 contracts were awarded in cases where competition existed between existing staff and outside contractors. However, the efficiency savings predicted from market-testing were greater than those actually realized. Savings of £100 million (14 per cent of the value of the work) were generated, compared with the targeted £375 million (25 per cent of the value of work).

As a result of this round of market-testing, 10,000 civil service jobs were to be cancelled, although the staff concerned would be mainly redeployed. However, there was a strong suspicion voiced by private bidders that the market testing programme had been undermined by the entrenched and complex procedures inhibiting a winning bid from outside contractors.

From October 1993 to September 1994, a further £286 million worth of contracts were being market tested across a wide range of defence activities, including, notably, the Defence Agencies (MoD, 1995). The most recent of the 22 Defence Agencies (employing approximately 40,000 civilians and 20,000 military personnel) are: the Disposal Sales Agency; the Logistic Information Systems Agency; the Defence Clothing and Textiles Agency; the Royal Air Force Signals Engineering Establishment; the Naval Recruiting and Training Agency; the Army Base Storage and Distribution Agency; the Defence Transport and Movements Executive; and the Defence Evaluation and Research Agency.

As is emphasized in the 1995 Statement (MoD, 1995, p. 99), 'The over-riding aim of the *Competing for Quality* programme is to secure long-term value for money, substantial savings in cost wherever possible, efficiency improvements and higher standards of service'. To achieve improvements in efficiency, the programme is but one of a number of initiatives designed to reduce x-inefficiencies in the organization, management and operation of the MoD. The 1994 Defence Costs study announced measures intended to reduce the costs of support and administrative functions throughout the MoD without diminishing the operational effectiveness or capabilities of the armed forces. Equally, the 'New Management Strategy' has focused upon the devolution of budgetary responsibility to top-level budget holders with the intention of sharpening financial management.

Notwithstanding these improvements, the MoD recognized that decision-making remained 'too bureaucratic, paper-dominated, hierarchical, and over-inclined to seek to make decisions through the formal agreement of everyone potentially concerned' (MoD, 1995, p. 94). The evidence, thus far, for efficiency gains through financial management strategies, or the creation of Executive Agencies, is modest, reinforcing the perception that market testing initiatives must be extended. During the period October 1993 to September 1994, the market testing programme identified, within the MoD, potential net savings of more than £90 million per annum. But the realization of these savings will be complicated by the inherent problems of establishing legitimate competition for contracts and avoiding the creation of cartels and collusive tendering (Sandler and Hartley, 1995).

Clearly, the scope of market testing and contractorization is not boundless. It is also important to recognize that in the procurement of weapon systems and related equipment, government has no alternative but to contract directly with a firm or firms. These contractual relationships are often complex and bedevilled by the type of problems that are common in principal-agent models. Imperfect and asymmetric information, problems of monitoring, implementing and enforcing contracts, together with coping with changing contract specification, can generate major difficulties in cost control and quality assurance.

Market-testing and the economic analysis of contracts

The arguments in the previous section might appear to apply, *a fortiori*, to contract formation in defence equipment, with less significance for contract specification in defence support services. The comparative value of such contracts might support such a dichotomy of argument but, in terms of the principles involved, there are similar methodological considerations.

What are the fundamental issues underpinning the economic analysis of contracts? Rosen (1985) has offered a concise definition:

> A contract is a voluntary ex-ante agreement that resolves the distribution of uncertainty about the value and utilisation of shared investments between contracting parties.

The reference to *ex ante* signifies the potential for *ex post* problems in the monitoring and enforcement of a contract, from the perspective of the contract provider (the principal). The theory of Agency (focusing upon principal-agent behaviour) is concerned with understanding the development of mechanisms that will resolve, in an optimal manner, conflicting goals of risk-sharing and incentives among principals (contract-providers) and agents (contract-purchasers).

Risk-sharing arrangements will seek to apportion the costs associated with the uncertainty accompanying the contract. In this context, uncertainty can take many forms with the contracting parties frequently having to cope with hidden information and hidden actions that come from information asymmetry (Rasmussen, 1991). As Rosen's definition implies, the value of the contract may be the outcome of the tendering process but its worth to the two parties may differ significantly *ex post* compared to *ex ante*.

In the process of competitive tendering, the auction process may result in the Winner's Curse phenomenon. If the contract is awarded to the highest bidder, many studies have demonstrated the tendency for systematic over-estimation of the value of the contract by the winning bid for, e.g., a government franchise, or the rights for oil or gas exploration in a designated area of land or sea, or the private provision of catering services for the Army.

However, the uncertainty does not reside exclusively in the pre-contractual behaviour of the agent. In inviting tenders for a government owned, contractor operated facility [GOCO], the Ministry of Defence may be mesmerized by low cost bidding and award a contract to the lowest cost bidder, only to discover subsequently that the through-life (life cycle) costs of reimbursement to the firm winning the contract are significantly greater

107

than specified in the initial contract specification.

The ability of the contract provider to differentiate between low cost and high cost contract purchasers exemplifies the classic problem of adverse selection (Akerlof, 1970). Even in cases where the principal is fairly sure of the quality of the contract provider, the contract specification may induce moral hazard behaviour, with the agent's performance and delivery of the contract altered, post-contract, to that signalled in the pre-contract negotiation.

The distribution of risks arising from contract formation in a market-testing environment will depend crucially upon the attitudes toward risk exhibited by principal(s) and agent(s). Drawing upon the theory of expected utility, attitudes toward risk can be summarized as: risk averse, risk preferring and risk neutral. A firm that is risk averse would always reject an actuarially fair gamble (for example, in participating in a contract where there was uncertainty surrounding the actual values of the contract awarded). In contrast, a risk preferring firm would always accept an actuarially fair contract gamble, whereas a risk neutral firm would be indifferent to any type of fair gamble.

The theory of principal and agent explores *inter alia* the implications of government and firms entering into bargaining over a contract with differing attitudes toward risk. A classic example of this type of analysis demonstrates that a risk neutral government and a risk averse firm would be party to an optimal contract that would impose the burden of risk upon the government. In this contract arrangement, the contract purchaser (the firm) would have a vested interest in making use of private information (regarding the efficient use of inputs and technological requirements) in order to misrepresent costs in the initial estimate and to behave x-inefficiently during the production stage (Braddon and Kendry, 1986).

Under these circumstances, the economic arguments for market-testing must take into account not only the transaction cost issues in support of the incumbent in-house contract provider, but also the considerable problems associated with the design, implementation, monitoring and enforcement of contracts with private firms.

One of the incentive arguments associated with market-testing is the impact of potential bidding and rivalry upon the performance of incumbent in-house teams. The injection of potential competition can reduce the moral hazard problem of shirking among existing teams of staff, but may also undermine motivation and morale by threatening to bring disruption and the disintegration of well-established teams. In this context, economies of performance (Radner, 1992) in the form of economies of decentralization of information and the decentralization of incentives, can be realized 'in-house' with the networks of information and coordination that reside in the existing teams. In the absence of taut contract conditions accompanying the specification of minimum quality, together with measures to contain costs, profit maximizing contract purchasers will have incentives to behave inefficiently and undermine the case for market testing.

Defence support services and contractorization in the USA

The particular focus of market testing in the defence sector in the USA and UK is upon improving efficiency within defence support services. One of the potential gains from such improvement during an era of significant decline in defence budgets is the ability to finance new weapon systems and equipment. Notwithstanding the efforts of the Republican-dominated Congress in the USA to halt the reduction in defence spending, it remains likely that US defence spending will remain stagnant until at least the end of the century. One of the consequences of budgetary erosion has been the increasing pressure on the new weapons budget. This has fallen, in 1995, to only 17 per cent of the overall budget and, since 1985, the spending of the Department of Defence (DoD) on procurement has fallen from over $136 billion to just under $43 billion.

Many US defence observers and analysts believe that the contractorization of defence support services and functions would, in the short term, be the only way to facilitate the financing of, for example, new aircraft carrier stealth strike aircraft for the Navy, a new stealth combat helicopter for the Army or the upgrading of bombers for the Air Force. The increasing commitment to contractorization in the DoD is prompted by the $50 billion allocated to the annual budget for operating and providing a range of functions that are not central to, nor at the core of, the competencies of the armed forces.

Among these functions, the Pentagon annually spends $10 billion to repair and maintain weapons in government-controlled shipyards and depots that are underutilized and poorly managed. The introduction of privately owned financial, inventory and personnel systems would promote productivity gains and cost reductions. US military supply centres employ in excess of 40,000 civilians and spend $5 billion annually to operate a system that has excessively long delivery times and costs more than 70 cents to deliver $1 worth of goods.

The centralization of management in the formation of many new agencies within the DoD has also attracted substantial criticism at a time when the barriers between commercial and military procurement are meant to be dissolving. Arguably, the adoption of commercial standards, practices and agencies would generate the support services for the Pentagon without extensive recourse to in-house monitoring agencies. For example, the DoD recently awarded a $500 million, eight-year, contract to Loral Federal Systems to install a new electronic mail and messaging system to 2 million users at 500 DoD sites, utilizing state-of-the-art technology.

The benefits of such contractorization in the USA depend upon the design and implementation of robust contracts, together with improvements in the quality of the internal management within the Pentagon. The UK experience is, in a number of respects, further advanced in both debate and design and offers a more detailed picture of the strengths and weaknesses of market testing and contractorization.

Market testing, 'value for money' in defence and the Conservative Government

From the outset of the Thatcher government in 1979, contractorization of public services was high on the agenda of reforms in the public sector. If the emphasis within the MoD, as well as other ministries, has often appeared to be on manpower savings, since the late 1980s the quest for efficiency has also focused upon the decentralization and devolution of budgets, permitting top-level budget holders to respond to incentives to introduce contractorization and market-testing.

For at least the last decade, the MoD has sought enhanced 'value for money' in defence procurement as its principal strategic goal. To achieve this objective, the drive to deliver 'front line military forces that are well equipped, properly manned and supported' had to be pursued while making 'every effort....to identify further areas where savings can be achieved without reducing front line forces' (MoD, 1994a).

Before 1983, the procurement policy which underpinned MoD's relationship with British industry had been characterized by non-competitive, cost-plus contractual arrangements which minimized risks for defence suppliers. The imbalance between reward and risk in MoD contracting needed to be corrected and, under the Levene reforms of the mid-1980s, competition and the entrance of new contractors to the defence supply market was positively encouraged. With respect to the provision of defence-related services by government, the new approach was clarified thus:

> It should be axiomatic that work is only carried out within the Defence Support Organization which is essential we carry out for proven operational reasons, or where there is significant financial advantage for the taxpayer. Where neither of these conditions obtains then....there is a prima facie case on grounds of competitive policy and in pursuit of the most accountable management for moving the activity into the private sector (MoD, 1992).

The switch to fixed-price contracts, supplemented by the subsequent shift in risk-bearing away from the MoD and towards suppliers, generated significant cost savings. The announcement in 1988 of MoD willingness to consider purchasing from foreign suppliers served to increase the contestability of the defence supply market and to erode further the market power of existing suppliers.

Defence services and competitive tendering

Such enhanced competition was perceived to offer the greatest potential for achieving the required value for money and quality maintenance in defence provision. With respect to 'defence services', the competitive goal was pursued through the application of market testing in order to compare the efficiency of MoD services and functions against that of outside competitors. In such a competitive bid, either the 'in-house' organization wins and retains the contract to provide the service or the contract is transferred to the successful external competitor. Where provision of defence services becomes a private sector operation, the design, implementation and monitoring of the associated contract becomes critical.

Much of the emphasis of recent MoD reorganization strategy has focused upon internal management and cost control measures. Initially, it was anticipated that such internal organizational reforms would enable the MoD to exercise effective budgetary control. Over time, however, the MoD was increasingly confronted by the growing awareness that without pursuing contractorization and out-sourcing of key support services, the long-term pressures on the defence budget would become even more problematic than had been anticipated by strategists in the early 1990s.

The Defence Efficiency Programme, launched in 1988, set targets for increased MoD efficiency of 2.5 per cent in each year (except 1991-92), targets which have been exceeded to date. The New Management Strategy (NMS) for Defence, implemented in April 1991, set specific targets for departmental and armed forces managers, introducing a devolved budgetary system with the allocation of specific managerial budgets and allowing managers a significant degree of flexibility in their use. Recently, NMS has been refined to include development of integrated management planning and budgeting processes, greater delegation of authority to budget holders and the improvement of management processes and systems. Furthermore, under the Government's Next Steps Initiative, the MoD has established several agencies to undertake a wide range of executive functions.

Competing for Quality and the Ministry of Defence

Perhaps the most important strategic component of the drive towards greater efficiency within government in general, and the MoD in particular, was introduced under the 1991 White Paper. Under the aegis of the Citizen's Charter, government departments were charged to:

a)   provide incentives to encourage managers to pursue competition;

b)   set targets and disseminate 'best practice' to promote competition;

c)   eliminate barriers to competition of all kinds in order to ensure fair competition; and

d)   encourage private sector organizations to seek new market opportunities to provide public services under contract.

The MoD responded to this strategic challenge by:

112

a) establishing a steering group of senior personnel to direct the market testing process across the MoD;

b) introducing new and enhanced management information systems, designed to provide a more comprehensive information database to support the market testing initiative in all key MoD budgetary areas;

c) appointing an external private sector adviser able to offer an independent view to Defence Ministers on the progress of the market testing initiative; and

d) improving guidance offered to managers internally within the MoD on the market testing procedure.

Before the 1990s, MoD market testing was applied principally to what may be termed 'traditional support services' (cleaning, catering, etc.). Under the new strategy, however, MoD managers were expected to identify new and imaginative functions to offer for market testing, thereby significantly broadening its scope and potential effectiveness. Among functional areas within the MoD considered appropriate for market testing were: resource intensive tasks, discrete self-contained functions, specialist services, temporary activities which would carry significant recruitment or training costs, new activities where private sector provision may offer cost savings, and re-location exercises. MoD activities subjected to market testing are now extensive and include: apprentice training, audit, banking, conservancy, dockyard operation, fire services, graphics, IT training, machinery maintenance, operational analysis, nursing services, parachute packing, printing, quality control, radar maintenance, simulator operation, tailoring, vehicle hire, and waste disposal.

The Defence Costs study

To augment the push towards greater 'value for money' in UK defence expenditure, the Defence Costs study was launched under the 'Front Line First' exercise in December 1993 to reduce support costs for the armed forces from 1996-97 onwards. All areas of administration and support for front line forces have been, and will continue to be, rigorously examined to ensure maximum cost-effectiveness. Over thirty key areas have been identified where significant cost savings may be attained, including major areas such as headquarters provision and administration; naval infrastructure; defence intelligence and medical provision, as well as a number of minor areas such as legal services, the meteorological office and catering and messes.

Internal reforms alone were not going to provide the efficiency gains required to enable the UK to sustain defence commitments in an uncertain post-Cold War environment and with a sharply constrained UK defence budget. Given the government's push towards privatization and contractorization in so many other areas of its activities, the MoD had little choice but to adopt a similar strategy and open up the provision of key support services to the private sector on a competitive basis. The package of reforms currently being implemented within the MoD, from revised budgetary procedures through to contractorization of key sectors, will fundamentally change the way the MoD operates. The MoD aims to be a more streamlined and responsive organization with simplified working procedures and flatter command and management chains, enabling optimum provision of effective defence while minimizing the drain this imposes on the nation's resources. To meet these strategic objectives and attain the enhanced efficiency and cost control standards required for the future, the MoD needs to attract experienced and flexible firms able to provide cost-effective service at the required quality.

The changing scope of contracting-out

Contracting-out in the defence sector is most appropriate for functions that can be clearly defined and operated under franchise arrangements, such as waste removal, cleaning services, accounting, and similar activities. In the United Kingdom, by 1993, over 100 Ministry of Defence functions had been contracted-out. These included such diverse activities as air traffic control, dockyard operation, gardening, lecturing, operational analysis, radar maintenance and waste disposal. In certain cases (for example the contracting-out of military hospital cleaning), significant cost savings of some 40 per cent were attained (Uttley, 1993).

While many MoD support services have been subjected to 'market-testing', actual contractorization has remained somewhat limited in practice. Uttley (1993) cites ancillary support services within the MoD (such as cleaning, laundry services and specialist management activities) as examples of successful contractorization with associated cost savings. To broaden the scope of contracting-out to encompass the more complex core areas of MoD operation, however, is likely to be more difficult for all parties involved.

Viewed from the perspective of the potential contractor/entrant, irrespective of current activity within the defence sector, the process of contracting-out offers a significant range of new market opportunities to explore. In the context of this chapter, two significant questions need to be addressed: what motives underpin their interest in entering potentially problematic and previously inaccessible markets? what forces determine or constrain the nature of that interest?

Economic theory, public choice and incentives for the private sector

Conventional neoclassical economic analysis sees the provision of defence goods and services as an optimization problem with output being maximised subject to the constraint of available resources. Alternatively, Marxist economic analysis considers defence expenditure to be an essential requirement for the continuation of capitalism allowing, as it does, demand to be continually expanded to absorb excess production and maintain profits (Hartley, 1991).

A third approach (and one viewed as particularly appropriate to understanding the scale and scope of the provision of defence goods and services) is public choice theory. Such an approach views decision-making in the defence sector as contingent upon the behaviour of at least four powerful groups, each seeking to maximize its objectives. In this approach, outcomes will depend upon the interplay between the vote-maximizing behaviour of governments, the welfare-maximizing behaviour of voters, the budget-maximizing behaviour of bureaucrats and the objective-maximizing behaviour of pressure groups.

In line with the standard literature on property rights and public choice (Williamson, 1975), private sector defence industry organizations can be viewed as groups of individuals, operating as a team, bound together by contractual arrangements (Hartley and Parker, 1991). If such defence companies (or networks) can be managed in such a way as to minimize waste and inefficiency, compared with their public sector counterparts within the MoD, superior performance in terms of reduced costs and operational capability can result. To deliver this outcome, the management process requires effective incentive mechanisms, with the profit motive best fulfilling this role.

Further sustaining the theoretical competitive advantage enjoyed by the private sector, public choice theory (Buchanan, 1978; Tullock, 1976) has long asserted the proposition that politicians and state-employed managers tend to focus more on their own self-interest, rather than the public interest which they are supposed to protect. Without the constraint of the profit motive, organizations within government will tend to pursue a range of strategies such as 'budget maximisation, risk aversion, over-manning and non-optimal pricing, employment and investment' (Ott and Hartley, 1991).

Defence privatization and economic efficiency

The crucial point, then, is that private sector defence industry organizations, where property rights underpin the profit motive, have a clear incentive to out-perform the Ministry of Defence in terms of allocative and productive efficiency. A stylized model of economic efficiency (allocative and productive) would analyse the choices for society in producing defence goods (warfare) and other goods and services (welfare) in the diagrammatic terms illustrated in Figure 5.2 below.

If the choices of society in allocating resources to the production of warfare goods and welfare goods were based upon the existence of well-informed and competitive markets, then it would appear reasonable to depict the crucial social choice, since the tearing down of the Berlin Wall, in terms of the mechanisms leading to a movement from C to B on the diagram, the fabled Peace Dividend.

Unfortunately, the defence market, as indicated above, cannot be described in these terms and the traditional non-competitive environment accompanying the disbursement of the military budget has promoted shirking, x-inefficiency and other disincentives, impeding the attainment of cost-minimizing production.

Putting to one side, temporarily, these arguments, the clamour for a peace dividend has been unrealistic, recognizing that the overall budgetary process does not permit a transfer of resources from defence to other items of public spending.

116

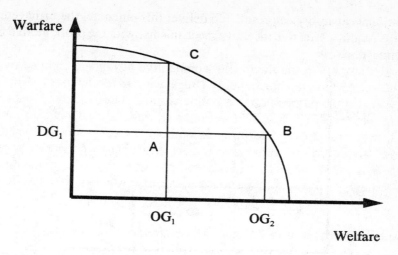

Figure 5.2 - Economic efficiency: the trade-off between warfare and welfare

Equally, the smooth substitutability of resources from warfare to welfare, as implied by the diagram, is an illusion; society's production possibility frontier is more likely to be non-convex rather than convex to the origin, suggesting that there will be significant obstacles (e.g. asset-specificity) and time lags in any readjustment of the warfare-welfare trade-off.

A pragmatic interpretation of the peace dividend might emphasize the benefits of reduced military spending in terms of an overall lower PSBR, with interest rates and the tax burden being commensurately smaller than would be the case in the absence of the reduced military spending. A problem with this type of argument is that it is based upon partial equilibrium analysis and does not incorporate the implications of reduced military spending for employment, output and tax revenue.

Hence, initiatives such as the New Management Strategy, the Defence Costs Study and market testing can be represented in the original diagram as measures that will improve productive efficiency and, in removing some of the endemic x-inefficiency within the organizational structure of the Ministry of Defence, enable society to move from A to C. Noting the earlier discussion regarding the limited degree of substitutability of resources between defence and non-defence goods, Figure 5.2 might be amended to suggest non-convexity in the production possibility frontier as

117

in Figure 5.3 below:

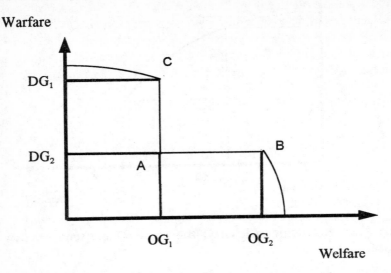

Figure 5.3 - Warfare versus welfare: non-convexities in the trade-off

As has previously been argued, allocative inefficiency can occur where public sector organizations lack a competitive environment that ensures efficient resource use. Productive inefficiency, on the other hand, can occur where an organization fails to minimize costs, often because incorrect internal organizational signals generate non-maximizing behaviour. The organization's performance is therefore adversely affected because its internal incentive and accountability structure is not designed to ensure an optimal outcome.

Evidence for efficiency

The international evidence comparing the relative efficiency attributes of public and private sector organizations is not conclusive. Borcherding *et al.* (1982), utilizing the results of more than fifty studies from five countries, argue that public sector organizations tend to display higher unit cost structures. Yet Millward (1982) was unable to find support for the superiority of the private organization, on efficiency grounds, from North

118

American studies.

There is some evidence from the defence sector, however, to suggest that the advantages of private sector provision may not be as significant as public choice theory might suggest. For example, important empirical work on the relationship between public and private sector organizations in the defence sector and their operational efficiency and overall performance calls into question the benefits of private sector provision.

Dunsire (1991) examined performance-based indicators of labour productivity and total factor productivity following changes in the status of three defence supply organizations: ROF (Royal Ordnance factories) from a government department to a trading fund in 1974; Rolls-Royce from private to public ownership in 1971; and British Aerospace from nationalization to privatization in 1981. While such an analysis inevitably confronts extremely complex problems (including the difficulty of accurately measuring performance and incorporating adjustments in enterprise objectives), several important findings emerged.

Measuring performance by changes in labour and total factor productivity, the transfer of Rolls-Royce to the public sector resulted in a significant improvement in performance. Similarly, contrary to the tenets of public choice theory, the move closer to a private sector trading organization by the Royal Ordnance factories resulted in a reduction in labour productivity although, in this instance, total factor productivity did improve overall. By contrast, the nationalization of British Aerospace does seem to have initiated a reduction in performance using these indicators, with a subsequent gain in performance following privatization in line with predictions of the established theory.

Synergy in defence and non-defence business

For a private sector defence organization, the untapped potential profits to be derived from implementing market-based efficiency measures in MoD contracts will attract those companies already performing a similar role in the defence industry or those wishing to diversify into new areas of business activity. As well as the profit motive, additional stimulants to market entry may include the potential for valuable synergy between a company's existing non-defence business activities and its intended role in the newly contractorized market.

119

Synergy of this kind can be manifested in the economies of scale, scope and experience, yielding lower production costs; the rationalization of market supply to secure a quasi-monopoly position for the most efficient firm in the new market in the longer term; and the opportunity to develop more focused and effective financial management.

Overall, within the market-testing and contracting-out approach, defence companies have to be able to demonstrate the capacity to offer defence support services more cheaply and more efficiently than MoD 'in house' providers. By offering flexible staff provision, efficiency gains from market-driven capital investment, and an improved factor-mix to achieve greater technical efficiency, private sector defence companies can, arguably, pursue cost-minimization strategies beyond the scope of their MoD counterparts.

Competing for MoD contractorization

Two types of private sector organization are likely to be interested in competing for MoD contractorization with the objective of attaining a quasi-monopoly supplier role for specific services following the competition phase. First, companies currently supplying the MoD with defence equipment and other services may possess both the managerial expertise and capacity to be able to switch business activities away from traditional areas and into those currently required from the market by the MoD. Analysis undertaken by the Research Unit in Defence Economics (Braddon *et al.*, 1991) suggested that major defence contractors, and many of their first tier suppliers, have been addressing the opportunities and threats that confront them as military expenditure declines, and are exploring precisely such new business opportunities. Many of these military-serving firms are adopting a corporate strategy for the future which includes:

a) the pursuit of collaborative business ventures in order to share, horizontally, the burden of costs and risks.
b) the enhancement of civil business, harnessing and transferring technology and other operational aspects.

In general, the emerging strategy from military-serving firms seems to be

120

one of long-range market positioning, while also targeting realistic short-term opportunities. Both elements of the emerging strategy, particularly for the largest defence contractors, are appropriate in switching the business focus from military production to the provision of MoD support services, while helping to meet the immediate diversification requirements of defence supply companies in the new post - 'Options For Change' commercial environment.

Second, private sector organizations that currently operate only in non-defence markets may be attracted into the MoD contractorization process if they identify cost advantages from the extension of existing managerial functions and capacity into new business activities. While a large private organization may have a business focus in pharmaceuticals, engine manufacture, power generation, food retailing or a range of such activities, the true business strength may reside in the 'managerial' skills and capacity that they can be brought to bear upon an organizational problem.

Expertise in facilities management

While the provision of many defence services may appear unlikely candidates for contractorization due to the specific nature, security and technical requirements of the work involved, this may be a misjudgement. Increasingly, many private companies have now developed expertise in 'facilities management' rather than performing individual business functions. Such companies operate with a broader business portfolio and can undertake a range of defence-related services provision, usually under a multi-activity contractual arrangement. While early experiments with contractorization in the MoD utilized single function contracts, these were found to be time consuming, cumbersome to operate and inflexible between functional areas.

Multi-activity contracts operated by facilities management companies, however, offer the MoD, as purchaser, advantages in terms of the enhanced flexibility of labour, permanent on-site presence of the contractor's management personnel and greater budgetary compatibility with New Management Strategy concepts. A further incentive from such contracts might be improved employment conditions for the contractor's employees. Examples of such multi-activity contractors include the provision of important support services by one company for the Ballistic

Missile Early Warning System at RAF Fylingdales, as well as the provision of more routine functions such as transport, accommodation and maintenance.

Barriers to entry

For any potential private sector entrant, however, considerable barriers to entry exist which may deter or delay entry into the market for defence support services. For the military-serving company which, traditionally, has tended to operate in a monopsonistic market producing sophisticated technical goods for the MoD, the principal barrier to market entry in a competitive contracting-out process is often 'cultural'. Although the reforms of the last decade have undoubtedly eliminated much of the historic tendency of, and incentives for, defence contractors to perpetrate cost-overruns, excessive profit-making, inefficiency, and, in extreme cases, fraud and corruption, limited experience of genuine open tendering in a new market, with many active competitors, may prove a significant barrier.

Companies which are primarily non-military in their business focus are clearly better positioned to take immediate advantage of new market opportunities in the defence sector. Managerial expertise is dedicated to ensuring a competitive edge in their principal markets on price, expected profit margins, quality, delivery time, after-sales service and other key respects. Costs are continually scrutinized to ensure that the competitive edge is maintained.

Nevertheless, several significant barriers to entry also exist to confront these companies. First, the transactions costs associated with gaining access through competition to a market, where conditions are set and monitored by a public sector monopsonist, could be considerable and may not be recouped, of course, should the competitive bid fail.

Second, having gained access to the new market, such firms may have to confront (perhaps for the first time) the critical requirements of the 'public interest'. This may include the need to operate within the constraints set by government-established regulatory bodies, limiting price and/or profit levels or, particularly in the defence sector, the need to meet stringent security requirements or life-critical quality and safety standards, both of which have significant cost implications. For example, in pursuing the contractor operation of the Atomic Weapons Establishment during the 1990s, the most stringent safety and security monitoring system was imposed on the successful contractor. A new Ministry of Defence Compliance Office was established to ensure contractor compliance with safety requirements with the authority to terminate immediately any activity deemed unsafe. At the same time, the MoD retained the power to set and monitor security standards to be maintained by private contractors.

Contracts and transaction costs

Wherever market relationships are formed, the conduct of transactions requires the formulation of appropriate contracts. In introducing contracting-in or -out to an area of government as sensitive and problematic as the provision of defence services, the adoption of particularly demanding contract procedures is required. Contracts have to be devised to cater for all future possibilities and have to be designed and applied in an environment which is constantly evolving. Such an all-embracing contract, usually termed a 'contingent claim contract', specifies what is required of all parties to the contract under any set of future conditions. Uncertainty about the future, however, imposes a 'bounded rationality' upon individuals in the contractual relationship, making the contract impossible to specify fully in practice.

An alternative approach is to adopt 'sequential spot contracting' under which a series of brief contracts is devised that attempt to incorporate all of the likely developments that may affect the contractual relationship. However, the central problem here is that, under this form of contracting, where the goods and services being exchanged are relatively unique, the supplier requires expert knowledge to meet the needs of his customer, knowledge that can only be acquired over a longer time period.

Existing suppliers will, therefore, gain a first mover advantage, thus enabling the incumbent to bid more effectively in each successive round of tendering than can any competitor. More important, once this outcome is appreciated by other potential market entrants, they will face a powerful disincentive to enter the competition. As a result, what is known as small numbers bargaining may occur in which there are few sellers and only one consumer. In essence, the competitive thrust of the newly-released market has been destroyed, with important consequences for costs and quality standards.

It is here that the bureaucratic organization, such as the MoD, may have an advantage over the competitive market, by virtue of being able to exploit an incompletely specified employment contract that reduces the scope for individual opportunism but, simultaneously, encourages trust in long-term working relationships that can promote higher reward for effective performance, leading to the development of 'goal congruence'.

Conclusions

Market testing and subsequent contractorization of defence services certainly appear to offer a range of significant benefits, The process carries with it, however, a number of important risks. On the positive side, private contractors tend to be more flexible in response to changing market conditions with greater delegation of decision-making authority to managers to respond quickly and effectively to requirements. Enhanced flexibility and a more efficient use of key resources (particularly personnel) should enable private organizations to attain greater cost-effectiveness in the delivery of defence services in an uncertain and rapidly evolving geo-political environment. On the other hand, these apparent benefits are not guaranteed and may also be perceived as risks. The contractorization process with respect to the provision of defence services may create risks in the form of:

a) limitations imposed by contractual arrangements on the MoD's capacity to adjust wider priorities as military requirements dictate.

b) the degree to which external private sector personnel can offer a reliable service.

c) the extent to which service quality and reaction time might be adversely affected.

d) the degree to which apparent cost savings can be maintained once the service is placed with a private contractor and prices increase in the future.

e) the consequences that might derive from contract failure.

f) the technical competence and financial viability of the potential contractors.

While the emerging markets in defence sector support services are clearly open to access by new entrants, the initial entry costs may be prohibitive to private sector organizations when set against the longer-term potential for profits. While such new markets may be opened up to competition, there is little chance that, in practice, the operation of these markets will remain genuinely open. In exchange for a quasi-monopoly position in the new defence market after the tendering process has ended, and the winning contractor has been selected, the government is certain to set tight safety, security and public interest constraints on the company's activities that inevitably, will limit its decision-making freedom in this most sensitive of operational areas.

References

Akerlof, G. (1970), 'The Market for Lemons: Quality Uncertainty and the Market Mechanism', *Quarterly Journal of Economics*, August, pp. 488-500.

Borcherding, T.E., Pommerehne, W.W. and Schneider, F. (1982), *Comparing the efficiency of private and public production: evidence from five countries*, Zeitschrift fur Nationalokonomie, Supplementum 2.

Braddon, D. and Kendry, A. (1986), 'The Defence Dilemma - Is Competition Enough?', *Occasional Research Paper in Economics*, Bristol Polytechnic, Bristol.

Braddon, D., Dowdall, P., Kendry, A. and Cullen, P. (1991), *The Impact of Reduced Military Expenditure on the Economy of South West England*, University of the West of England, Bristol.

Buchanan, J.M. (1978), *The Economics of Politics*, Institute of Economic Affairs, London.

Dunsire, A. (1991), 'Organizational Status Change and Performance: the Significance of Internal Structure', in Ott, A.T. and Hartley, K. (eds.) *Privatization and Economic Efficiency: A Comparative Analysis of Developed and Developing Countries*, Edward Elgar, Aldershot.

Hartley, K. (1991), *The Economics of Defence Policy*, Brassey's, London.

Hartley, K. and Parker, D. (1991), 'Privatization: A Conceptual Framework', in Ott, A.T. and Hartley, K.(eds.), *Privatization and Economic Efficiency: A Comparative Analysis of Developed and Developing Countries*, Edward Elgar, Aldershot.

Her Majesty's Government (1984), Eighth Report of the Public Accounts Committee, *The Proper Conduct of Public Business*, HMSO, London.

Her Majesty's Government (1991), *Competing for Quality* (Cmnd 1730), HMSO, London.

Jackson, P.M. (1994), 'The new public sector management: surrogate competition and contracting out', in Jackson, P.M. and Price, C.M. (eds.), *Privatization and Regulation: A review of the issues*, Longman, London and New York.

Millward, R. (1982), 'The comparative performance of public and private ownership', in Rolls, E., *The Mixed Economy*, Macmillan, London.

Ministry of Defence (1992), *The Guide to Competition in Defence Services*, The Market Testing Service, London.

Ministry of Defence (1994), *Front Line First: The Defence Costs Study*, HMSO, London.

Ministry of Defence (1994), Statement on the Defence Estimates (Cmnd. 2550), HMSO, London.

Ministry of Defence (1995), Statement on the Defence Estimates (Cmnd. 2800), HMSO, London.

Ott, A.T. and Hartley, K. (1991), *Privatization and Economic Efficiency: A Comparative Analysis of Developed and Developing Countries*, Edward Elgar, Aldershot.

Radner, R. (1992), 'Hierarchy: the Economics of Managing', *Journal of Economic Literature*, September.

Rasmussen, E. (1991), *Games and Information*, Basil Blackwell, Oxford.

Rosen, S. (1985), 'Implicit Contracts: A Survey', *Journal of Economic Literature*, September, pp 1144-1175.

Sandler, T. and Cauley, J. (1975), 'On the Economic Theory of Alliances', *Journal of Conflict Resolution*, vol.19, no. 2, pp. 330-348.

Sandler, T. and Murdoch, J.C. (1990), 'Nash-Cournot or Lindahl Behaviour?: An Empirical Test for the NATO Allies', *Quarterly Journal of Economics*, vol.105, no. 4, pp. 875-894.

Sandler, T. and Hartley, K. (1995), *The Economics of Defense*, Cambridge University Press, Cambridge.

Tullock, G. (1976), *The Vote Motive*, Institute of Economic Affairs, London.

Uttley, M. (1993), 'Contracting-Out and Market-Testing in the UK Defence Sector: Theory, Evidence and Issues', *Public Money and Management*, January - March; pp. 55 - 60.

Williamson, O.E. (1975), *Markets and Hierarchies: Analysis and Anti-Trust Implications-A Study in the Economics of Internal Organization*, Free Press, London.

Wulf, H. (1993), 'Arms Industry Limited: The Turning Point in the 1990s', in Wulf, H. (1993), *Arms Industry Limited*, Oxford University Press, New York.

6 The Privatization of Social Housing

ANTHONY PLUMRIDGE

Introduction

The privatization of social housing in the UK stands apart from other privatizations of the post-1979 Tory government. Housing has a central role in the lives of the typical household, both economically and socio-culturally. Major shifts in housing tenure and management have potential consequences of great significance in terms of welfare and economic behaviour. Lifestyles are much more likely to be altered by the privatization of housing than by the combined effects of all other privatizations. Moreover, the value of housing assets transferred to date amounts to some 50 per cent of the total value of assets transferred in the course of other privatizations. It is thus by far the largest single privatization. Finally, the origins of social housing privatization stretch back to the beginning of the twentieth century and its dominant component, the sale of council houses, has been high on the political agenda throughout the post-war period.

In addition to the sale of council houses to their tenants, there have been other methods of transfer of houses to private ownership, as well as changes in financing, management and production policies which can be classified as privatization. A brief history of the evolution of housing privatization policies is given in the first section. The second section examines some of the macro-scale consequences for the economy as a whole. Next, the typical experience of households purchasing their council houses is compared with those still renting. Then the impact of privatization on the supply and stock of dwellings is reviewed. Finally, current policy proposals are examined and lessons for the future drawn.

History of the privatization of social housing

The sale of council housing up to 1979

The sale of housing built by the public sector dates back to late nineteenth century slum clearance programmes. Some 24,000 dwellings constructed by municipal authorities under the 1890 Housing and Working Classes Act had been sold by 1914. After the first world war, a succession of Housing Acts designed to produce 'homes fit for heroes' resulted in a massive output of some 3.8 million houses by 1938, of which some 1.1 million were built by local and new town authorities. During this period, there were sales by some local authorities on a 'best price obtainable' basis. In 1938 the composition of the housing stock was 32 per cent owner occupied, 10 per cent public sector and 58 per cent private rented. Owner occupation had grown rapidly in the inter-war period through new construction and purchases, especially from the private rented sector. Council housing was predominantly for the respectable working class and lower middle classes. The most disadvantaged sections of society tended to be housed in the private rented sector. After the second world war a serious housing shortage emerged as a result of slum clearance and the decline of the private rented sector, as well as a result of bomb damage. Some 3.7 million new homes had been constructed by 1960, 2.3 million by the public sector. Owner occupation continued to grow, partly through new construction and partly by purchases from the private rented sector, which declined by some 2 million units.

There was some support for council house sales in the 1952 Housing Act introduced by the new Conservative government. The previous requirement for sale at 'the best price obtainable' was dropped, although sales were entirely at the local authority's discretion. Some 9,000 council houses had been sold by 1957, but the demand then fell as private development expanded.

Between 1960 and 1975, the rate of private development increased: some 2.6 million houses were built, mainly for owner occupation. A prominent political debate on the issue of council house sales took place during the 1960s, with Labour at first opposing, but then capitulating to Conservative views a few years later. Sales remained steady during the early 1960s (see Table 6.1) but began to grow from 1966. The Labour government followed somewhat inconsistent polices, reflecting a lack of any overwhelming commitment either to support or oppose the principle of discretionary sales. In 1967 a 20 per cent discount off the price was allowed, but this discount had to be related to the open market price. This could be seen as acquiescing to the reality of sales at below the market price. Sales doubled in 1968. As a reaction, quotas were introduced by Labour setting a maximum ceiling to the volume of permitted sales.

Table 6.1

Sales of local authority dwellings 1960-93, England and Wales

Year	Number sold	Year	Number sold
1960	2,889	1977	13,020
1961	3,795	1978	30,045
1962	4,404	1979	41,665
1963	3,673	1980	81,485
1964	3,817	1981	102,835
1965	3,590	1982	201,880
1966	4,906	1983	145,585
1967	4,867	1984	103,180
1968	9,979	1985	92,295
1969	8,590	1986	88,410
1970	6,816	1987	108,178
1971	17,214	1988	160,128
1972	45,878	1989	187,169
1973	34,334	1990	145,402
1974	4,657	1991	80,120
1975	2,723	1992	72,034
1976	5,793	1993	74,723

Includes sales by local authorities and new towns to owner occupiers, housing associations and others.

Source: Housing and Construction Statistics, HMSO.

Sales fell in 1969 and 1970. The quotas were removed by the Conservatives in 1970 and the permitted discount increased to 30 per cent. Sales increased dramatically as a result. The 1973 Housing Act allowed further increases in discount and extended discretionary sales to Scotland. Paradoxically, sales fell in 1973 and collapsed subsequently, in spite of the new Labour government continuing Conservative policies. Forrest and Murie (1991) suggest that soaring prices took council house prices beyond the affordability of many potential purchasers.

Sales picked up again from 1976 to 1979, approaching the early 1970s peak by the end of the decade. During this period the economy recovered somewhat from the medium term effects of the oil crisis and the three day week and at the end of the period nominal house prices increased rapidly. Forrest and Murie (*ibid.*) account for the increase in sales in terms of improving affordability and local authorities becoming sympathetic to purchase following Conservative successes in local elections. In 1979 the Labour government responded by restricting eligibility to those tenants of more than two years' standing and by forbidding the sales of vacant council houses. The latter was revoked by the Conservative Government in the 1980 Housing Act, which introduced the 'Right to Buy'.

The 'Right to Buy'

During the 1970s, there was much debate on the policy of local authority discretion over council house sales. The opportunity for the further expansion of owner occupation came to rely more on new building as the size of the private rented sector shrank to some 12 per cent of the total housing stock by the end of the decade and sales into owner occupation, 'gentrification' as it had come to be called, slowed down. Moreover, council house building had been in competition with private residential development for the resources of the construction industry and thus was at the expense of growth in owner occupation. The 'Right to Buy', ending the discretion of local authorities over council house sales, together with policies reducing the rate of construction of social housing, served the objectives of the new Conservative government of increasing owner occupation.

The 1980 Housing Act included a uniform statutory procedure to be followed by all local authorities in implementing the 'Right to Buy' provisions, backed up by very strong intervention powers for the Secretary of State to ensure compliance. Only tenants of at least three years' standing were eligible to buy. The minimum discount was set at 33 per cent with an extra per cent discount for each year of tenancy over three years up to a maximum of 50 per cent. Repayment of a proportion of the discount was enforceable if resale took place within five years. The Act granted a legal right to a mortgage on terms set by the Secretary of State and gave potential purchasers a two-year option to buy on the basis of the initial valuation in return for a deposit of £100. A discretionary scheme for sale to those not qualifying under the 'Right to Buy' was also introduced. The impact of the new legislation on sales was dramatic (see Table 6.1). During the early years there was considerable resistance from a few local authorities. The resolve of the government to force through this highly centralist interventionist policy was demonstrated in the case of Norwich City Council. The 'Right to Buy' policy was challenged in the courts, but the Department of the Environment triumphed. The UK economy was only just emerging from the deepest recession since the second world war. Unemployment was rising sharply, recent public spending cuts had been so severe as to cause riots, and interest and mortgage rates were only just falling after having reached historically exceptionally high levels. In spite of these difficult conditions, large numbers of tenants took advantage of the 'Right to Buy', suggesting that there were significant factors in the legislation that made purchase possible. After their election defeat in 1983, even the Labour Party ceased to oppose the 'Right to Buy' in principle.

However, by 1983, the rate of sale was beginning to slow down. This coincided with an overall increase in the level of economic activity, although unemployment continued to rise for some time to levels comparable with those experienced in the slump of the pre-war years. The diminishing supply of both desirable properties and sufficiently prosperous tenants to buy them no doubt contributed to this decline. Measures were introduced in the Housing Acts of 1984, 1985 and 1986 intended to stimulate sales. The qualifying period of tenancy was reduced from three to two years and the maximum discount extended to 60 per cent for tenants of 30 years standing or more. Discounts on flats started at 44 per cent and increased to 70 per cent after only 15 years tenancy. Early resale penalties were reduced and there was protection against unforeseen structural defects and excessive increases in service charges.

The majority of housing association tenants, although nominally covered by 'Right to Buy' legislation, were prevented from buying by the charitable status of most associations. The Housing Acts entitled such tenants to cash grants to enable them to buy a home in the private market. In addition, home purchase was brought within the reach of council tenants on lower incomes by the introduction of shared ownership schemes.

The rate of sale increased again after 1986, probably due to the combined effects of sharply improving employment prospects and the capital gains tenants perceived they might make in a buoyant housing market during the boom years at the end of the decade. The 1988 Housing Act attempted to further increase affordability with the introduction of the Rent to Mortgage scheme. This allowed a progressive process of equity acquisition. It was piloted in a few trial areas with a disappointing response, possibly because of lower discount rates than under 'Right to Buy' and the general difficulties in the housing market.

After falling from 1990, sales figures in Table 6.1 level off. The continuing decline in individual sales is disguised by increasing Large Scale Voluntary Transfers (LSVTs) from 1990. The downturn in the economic cycle and a sharp reduction in affordability are partly responsible. So too is the further decline in the remaining numbers of eligible tenants and suitable properties in the local authority sector. The current policy responses to this situation are considered at the end of this chapter.

Large Scale Voluntary Transfers

LSVTs were facilitated by the 1980 Act. Local authorities could elect to transfer part of their stock to housing associations or private landlords. Where the estates needed refurbishment, the original tenants were 'decanted' into alternative accommodation and paid compensation. The dwellings on the refurbished estate were then offered for sale or for rent to new tenants. Tenants of local authority properties could transfer their 'Right to Buy' discounts to such schemes.

Legislation introduced in the 1985 Act allowed local authorities to transfer all or a substantial part of their housing with sitting tenants to another landlord, provided the agreement of a majority of the tenants was obtained. Guarantees of very favourable future rents have often been the price for tenant support. Whole housing departments of local authorities have reconstituted themselves as new housing associations for the purpose of taking over the council housing stock. A result has been that the stock taken over remained in the social rented sector as the 'Right to Buy' did not extend to the new tenants.

The 1988 Housing Act introduced two new initiatives. 'Tenants Choice' allowed the initiative for large-scale transfers to come from a prospective new landlord or the tenants themselves. The legislation requires a ballot of tenants to be held and, unless a majority of tenants eligible to vote object, the transfer proceeds. The minority objecting can remain as council tenants. To date the impact of this policy has been limited. Housing Action Trust legislation allowed central government to takeover run-down estates for refurbishment in the absence of any local authority or Tenants Choice initiative. Such estates would then be transferred to a new landlord. Contrary to the government's expectations, pilot schemes met with considerable tenant resistance arising out of a concern over future rents under a private landlord. Consequently, current proposals involve the passing of estates back to the local authority. The volume of all such large-scale transfers was small until 1988, since when it has been averaging some 20,000 dwellings a year, reaching a total of about 180,000 by 1995.

The privatization of housing production

There has been a considerable shift away from the provision of new housing by the state to provision by the private and voluntary sectors, and at the same time a shift away from the funding of the voluntary sector by the state to funding by the private sector. Table 6.2 shows how housing associations have become dominant in the production of social housing, although local authorities have increased capital expenditure on refurbishing their retained housing stock. In addition, since the 1988 Housing Act, the Housing Corporation grant to housing associations has fallen as a proportion of total development costs, the balance being increasingly funded by private sector finance. The effective grant rate in 1990-91 was some 80 per cent. This is forecast to fall to some 55 per cent for 1995-96 (The Housing Corporation, 1994).

The macro-economic impact of privatization

Table 6.6 below (discussed in detail later) shows that the proportion of the housing stock accounted for by owner occupied dwellings increased by some eleven percentage points between 1979 and 1993, while the decline in the proportion accounted for by local authority housing declined by some eleven percentage points. It does not follow, of course, that all the increase in owner occupation came from the sale of council houses, as the housing stock was increasing over the period. The sale of some 1.5 million council houses accounted for some 35 per cent of the increase in the number of owner occupied dwellings. The remaining increase came predominantly from new construction by the private sector. However, not only were council houses sold, they were not replaced, forcing many new households to consider purchasing in the private sector. Thus housing policy as a whole was responsible for much of the increase in owner occupation.

Important macro-economic consequences flow from this: an increased sensitivity of consumer expenditure to changes in the mortgage interest rate and house price fluctuations; an enhancement of the potentially destabilizing effects of equity withdrawal and equity replenishment; a growth in the potential demand for home-centred goods and services; a shift in the economic behaviour of those socio-economic groups and cohorts where households entering the housing market are concentrated.

The late 1980s demonstrated the destabilizing effects of equity withdrawal, amounting to some £25 billion in 1987-88 and a major factor in the consumer boom at the end of the decade (see Holmans, 1994). The collapse in house prices, the resulting negative equity and consequent equity replenishment or repossession, has been shown to have been a major factor in the collapse of consumer expenditure in the early 1990s (see Mean, 1994). This medium-term volatility in the housing market has led to widespread calls in trade journals and the press for a fundamental reassessment of housing policy (see, for example, Bevins, Garrett and Oulton, 1995; MacEarlean, 1995; Foster, 1995; and Stewart, 1995).

Impact on housing finance

There have been major consequences for the government's overall housing budget and thus for the financing of public sector expenditure. The impact of privatization is complex and there are many implications for the exchequer. The overall value of council house sales depends on the numbers sold, movements in house prices and the level of 'Right to Buy' discounts offered.

These discounts lead to a capital loss for local authorities. Council house sales to tenants lead to a flow of payments to the local authority comprising initial deposits securing the 'Right to Buy', deposits paid by those taking out a local authority mortgage, repayments made on such mortgages and capital sums received from those tenants taking out a private sector mortgage (an increasing proportion over time).

Table 6.2

Housing production: permanent dwellings completed (UK)

Year	Private sector	Housing assn.	All Public sector	Total
1971	52,166	22,779	113,658	288,603
1979	143,949	18,055	89,691	251,695
1980	131,974	21,422	88,590	241,986
1981	118,579	19,420	68,567	206,566
1982	129,004	13,506	40,309	182,819
1983	153,038	16,777	39,218	209,033
1984	165,574	17,282	37,638	220,494
1985	163,395	13,664	30,422	207,481
1986	178,017	13,161	25,416	216,594
1987	191,212	13,117	21,833	226,162
1988	207,387	13,496	21,451	242,334
1989	187,504	14,619	19,323	221,446
1990	166,655	17,353	17,879	201,887
1991	159,290	20,469	11,211	190,970
1992	147,094	25,899	5,740	178,733
1993	144,604	34,409	3,248	182,261

Source: DoE Housing and Construction Statistics, 1994, Table 6.1 and earlier equivalents.

Clearly, the cash flow emanating from council house sales will not bear a simple proportional relationship to the value of those sales. LSVTs lead to a different pattern of payments to those emanating from tenant purchasers as the purchase funding arrangements are not comparable.

Council house sales lead to a loss of rental income. Against this must be offset a reduction in management and maintenance costs that have been borne by the local authority.

The reduction of public sector housing production results in a reduction in capital expenditure against which must be offset increased Housing Corporation funding and tax allowances made available to the private sector, such as those under the Business Expansion Scheme.

The shift from council renting to owner occupation reduces the number of households entitled to rent allowances, rent rebates and housing benefit, as owner occupiers do not qualify for such support. Offsetting this there is an increase in the number of households qualifying for unemployment mortgage assistance and for mortgage interest tax relief (MIRAS). The impact of all these vary as rates of benefit and the rate and basis of tax relief change.

The movement of council rents towards market levels increases local authority revenue but increases expenditure on rent rebates and allowances paid to those tenants who cannot afford the increased rents. The picture is complicated by the replacement of these rent subsidies by housing benefit, which falls within the social security programme rather than the housing programme. Further, it is arguable that the growth in housing benefit expenditure and the high level of such expenditure, compared with the equivalent benefits in other countries, is more the consequence of the inadequacy of unemployment benefit and income support rather than the consequence of changes in the system of housing provision in the UK. There may be further indirect costs to the Exchequer as a consequence of reduced incentives to work, increases in the Retail Price Index and reduced employment flexibility (see National Federation of Housing Associations, 1994).

It is beyond the scope of this chapter to evaluate in money terms the impact of this complex web of financial consequences of privatization. Forrest and Murie (1991, ch.5) attempt such an exercise. They include the following figures for capital receipts from property sales by the public sector as a whole, the bulk of which emanate from 'Right to Buy' sales, from 1979-80 to 1987-88:

The direct impact of these receipts on the PSBR was through reductions in grants paid by central government to local authorities. Overall, local authority capital expenditure on housing was determined within the national Housing Investment Programme (HIP).

The aggregate funds made available to local authorities under this programme during the 1980s was determined taking into account estimated 'Right to Buy' receipts. The overall HIP was thus less than it would otherwise have been in the absence of the 'Right to Buy'. The basis of allocation to individual local authorities did not take into account the extent to which that authority's 'Right to Buy' receipts departed from the national average. As it turned out, the flow of 'Right to Buy' receipts was much greater than anticipated by the Department of the Environment in their 1980-81 forecast.

Table 6.3

Capital receipts by the public sector from the housing programme
(£ million cash)

Year	79-80	80-1	81-2	82-3	83-4	84-5	85-6	86-7	87-8
Total receipts	472	603	1,045	1,877	1,955	1,804	1,771	1,886	1,702

Source: Forrest and Murie (1990b), Table 5.4.

This was due to a higher level of sales and, from the mid 1980s on, the higher proportion of private sector mortgage finance as a result of financial liberalization. Local authorities were limited in the use they were permitted to make of this 'windfall'. Initially only 50 per cent and after 1987 only 20 per cent of council house sale receipts could be used to top up the HIP allocations. The remainder had to be held on deposit by local authorities and interest used to reduce current expenditure. Thus the requirement for grants towards local authority current deficits was reduced.

In summary, therefore, the direct impact of council house sales on the PSBR is a reduction in the capital cost to central government of the HIP and a reduction in the current grants to local authorities. These together might have reduced the PSBR by some £14 billion over the period from 1980 to 1994 inclusive. In addition, some £6 billion of sale proceeds are held currently by local authorities.

The typical experience of privatization

The political context

It is often suggested that the motives for the vigorous implementation of 'Right to Buy' policies were based on political rather than welfare considerations. These policies were very much a key component of the 1980s Thatcherite crusade. Home ownership is seen by those on the centre/right of the political spectrum as a major component of popular capitalism together with wider share ownership (Saunders and Harris, 1994, p. 27). There is thus a certain circularity in some of the political arguments justifying policies which lead to an increase in home ownership: owning one's own home is part and parcel of popular capitalism and desirable because home owners tend to support popular capitalism.

Marxists and the traditional left, on the other hand, have a deep resentment of home ownership and the associated homecentredness. As Colin Ward (1983) puts it: '(they) fear that the workers will be at home papering the parlour when they ought to be out in the streets making a revolution'. The evidence for shifts in political allegiance from Labour to Conservative following council house purchase is not strong. Saunders (1990) reviews many surveys in an attempt to present a convincing case. Forrest and Murie (1990) point out that there is little evidence for a direct causal relation between changes in tenure from council renting to owner occupation and changes in political allegiance. Rather, they suggest that there may be independent attitude factors which predispose certain households both to purchase their council houses and to switch from traditional Labour support to voting Conservative.

Housing tenure and welfare

The welfare implications of social housing privatization will depend in part on whether the shift in tenure to owner occupation has been in line with household preferences. An example of stated preference data is that given in the Housing and Saving survey by BMRB in 1989. (Table 6.4)

Saunders describes a 'crippling and frustrating sense of powerlessness' amongst respondents renting council houses. He postulates that the reference group for council tenants used to be those renting in the private sector but has now become owner occupiers. With this change has come

140

increasing dissatisfaction.

Table 6.4

Type of accommodation in which would most like to live in two years time, by present tenure, per cent of total

	A	B	C	D	E	F	G
Total	100	70.5	22.1	1.7	2.4	2.2	1.1
Preferred tenure							
Owned	81	95	47	18	69	31	67
Council	12	1	48	7	9	11	10
H. Assn.	2	-	2	68	1	-	8
Prvt fn.	1	1	1	-	17	3	-
Prvt. unf.	2	-	1	2	4	52	5
D/K	1	1	1	5	-	2	10

Source: BMRB Housing and Saving (1989).

Key: A = Total   E = Private rented furnished
      B = Owner-occupied F = Private rented unfurnished
      C = Council rented   G = Other
      D = Housing Assn rented

From the three towns survey, Saunders concludes that there are high levels of preference for owner occupation irrespective of age, ethnic origin or current tenure.

There has been a lengthy debate over the reliability and significance of such stated preferences. Saunders (1990) summarizes the findings of studies of tenure preferences between 1967 and 1988 showing a growing popularity for home ownership.

Saunders and Harris conducted a survey of 450 owner occupier and council renting households in three towns, Slough, Derby and Burnley, in 1986.

On the basis of this, Saunders (1990) suggests reasons for a preference for owner occupation, which are summarized here as follows:

Financial: mortgage payments work out in the long run to be cheaper than rents; there is the prospect of a capital gain; the property can be bequeathed.

Control: home can be modified and personalized; there is the freedom to make use of it indefinitely in any way one wishes; there is security of tenure.

Achievement: pride accompanies ownership; owning property confers status.

These advantages are compared with the disadvantages of renting a council house identified by Saunders:

Financial: rent is perceived as wasted, throwing money away; rents are increasing at a much faster rate than earnings.

Control: maintenance is inefficient; decoration is restricted; mobility to another area or type of property is difficult.

Forrest and Murie (1990) take issue with Saunders regarding high levels of dissatisfaction among council tenants and point to methodological factors that account for the failure of Saunders and Harris to identify a general level of satisfaction amongst council tenants as revealed in other studies. They cite studies prompted by the Tenants Choice legislation in the 1988 Housing Act. These show a more frequent majority preference among tenants for retaining the council as landlord rather than entrusting management to either a private landlord or to a tenants' cooperative. Forrest and Murie also use their own data from research carried out in London and Birmingham in 1988 to support their position. This was a longitudinal study of council house purchasers.

Forrest and Murie (1990, p. 86) stress that tenure preferences change over time in response to changes in:

the current realities of the stock of dwellings, the means of access to them, the way in which they are managed and the financial and policy framework.

With uncanny foresight of what was to occur in the UK, they describe how changes in the preference for renting in the Netherlands reflected the 'collapse' of home ownership in the early 1980s. The proportions were 60.7 per cent, 72 per cent and 61.5 per cent in 1977, 1981 and 1985 respectively.

Forrest and Murie also refer to pre-war and wartime housing studies showing very different attitudes to tenure in the UK in the past. Tenure was not seen by the researchers or respondents as important compared with the attributes provided by dwellings. Forrest and Murie conclude that there is nothing natural, inherent or cultural in a preference for home ownership.

Further evidence is provided by a study of households involved in LSVTs. A survey of the new residents in fifteen such schemes and some of the original tenants displaced (Glendenning, 1989) gives some interesting results relevant to some of the issues raised here. Some 88 per cent of respondents were very or fairly satisfied with their new accommodation, irrespective of whether they were renters or owners. There was a wide variation in the perceived quality of council accommodation. The Glendenning study interviewed former tenants of some of the least desirable council dwellings - tenants who chose to move rather than purchasing as sitting tenants and tenants decanted from estates in need of renovation. Tenure did not emerge as a factor influencing reported overall satisfaction, whereas the rate of discount enjoyed by purchasers did.

Coercive factors

A preference for owner occupation is revealed by over one million council tenants exercising their 'Right to Buy' as shown in Table 6.1 above. This has been seem by some as 'coerced', in the sense that tenants have been driven to move by policies that exploit the stick of council house squalor or the carrot of pecuniary gain. If this is true, it undermines arguments that welfare is enhanced purely as a result of the shift to owner occupation through tenants buying their council houses.

Negative coercive factors

Forrest and Murie's work discounts the proposition that there is widespread dissatisfaction amongst council tenants and this suggests that the concept of a stick of squalor has not been a widespread motivation. The authors do, however, acknowledge that there is research evidence that rising rents constitute a negative factor encouraging council house purchase (1990, p. 88). In addition, Saunders (1990, p. 108) refers to evidence of another negative factor: the lack of choice facing new households. Those who could afford to buy had to buy, those who could not could only hope to be housed by the council.

Positive coercive factors

The perceived benefits of purchase in the predominantly strong housing market of the 1980s were significant (see for example Saunders, 1990). The carrots of pecuniary gain consisted of an instant capital gain of up to 70 per cent (on average some 43 per cent) of valuation due to discount; a future anticipated capital gain as house prices increased in real terms; and a build up of equity in the property over 25 years as opposed to rent payments until death or the end of the tenancy with nothing to show.

Even set against the negative factor of rents increasing rapidly in real terms, these inducements turn out to be significant. Saunders in his three town survey estimated the real (1986 prices) annual gross gain for the households who had purchased their homes from the council. This averaged in excess of £2,500 per annum up to spring/summer 1986. There was a wide spread of experiences, from the lowest decile averaging a gain of only some £400 per annum to the highest averaging over £5000 per annum. It should be noted that these figures omit mortgage repayments, transaction costs and all current expenditure.

A full picture can only be achieved by taking into account current expenditure, comparing council rents with the mortgage interest payments net of tax relief, repair and maintenance costs borne by purchasers. This is a complex exercise, and Saunders attempts only a crude estimation. He works out a nominal annual average net rate of return on capital invested (the deposit, not the full purchase price) of 37.5 per cent per annum to over 60 per cent, depending on gearing. What emerges is that the exceptionally high rates of return and capital gains accruing to purchasers of council houses is largely due to the initial discount on valuation, averaging 44 per cent in the Saunders study. It is arguable that the rate of discount has been set too high.

Hills (1991) considers whether the level of discount results in a 'fair price' to the local authority and the purchaser, reflecting the discounted stream of benefits and costs transferred. On reasonable assumptions Hills shows that, for a (young) tenant expecting 45 years of occupancy and not entitled to housing benefit, the discount should stand at around 25 per cent and fall each year until it reaches zero at the end of the tenancy. This is, of course, a much lower level of discount than that offered under 'Right to Buy' legislation where after the qualifying two years the discount is 32 per cent and thereafter increases to a maximum of 60 per cent, rather than falling to zero!

Saunders (1990) shows that the mortgage outgoings of council house purchasers are likely to be higher, and in some case very much higher, than they were paying as tenants. He shows that, in principle, as a result of the mortgage debt being fixed in money terms and declining in real terms, rents fixed in real terms will, in his typical example, overtake mortgage outgoings after 19 years. After 25 years the mortgage will be repaid and the undiscounted lifetime housing costs after 50 years will be some three times greater for the tenant.

Although Saunders ignores the other outgoings which the purchaser has to bear, such as maintenance and insurance, a thorough analysis taking these into account, discounting all the costs and bringing in the substantial capital gains on some reasonable discounting assumptions, would be certain to show substantial financial benefits to the majority of sitting tenant council house purchasers during the period up to 1986.

Those purchasing after 1986 may not have fared so well in financial terms. It is likely that those purchasing at the top of the market in 1988-89 would be in a far stronger financial position by 1995 had they remained as council tenants. A simple illustration is given in Table 6.5 below based on a typical council house worth £36,000 in 1988 purchased by a young tenant.

The illustration below shows the purchaser to be some £12,500 worse off than if he/she had remained renting. This ignores discounting which would increase the capital loss significantly. On the simple assumptions made, outgoings would increase from some £300 per month in early 1988 and peak at £420 in 1991 compared with £100 per month immediately before purchase when still renting. A typical family on, say, two-thirds average earnings facing such a steep rise in outgoings would be very likely to run up mortgage arrears in the event of any disruption of earnings or unexpected expenditure. Clearly, it is likely that a significant number of purchasers at the end of the 1980s could have had their initial financial benefits wiped out and some of these will have found themselves facing repossession. Such experiences may well have changed the attitudes to owner occupation discussed above.

There is ample anecdotal evidence for increasing financial problems facing tenants who purchased at the peak of the market. Empirical evidence for the impact of such problems on attitudes to tenure is less clear cut. A follow-up survey by Lynn (1991) interviewed part of the sample studied in 1985-6 by Kerr (1988). This showed an increase, from 33 to 39 per cent, of tenants citing inability to afford the mortgage as a reason for not buying. The proportion of buyers facing problems in keeping up with payments increased from 9 to 18 per cent. However, the fieldwork was conducted prior to mortgage rates reaching the 1990-91 peak and prior to the collapse of house prices. Respondents showed a lack of knowledge of relative rent and mortgage cost movements and attitudes to tenure had not changed significantly between the two surveys.

A more recent study by Hedges and Clemens (1994) was based on fieldwork carried out early in 1992, too early to fully reflect the degree of gloom in the housing market apparent three years later. Of those interviewed with a mortgage, 26 per cent expressed worry over their ability to make payments and the threat of repossession. Attitudes to tenure were largely assessed on the basis of actual moves made in the past and thus that part of the study is of little help in reflecting the impact of 1992 housing market conditions. Even so, the results show a marked decrease over time in moves from renting to owner occupation and a marked increase in moves from owner occupation to renting, although the proportion making the latter change in tenure was still only some 4 per cent. Responses on likely future tenure among those likely to move do reflect 1992 conditions and do show some reduction in the proportion anticipating owner occupation (76 per cent) and an increase in those anticipating renting (24 per cent) compared with the preferences shown in the 1989 BMRB survey (Table 6.4). Naturally, such comparisons between studies must be made with caution.

Housing decisions are based on a wide range of factors. These factors include the attributes of the available supply, together with financial and employment considerations.

Households are not influenced mainly by ideological and tenure-centred factors. It seems reasonable to conclude that the majority of households have experienced an increase in welfare as a result of exercising their 'Right to Buy', although in large part due to the carrots of discounts and capital gains. However, more recent purchasers may not have prospered to the same extent.

Forrest and Murie (1990) hold the view that council renting and owner occupation are complementary and that council renting forms a stepping stone to owner occupation. The implication is that the success of many local authority housing programmes has led to the success of the 'Right to Buy'.

The evolution of the housing stock

This section reviews the consequences of the privatization of social housing for the overall supply of housing in the UK in terms of quantity, quality, and choice. Table 6.6 below gives a general picture of the evolution of housing stock analysed by tenure over the last two decades.

Table 6.2 above showed the overall decline in housing production and changes in the composition of that output. As Table 6.6 shows, the overall housing stock has been increasing over the period. The number of households was 20,695,000 in 1984, 21,766,000 in 1989 and 22,503,000 in 1992 (DoE, 1994). The extent to which the housing stock exceeded these figures was 1.0 million in 1984, 0.9 million in 1989 and 0.8 million in 1992.

Quantity

It is to be expected that there are more dwellings than households due to concealed households not isolated by the census, voids between lets in the rented sectors and the significant number of holiday homes and properties let to holidaymakers. Thus the 'excess' housing stock is not inconsistent

147

Table 6.5

A hypothetical illustration of tenant purchaser losses

Capital position in 1995:	£	£
Purchase price in 1988 (33% discount)		(24,000)
Value in 1995 (after 40% market decline)	21,600	
Value of With-Profits Endowment policy	2,000	
Total Assets		23,600
Capital Gain/(Loss)		(400)
Revenue position from 1988 to 1995	£	£
Mortgage payments (net of tax relief)	(15,000)	
Endowment premiums	(4,000)	
Maintenance and insurance	(4,200)	
Total outgoings		(23,000)
Council Rent saved		10,850
Profit/(Loss)		(12,150)

Notes
1. 100 per cent endowment mortgage assumed.
2. Endowment premiums are £50 per month; the policy bears £2,200 front end loaded commission and charges.
3. Maintenance assumed at £10 per week.
4. Buildings insurance assumed at £100 per annum.
5. Rent starts at £25 in 1988 rising to £37 a week by 1995.

with a housing shortage. The margin of dwellings over households declined over the period. This could be partly explained by increasing efficiency in the rented sectors. There is evidence of falling voids in the local authority rented sector.

However, the number of second homes and holiday homes is increasing. There may well have been an increasing housing shortage as a result of policies pursued in the 1980s. Hills (1991) gives some anecdotal evidence for this view. The shift in production from the public to the private and voluntary sectors tends to result in output moving in line with the economic cycle, rather than in response to housing need. Table 6.2 above showed total production following the 'boom-bust' cycle of the 1980s.

If steady economic growth without excessive inflation is sustained into the next millennium, the private and voluntary sectors may be able to

Table 6.6

Stock of dwellings by housing tenure
Great Britain

Year	Owner occupied %	Private rented %	Hsng Ass. rented %	Lcl Auth. rented %	Total Stock thousands
1974	53.0	16.3		30.7	19.6
1979	54.7	13.8		31.4	20.7
1984	59.6	10.6	2.4	27.4	21.7
1989	65.2	9.1	2.9	22.8	22.7
1993	66.4	9.7	3.7	20.1	23.5

Source: DoE, *Housing and Construction Statistics*, 1994, Table 9.3 and earlier equivalents.

respond to demand without being alternately held back or encouraged by fluctuations in confidence or the availability and cost of funding. Past experience suggests that economic management, even of the 'sound money and sound public finances' variety, is unlikely to achieve such stability in the economic environment in the long run. It is also likely that exogenous shocks and international structural adjustments will have an impact on the equilibrium of financial markets, with repercussions for the private sector funding of housing production in the UK. As the Managing Director of a finance company active in lending to the voluntary sector put it:

> All debt depends on world economic issues, and I am not sure that housing should depend on interest rates and inflation in that way. (*Inside Housing*, 7 April 1995)

A case could be made for countercyclical public housing investment, compensating for fluctuations in private sector production, so that output maintains a stable relationship to demand. This might be best achieved by a combination of measures, applied to refurbishment as well as new construction and to housing association subsidies as well as to local authority capital grants.

Quality

The debate as to whether the social or private sector produces better quality housing is long established. The private sector is capable of producing some of the worst housing (for example nineteenth century slums) and some of the best (for example Unwin and Parker's Letchworth). The public sector has the same mixed reputation: contrast the discredited high rise developments of the 1960s with some of the low density Parker Morris standard homes built in the post-war New Towns. Coming up to date, of the ten winners of the 1995 Housing Project Awards, five were within the social sector, three within the private sector and two were partnership schemes. Thus, on the evidence, there is no reason to conclude that a shift from social to private sector provision will necessarily increase quality.

Quality of housing has many components. An economist might argue that private provision within a free competitive market should result in a wide choice of housing tailored to meet consumer needs at the lowest possible cost. This proposition is more applicable to regularly purchased

150

widely marketed consumer goods and services, such as those which have been the subject of other privatizations discussed in this book. In the case of housing, the market is awash with imperfections. House purchase (or the agreement to a lease) is an infrequent occurrence and a major financial commitment. Transaction and search costs are high. The purchase (or renting) decision is a complex one involving the appraisal of many product qualities in addition to price or rent: size; style; internal layout; specification; running costs; garden; privacy; setting; neighbourhood and community; access; availability and quality of essential services; availability of leisure facilities; employment opportunities. Some of these qualities will not be capable of a fully informed assessment. The welfare implications of making the wrong decision are great. The financial and other costs of attempting to effect another choice of product are considerable. Further, there are considerable externalities of both housing production and consumption. It is not inconceivable that the most enlightened system of public sector provision, with planners and architects making full use of techniques of consultation and allowing consumer participation wherever possible, could attain higher standards of product quality than could be attained by private provision.

There are further aspects of quality associated with tenure. Evidence from Forrest and Murie (1990) suggests that the maintained condition of former council houses that are purchased is marginally superior to that of similar properties still in local authority control. The evidence of this and other surveys (Saunders, 1990; Glendenning, 1989) is that the opportunity to modify and personalize enjoyed by owner occupiers brings a real increase in perceived quality. However, more fundamental tenant participation in management could result in similar benefits to the rented sector. Finally, quality may be prejudiced by the process of residualization of council housing. There is a tendency for remaining council property to become increasingly occupied by the marginal poor. The deterioration in both the physical fabric and the social conditions on such estates may well constitute negative coercive factors for the minority of residents in a financial position to be able to move to owner occupation. It is unlikely that they will choose to do so as sitting tenant purchasers, but may avail themselves of other opportunities for low-cost entry into owner occupation, such as shared ownership schemes. The processes of residualization, polarization and marginalization are considered in detail by Forrest and Murie (1990) and the financial aspects by Hills (1991). The implications

151

for housing quality are well examined and described by Forrest and Murie (1990). They argue that a combination of low wages, unemployment, benefit dependency and a lack of prospects shared by such households reduces their ability to maintain or improve the standards of their council housing.

There is a growing appreciation of the need to resist the further degradation of the rump of public housing stock in certain areas of the UK. Refurbishment programmes have been widely implemented. The danger is that the essence of the problem may not merely be the physical condition and uninspiring appearance of such estates. It may lie in the very process whereby council housing has become residual accommodation for marginal groups.

Choice

It is generally agreed that the sale of council houses at discounted prices has made possible owner occupation for many additional householders Table 6.7 below illustrates the impact at a national level. On the other hand, the supply of dwellings available to rent has been much diminished in quantity, quality and variety. The possibilities of new council tenants progressing through the council stock as their needs evolve, terminating with a purchase, are much diminished (Forrest and Murie, 1990).

Hills (1991) surveys studies of the impact of council house sales on the availability of houses to rent. Clearly the number of new dwelling lets has fallen drastically over the 1980s with the reduction in local authority production.

What is more difficult to assess is the impact on re-lets. Forrest and Murie suggest that some 36,000 re-lets a year were being lost in 1991. During the period covered in Table 6.8, the production of dwellings by local authorities had fallen to very low levels (see Table 6.2). Most of the lettings were thus re-lettings. This suggests that the sale of council houses is yet to have much impact on the availability of houses to rent. This is the result of the age profile of council house purchasers and the low turnover rates among tenants (see Forrest and Murie, 1991).

Census data suggests that the middle aged are under-represented among council tenants, compared with the age distribution prior to the 'Right to Buy'.

Table 6.7

**Owner-occupation by socio-economic group (per cent),
Great Britain**

Socio-economic group	1979	1993
Professional	86	90
Employers and managers	78	89
Intermediate non-manual	70	83
Junior non-manual	56	67
Skilled manual	47	72
Unskilled manual	19	42
Economically inactive	n.a.	55
TOTAL	52	67

Source: General Household Survey.

The impact of sales on lettings will be felt in the first decade of the next millennium, as the depleted age groups come to the natural end of their tenure. This imminent decline in the number of local authority properties available to rent is likely to be accompanied by a decline in housing association lettings. Figures for Great Britain in recent years are shown in Table 6.8.

It is unlikely that the small expansion in private lettings will compensate unless much stronger incentives are provided to private developers and management enterprises. On the contrary, in the foreseeable future the private rented sector may go into decline once again (see NFHA, 1994).

The future of social housing privatization

Housing tenure preferences in a deflating market

The majority of former council tenants faced substantial increases in outgoings following purchase but made substantial capital gains. Some, however, have made substantial capital losses and have been forced to return to the rented sector. The privatization of housing has brought more households into a position where the very locus of their lives is susceptible to the economic cycle.

Table 6.8

Local authority lettings to new tenants

Year	Lettings to new tenants (thousands)	
	England	**Great Britain**
1987/8	241.9	299.7
1988/9	236.3	296.7
1989/90	228.6	286.0
1990/1	239.6	298.1
1991/2	238.6	294.3
1992/3	230.2	282.5

Source: DoE, *Housing and Construction Statistics*, 1994.

This prompts a questioning as to how real the advantages associated with owner-occupation prove to be. It can be argued that in the circumstances of the mid-1990s many factors circumscribe the supposed benefits of this form of tenure: use is subject to planning controls and often subject to insurer and mortgager consent; security of tenure is threatened by repossession; financial advantages are threatened by negative equity, the ongoing prospect of real falls in house prices, the withdrawal of mortgage interest tax relief, the reduction in social security benefits for mortgagers, increasing buildings insurance costs and poor endowment policy performance; the ability to bequeath is threatened by the need to liquidate the asset to finance care in geriatric incapacity.

Some empirical evidence and extensive anecdotal evidence of a disenchantment with owner occupation on the part of a significant minority of households point to the need for an alternative: an adequate supply of rented housing.

Much of the success of the 'Right to Buy' is due to the solid quality of the public housing that has been purchased. The impact on the availability of property to let has yet to be felt. Moreover, the supply of property to rent in the voluntary sector is also set to fall. There is no clear advantage to private as opposed to public production of housing. It would be wise for policy makers to be open minded on the question as to which is the most effective system of provision, given that the concentration of production in the private sector results in output moving in line with the economic cycle, rather than in response to housing need. Maclennan (1994) gives fuller discussion of housing policy and the need for a larger social and private rented sector.

The evolution of privatization policies

Clearly the prospects for further sales of local authority houses to tenants are limited as most of the marketable stock has already been sold. The sale of housing association stock to tenants is now being advocated, in addition to policies subsidizing the purchase of properties by tenants outside the sector (DoE, 1995). This can never match the scale of council house sales, as the size of the housing association stock is comparatively small. Further, there are difficulties in finding a financial formula that housing association tenants will consider affordable and which will make sense in terms of the overall structure of social housing finance. The demographic and socio-economic profile of these tenants is very different from that of former council house purchasers.

Current policy pronouncements foresee a continued growth in owner occupation by some 1.5 million households over the next ten years. This is largely to come from new production by the private sector (DoE, 1995). At the same time, subsidies and safety net benefits for owner occupiers are being phased out. Private housing starts fell by 14 per cent in 1994 and are still falling. Although macro-economic stability is seen as a component of the policy of increasing owner occupation, it has been widely recognized that increasing levels of owner occupation bring increased macro-economic volatility. There are thus fundamental inconsistencies at the core of these policies.

Decisions on future housing policy may be made in a context where it is increasingly recognized that the need for physical mobility must be reduced and a sense of belonging to local social structures increased. Policies towards the residual rump of public housing, increasingly the dwellings of marginal groups, need to take this context into account. There may well be a case for a policy of countercyclical public housing investment, both in refurbishment and new construction, to complement the output of an increasingly enlightened and responsive private sector.

References

Bevins, A., Garrett, A. and Oulton, C. (1995), 'Can't buy, can't rent', *The Observer*, 4 June, p. 9.

Department of the Environment (1994), *Housing and Construction Statistics*, HMSO, London.

Department of the Environment (1995), *Our Future Homes*, HMSO, London.

Forrest, R. and Murie, A. (1990), *Moving the Housing Market: Council Estates, Social Change and Privatization*, Avebury, Aldershot.

Forrest, R. and Murie, A. (1991), *Selling the Welfare State*, second edition, Routledge, London.

Foster, M. (1995), 'Housing: No room at the inn', *The Observer*, Business Section, 4 June, p. 8.

Glendenning, R. (1989), *Sale of Local Authority Housing to the Private Sector*, Department of the Environment, HMSO, London.

Hedges, B. and Clemens, S. (1994), *Housing Attitudes Survey*, Department of the Environment, HMSO, London.

Hills, J. (1991), *From Right to Buy to Rent to Mortgage: the privatization of council housing since 1979*, Joseph Rowntree Foundation, York.

Holmans, A. (1991), *Estimates of Housing Equity Withdrawal by Owner Occupiers in the UK*, Department of the Environment, HMSO, London.

Housing Corporation (1994), *The Next Three Years*, The Housing Corporation, London.

Kerr, M. (1988), *The Right to Buy: a National Survey of Tenants and Buyers of Council Houses*, Department of the Environment, HMSO, London.

Lynn, P. (1991), *The Right to Buy: a National Follow-up Survey of Council Houses in England*, Department of the Environment, HMSO,

London.

MacErlean, N. (1995), 'As safe as houses?' *The Observer* 28 May, p. 6.

Mean, G. (1994), *Changes in the Relationship Between Housing and the Rest of the Economy*, Joseph Rowntree Foundation, York.

National Federation of Housing Associations, (1994), *Working Households: Affordable Housing and Economic Needs*, NFHA, London.

Maclennan, D. (1994), *A Competitive Economy: The Challenges for Housing Policy*, Joseph Rowntree Foundation, York.

Saunders, P. (1990), *A Nation of Home Owners*, Unwin Hyman, London.

Saunders, P. and Harris, C. (1994), *Popular Capitalism*, Open University Press, Buckingham.

Stewart, J. (1995), 'Is the Government Abandoning Home Owners?', *The Housebuilder*, May.

Ward, C. (1983), *Housing, An Anarchist Approach*, Freedom Press, London.

7 Pensions Privatization: a response to the crisis in Public Policy

MARTIN SULLIVAN

Introduction

The idea that the state has an important role to play in providing financial security for people in their old age is not, in itself, particularly controversial. The economic justification for state involvement in the area of pensions provision rests on the view that people typically have a short time preference. That is, people value immediate consumption more highly than consumption in the future. Left to themselves, therefore, myopic individuals would fail to make adequate provision for their old age in the form of saving during their working lives. Moreover, it is likely that there will always be some individuals who simply cannot afford to save enough during their working lives to adequately provide for their retirement.

Whether individuals fail to make proper provision for their old age from fecklessness or lack of resources, the outcome will be the same: a socially unacceptable level of poverty among the elderly. One solution to this problem is for the state itself to make pension payments to the elderly, funded by a tax on the working population - the redistributive approach. Alternatively, the state has the power to overcome people's time preference by either compelling or encouraging individuals to save for their old age - the paternalist approach. Personal saving for retirement could be conducted through private sector organizations such as insurance companies, or through a state-administered savings scheme.

Although there is a large measure of agreement that the state has a role to play in the area of pensions provision, the question of what precise form that role should take is far more contentious. For example, should the government itself provide financial security for the elderly through some form of state-administered pension scheme and, if so, what type of scheme should this be? Or should governments simply ensure that the appropriate conditions exist within which individuals can make their own private pension arrangements? If, on the other hand, some combination of both state and private pension provision is thought to be desirable, where does the state's responsibility end and the individual's begin?

Whilst such questions are philosophically interesting, raising as they do issues of paternalism and individual responsibility, they assumed an altogether more practical importance in the 1980s. There was a growing recognition, in the first half of the decade, that the existing UK pension arrangements were becoming increasingly anachronistic. Long-term trends, not anticipated when the current pension arrangements were put in place, were giving rise to significant inequalities of treatment among a variety of socio-economic groups. At the same time, labour market flexibility was thought to be undermined by a set of pension arrangements which often discouraged workers from changing jobs. Most worrying of all - especially for a government which, along with monetary stability and a declining public sector share of GDP, regarded balanced budgets as the hallmark of competent economic management - was the soaring cost to the Exchequer of the state pension scheme.

The current state pension arrangements in the UK date back to the Social Security Act of 1975, when the State Earnings Related Pension Scheme (SERPS) was added onto the existing basic state pension, which had been in place since 1946. This two-tier system provides for a flat-rate old age pension to be paid on retirement according to the principle of universality, subject to individuals having made National Insurance Contributions (NICs) for roughly nine tenths of their working life. In order to maintain the value of pensioners' incomes, relative to prices and incomes from employment, the basic pension needs to be regularly uprated. This means that the cost of the state pension scheme inevitably increases over time.

In addition to the basic state pension, SERPS requires all employees and their employers to make additional NIC payments based on earnings. These additional NICs entitle workers retiring after 1978 to receive a supplementary earnings related pension from the state. The purpose of introducing SERPS was to more closely match an individual's retirement income to his or her earnings from employment. Concerns about the enormous budgetary impact of the new scheme, however, led the then Labour government to restrict full entitlement to SERPS to those retiring from 1998 onwards. Individuals retiring during the two decades up to 1998 would still be entitled to receive an earnings related pension, but at a reduced rate. Thus the full cost of SERPS to the Exchequer was postponed for twenty years, after which it will rise very rapidly.

The spiralling cost of state pension provision was by no means a uniquely British phenomenon. On average, state pension expenditure more than doubled its share of GDP in the member countries of the Organization for Economic Cooperation and Development (OECD) between 1960 and 1984. Although the rate of growth of state pension expenditure exhibited considerable variation, between countries and over time, by the mid 1980s such expenditures were becoming the largest single budgetary item in most OECD countries.

In 1985, the government published detailed proposals for pensions reform in a Green Paper (Secretary of State for Social Services, 1985) presented to Parliament that summer. Whilst the Green Paper reaffirmed the central role of the state with regard to the financial well-being of the elderly, it contained proposals to radically redefine that role in terms of the balance of individual and collective responsibilities and obligations. In addition to some far-reaching alterations to SERPS, the government announced its intention to enact legislation that would significantly extend the provision of private pension arrangements. By permitting private sector organizations to sell personal pension plans directly to the public, as an alternative to SERPS and occupational pension schemes, the proposed legislation would have a number of beneficial outcomes. First, since individuals would have the right to opt-out of SERPS altogether, the expected future cost of state pension provision would be reduced. In addition, personal pensions would also extend consumer choice, remove the inequalities that had emerged under the existing arrangements and facilitate greater flexibility in the labour market.

Although the enabling legislation was contained in the 1986 Social Security Act, it was not until mid 1988 that individuals were able to begin contributing to their own personal pension plans. Once on sale, the combination of a generous package of financial inducements offered by the government, and an aggressive marketing campaign mounted by the new pensions providers, saw the number of individuals opting for personal pension plans dramatically exceed official expectations. By 1990 some four million people had opted for a personal pension, rising to around eight million by the end of 1994. By 1992, however, it had become apparent that large numbers of individuals stood to lose out as a result of being persuaded to leave perfectly good occupational pension schemes and purchase less favourable personal pension plans.

Notwithstanding the mis-selling scandal, the partial privatization of old age pension provision in the UK, through the introduction of personal pension plans, does represent a genuine and timely attempt by the government of the day to reform the state pension system. The enormous social and economic changes that had taken place in the preceding four decades meant that the prevailing set of state pension arrangements, which had been designed to meet the particular needs of the immediate post-war generation, were no longer appropriate for the 1980s and beyond. The remainder of this chapter is given over to a more detailed analysis of the 1986 reforms and to a consideration of some proposals for further reform.

Paying for the elderly

In Britain today there are more than ten million men and women of pensionable age, representing over 18 per cent of the total population. Moreover, as Tables 7.1 and 7.2 show, the size of the pensioner population is projected to increase significantly in both absolute and relative terms over the next few decades. If current estimates are correct,[1] there will be around fourteen million pensioners in Britain, 23.5 per cent of the population, by the year 2030. Although the number of pensioners and their share of the total population is expected to decline slightly thereafter, by the year 2050 the support ratio - the number of people of working age for every pensioner in the population - will have fallen to 2.6 compared to 3.3 today.

During the first half of the 1980s, concern began to mount that the enormous growth in the pensioner population would place an intolerable burden on future taxpayers and that, in their present form, the existing state pension arrangements would be just too expensive. The annual cost to the Exchequer of the basic state pension was already more than £15 billion. Taken together, the expected increase in demand and the need for the basic pension to be annually uprated, in order to preserve its real

162

value, meant that the pensions bill would inevitably spiral upwards.

Since different methods of uprating can be applied, the rate at which pensions costs would rise depended upon the actual method used. During the 1970s, the usual approach was to increase the basic state pension in line with changes in either average earnings or average retail prices, depending on which was the greater.

Table 7.1

Population projections for Great Britain (numbers in millions)

Cohort	1990	2010	2030	2050
Children	11.2	11.8	11.9	11.2
Working age	34.3	35.3	33.7	33.7
Pensionable age	10.3	11.2	14.0	13.2
Total	55.8	58.3	59.6	58.1

Source: Dilnot and Johnson (1992, p. 4).

Table 7.2

Percentage share of GB population by cohort

Cohort	1990	2010	2030	2050
Children	15.0	20.1	20.2	19.9
Working age	61.5	60.6	56.6	58.0
Pensionable age	18.4	19.2	23.5	22.7
Total	100.0	100.0	100.0	100.0

Source: Dilnot and Johnson (1992, p. 4).

Since the beginning of the 1980s, however, price uprating has been the only method used to revalue the state pension.

Table 7.3 shows the Government's own estimates from the mid-1980s of the future cost of the basic state pension. Assuming that price uprating continued to be used, where pensions are annually revalued in line with

163

changes in the retail prices index, by the year 2033 expenditure on the basic pension was expected to amount to £45 billion. If income uprating was applied, where pensions are annually revalued in line with changes in average male earnings, the projected increase in expenditure on the basic state pension between 1985 and 2033 was £50.1 billion. Although the cost of SERPS was trivial in the mid-1980s, it was set to rise rapidly after 1998. The scheme was expected to mature[2] by the year 2030, with an estimated annual cost to the Exchequer of £15 billion.

Table 7.3

Projected increase in the cost of the basic state pension according to the method of uprating used

	1985	1993	2003	2013	2023	2033
Price uprating	15.4	17.9	21.0	27.7	35.7	45.0
Income uprating	15.4	20.0	25.9	36.4	49.8	66.5

Source: Secretary of State for Social Services (1985).

The state's financial commitment to the elderly is not confined solely to pension expenditures. Large numbers of pensioners - 1.5 million in 1992 - are also entitled to receive income support, since this means-tested benefit is provided at a slightly more generous level than the state pension. Other income-related benefits such as housing benefit and council tax benefit are also available to pensioners. As Table 7.4 shows, older pensioners derive a much larger proportion of their total income from social security compared to those who have recently retired. In 1992, around 3.1 million pensioner units[3] were in receipt of means-tested benefits to supplement their pensions. The cost to the Exchequer of additional social security payments to pensioners was around £11 billion in 1994-95. (Dilnot *et al.*, 1994).

The state pension system

Although the origins of occupational pension schemes in Great Britain can be traced back to the first half of the 19th century, state provision of old age pensions was not introduced until 1908. The Pension Act of that year had the rather limited objective of alleviating financial hardship amongst only the most elderly members of the population who had no alternative means of support.

Table 7.4

Real income of pensioner units: by source, 1992

	Recently retired	Other pensioners
Social security benefits	41	55
Occupational pensions	25	23
Investment income	19	20
Earnings from employment	13	2

Source: Central Statistical Office (1995).

Entitlement to a pension was, therefore, restricted to individuals aged seventy or over with a weekly income of less than twelve shillings (60 pence). Given these age and income criteria, the financial implications for the Exchequer were comparatively modest, since only a small number of individuals qualified for the non-contributory benefits made available under the legislation. A progressive broadening of the scheme's coverage through periodic alterations to the eligibility criteria was, however, to have much greater fiscal implications.

The Widows', Orphans' and Old Age Contributory Pensions Act of 1925 reduced the pensionable age for men and women by five years to sixty-five. The Act also abolished means-testing and introduced the insurance principle,[4] which has remained an important feature of the state pension system ever since. The switch from means-testing to insurance meant that entitlement to a pension was determined not by reference to some minimum income level, but rather on the basis of an individual's contribution record during his or her working life. Although the new scheme only applied to workers in a small number of industries, the effect of the 1925 Act was to significantly extend the coverage of state pension provision. Coverage was extended still further when, in 1937, membership of the scheme was granted to black-coated workers and, in 1940, the age at which women were entitled to a pension was reduced to sixty.[5]

The publication of the Beveridge Report (Beveridge, 1942) laid the foundations for the most radical expansion of state pension provision so far. Along with the low incomes earned by some groups of workers, Beveridge saw individual income loss as a major cause of poverty in Great Britain. Since income loss was usually the result of redundancy, invalidity or old age, a system of national insurance was envisaged in order to safeguard all workers against these contingencies. In view of the potentially enormous cost to the treasury, it was never Beveridge's intention that the state should take on the role of sole provider of retirement incomes. He proposed, instead, that a system of social welfare provision be put in place, based on a minimum income level below which no individual should be compelled to sink. Those wishing to receive a retirement income, above the bare minimum provided by the state, would be free to make additional private pension arrangements through their employer or with an insurance company. Thus, the resulting National Insurance Act of 1946 introduced the principle of universality into the state pension arrangements.

The old age pension scheme devised by Beveridge was to be funded on a pay-as-you-go (PAYG) basis and relied upon an implicit contract between the working and retired generations. Under the scheme, eligible individuals were entitled to receive a flat-rate weekly pension on retirement, to be paid for by a special tax, national insurance contributions, levied on all employees and their employers. In return for having paid NICs for the qualifying period during their working lives - forty four years for men and thirty nine years for women - employees would have earned entitlement to a retirement pension which the next generation of workers would provide. Women who temporarily left the workforce to care for young children could have their NICs credited under a system of home responsibility protection.

Viewed from the perspective of the mid 1990s, with the contemporary emphasis on budgetary restraint and targeted public expenditures, the 1946 scheme with its universal retirement benefits and PAYG financing arrangements appears to be both excessively broad and fiscally reckless. Seen from the perspective of its architects, however, the scheme was an eminently sensible one, given the prevailing social and economic conditions. Despite the universal nature of the benefits provided, there were two important reasons for believing that the cost to the Exchequer could be kept within acceptable limits. First, the value of the old age

166

pension was not intended to be particularly generous, being set close to the subsistence level. Second, the demand for pensions was expected to be modest, given that a significant proportion of the population would not reach pensionable age. The average life expectancy at the time was only 62 for a man and 67 for a woman.

Since the government was committed to the maintenance of a high and stable level of employment, it made good sense to finance state pension provision on a PAYG basis. Under conditions of near full employment, the government could expect to generate sufficient revenue in the form of NICs to meet current pension expenditures without the need to set an unacceptably high contribution rate. However, the successful management of the British economy, upon which the new pension arrangements were largely dependent, was soon to prove problematic for the scheme.

The three decades from the end of the second world war to the mid-1970s were, notwithstanding the occasional dip into recession, characterized by sustained economic growth. The living standards of those in employment rose rapidly as the annual rate of growth of average earnings typically exceeded that of prices. At the same time, the real value of the state pension was also increased, albeit in a somewhat ad hoc fashion. Despite Beveridge's original proposal that the state pension should be uprated in line with price inflation, its value increased more rapidly than prices during the 1950s and 1960s, but at a slower rate than average earnings. High rates of inflation in the 1970s, coupled with the practice of uprating the state pension in line with either changes in prices or earnings, depending on which was the greater, saw the value of the pension relative to earned incomes reach an all-time high of 20 per cent in 1977. The exclusive use of price indexation, since 1980, has reduced the value of the basic pension by about 2.4 per cent per annum compared to what it would have been had the formula used in the 1970s still applied.

The rapid growth in average earnings meant that supplementary pensions were becoming increasingly important in order to provide individuals with a realistic replacement income on retirement. Although workers were free to make their own arrangements to supplement the state pension by joining an occupational scheme, only just over half the workforce had actually done so by 1967 despite the proliferation of such schemes during the 1950s and 1960s. The number of individuals contributing to private annuities - for more than a decade the only alternative private supplement to membership of an occupational scheme - represented only a tiny fraction of the workforce.

By 1959, the low take-up of private supplementary pensions and the growing inadequacy of the state pension led the government to introduce a supplementary scheme of its own, the Graduated Pension Scheme. The aim of this new scheme was to more closely link a worker's income at retirement to that achieved during his or her working life by allowing individuals to purchase units of graduated retirement benefit based on their current earnings. The Graduated Pension Scheme was abolished in 1975 and replaced by SERPS.

In its original form, SERPS, which came into effect in 1978, was to provide all employees retiring after 1998 with a supplementary pension equal to 25 per cent of earnings between a lower and an upper weekly limit, averaged over their best 20 years. Individuals retiring after 1978, but before 1998, are, however, only entitled to receive a supplementary pension equal to 1.25 per cent of eligible earnings for each year covered by the scheme. In this way the full burden of financing SERPS was postponed for twenty years.[6] To pay for SERPS, employees and their employers are obliged to make additional NICs on earnings between the lower limit, currently £57 per week, and the upper limit of £430. Because SERPS is only available to employees with an income above the lower earnings limit, the very lowest paid workers - usually part-timers working just a few hours each week - are excluded from the scheme.

Occupational pension schemes

Apart from SERPS, occupational pension schemes represented the only significant source of supplementary retirement income available to large numbers of pensioners during most of the 1980s. In their modern form, these schemes appear to have been introduced into the UK as a means by which public and private sector employers could reward their employees for long and loyal service. Although the Metropolitan Police Force established what was probably the first such scheme in 1829, the civil service pension scheme, introduced in 1834, was the one on which numerous other public and private sector schemes were subsequently modelled. On reaching the age of sixty-five and having served for forty-five years, civil servants were entitled to retire with a pension equal to two-thirds of their final salary.

An important feature of final salary occupational pension schemes is that the income replacement rate - the proportion of an individual's earned income represented by the pension they receive - is determined in advance according to the rules of the particular scheme to which they belong. In general, pension entitlement is usually defined as a fixed fraction of an individual's final salary multiplied by their length of service. Such schemes are, therefore, known as defined benefit schemes. A typical example of a defined benefit scheme would be one that offered members an income on retirement equal to one-sixtieth of their final salary for each year of service. At the end of forty years service, therefore, an employee would be entitled to a pension income equal to two-thirds of their final salary. Because workers' incomes tend to increase with length of service, final salary schemes are back-loaded, since their accrual rate - the rate at which the value of pension entitlement is increased - will be greatest towards the end of an individual's career.

SERPS was never meant to be a substitute for occupational schemes. Rather, it was intended to provide an earnings related top-up to the state pension for those individuals who, perhaps because no occupational scheme was available to them, had no alternative supplementary retirement income. To stimulate increased membership of occupational schemes, and thereby limit the state's future SERPS liabilities, employees were encouraged to surrender their SERPS entitlement, in return for a lower rate of national insurance contributions by joining an approved employer-provided, or industry-based, occupational scheme. To be approved, these so-called contracted-out schemes were required to provide employees with retirement benefits which were at least as good as could be obtained from membership of SERPS, the so-called guaranteed minimum pension. In addition, the minimum contributions to such schemes made by both the employee and the employer had to equal those required by SERPS. In practice, contracted-out schemes typically provide members with a level of retirement income well in excess of that offered by SERPS. Moreover, membership of contracted-out schemes was often made a condition of employment, since a large contributions base was required if the contribution rate was to be acceptable to both the employer and the employees.

Membership of occupational pension schemes grew rapidly during the 1950s and 1960s, largely as a result of the post-war expansion of the public sector. Many private sector firms were simply too small to be able to offer a company pension scheme. Others either lacked the resources or were unwilling to take on the financial commitment. Workers in the public sector were thus much more likely to be members of an occupational scheme than those in the private sector. In fact, as Table 7.5 shows, less than half the workforce was actually covered by an occupational pension scheme throughout most of the 1980s. The table also shows that women were much less likely than men to be members of occupational schemes.

Whilst occupational pension schemes represent an important source of supplementary retirement income for a sizeable portion of the workforce, and, in the case of contracted-out schemes, are almost always superior to SERPS, they are not free from risk. Since the value of pensions derived from these schemes is linked to an employee's years of service, redundant workers or those who retire early will have a reduced pension entitlement compared to what they would have received had they continued in employment.[7]

The same is true for women who leave a job that provides them with an occupational pension in order to raise a family. Even if redundant workers or women returning to the workforce are able to gain employment with another organization offering its own occupational scheme, the costs associated with transferring their accrued pension entitlement from the old to the new scheme, can further reduce the value of the pension that is ultimately received.

Table 7.5

Percentage of all employees covered by occupational pension schemes

	Men	Women	Total
1953	34	18	28
1963	63	21	48
1971	62	28	49
1983	64	37	52
1987	60	35	49
1991	57	37	48

Source: National Association of Pension Funds

A system under strain

The cost of a PAYG state pension scheme is very sensitive to changes in both the demand for pension expenditures and the size of the contributions base. If the demand for pension expenditures rises, with no over-funding prior to the increase, either the contribution rate would have to increase or the government would be required to fund the additional spending out of general taxation. Likewise, a contraction in the contributions base with demand either unchanged or rising would have similar implications. Changes in the base and the demand for pension expenditures can arise either from political choice - for example, governments fix the level of state pensions, set the eligibility criteria and decide who shall foot the bill - or as a result of changes in social and economic circumstances. Since the early 1950s, a number of long-term social and economic trends have emerged that have dramatically increased the demand for pension expenditures and undermined the contributions base.

During the last 50 years or so, the life expectancy of men and women has increased by around two years each decade. The average life expectancy of a man is now 74, compared to only 62 in 1944. Likewise, women can typically expect to live to 79 today, compared to 67 half a century ago. The consequence of improved longevity is that most males can now expect to reach the age at which they become eligible for a pension from the state. Furthermore, the proportion of an individual's life spent in retirement, and hence drawing a pension, has also increased.

At the same time as longevity was increasing, changes were also taking place in economic activity rates.[8] The general trend has been for the growth in the number of older people in the population to be associated with a decline in the age at which individuals effectively leave the workforce. Within this general trend, however, there are important differences between the sexes. From the early 1960s, economic activity rates among females increased steadily until 1975, after which they began to decline. Economic activity rates among males, on the other hand, have exhibited a consistent and steep downward trend (Mailer and Shafto, 1992). Table 7.6 shows that, in 1992, nearly half of all males aged between 60 and 64 had either retired early or were unemployed, compared to only 16 per cent in 1975.

Unemployment and inflation, both of which had been relatively low since the end of the second world war, began to accelerate in the late 1960s. Unemployment, especially long-term unemployment, is problematic for a PAYG pension scheme, since it represents a reduction in the size of the contributions base. The need to uprate pensions, in order to maintain their real value, means that the rate of inflation is also an important determinant of state pension expenditures. Moreover, since higher rates of inflation are also associated with increased volatility, forecasting future pension expenditures - an imprecise activity at the best of times - becomes much more difficult.

While price indexation of the basic state pension in the 1980s was gradually eroding its value, relative to earned incomes, the casualization of employment relationships was also undermining the usefulness of the existing set of supplementary pension arrangements. High rates of unemployment and a rapid increase in the number of part-time and temporary jobs in the economy, meant that full-time and continuous employment was no longer the norm for a large and growing section of the workforce.

Both SERPS and occupational pension schemes were poorly suited to the needs of the casualized workforce. While low earned incomes from part-time employment kept large numbers of workers out of SERPS, members of occupational schemes often found their future pension entitlements reduced by frequent and/or lengthy periods of unemployment.

Table 7.6

Male and female economic activity rates: 1975-92

Age	Male 1975	Female 1975	Male 1992	Female 1992
18-24	91	71	89	75
25-34	98	55	95	70
35-49	98	68	95	78
50-59	96	60	83	64
60-64	84	29	52	23
65+	15	6	7	3

Source: National Association of Pension Funds.

Privatizing pension provision

Through a wide-ranging series of reforms contained in the 1986 Social Security Act, the government sought to remove the anomalies and inconsistencies of treatment that had developed under the old pension arrangements and, more importantly, to limit the state's future SERPS liabilities. These reforms can be seen as consisting of two broad elements. First, the government aimed to limit the future cost of SERPS through a revision of the rules under which the scheme operated.[9] Instead of an individual's SERPS entitlement being 25 per cent of their best 20 years earnings, benefits would, in future, be calculated as 20 per cent of eligible earnings averaged over the years preceding retirement. The future value of individual SERPS entitlements was thus significantly downgraded and the attractiveness of the scheme much reduced.

While the government was committed to providing the basic old age pension as before, the second element of the 1986 reforms was intended to shift the responsibility for supplementary pensions from the state to the private sector. This was to be achieved through the wide-spread take-up of personal pension plans. Changes in the existing rules governing the provision of private pensions were, therefore, required i
n order to permit organizations, other than insurance companies, to offer personal pensions to the public. In addition, an effective system of regulation was also needed to give the new plan-holders an adequate level of investor protection. Although the original aim had been for personal pensions to be available from April 1988, difficulties relating to the investor protection requirement meant that they did not actually go on sale until July that year.

Unlike SERPS or final salary occupational schemes, personal pension plans offer an income that is completely unrelated to an individual's earnings. Contributions to these plans accumulate in an individual's own fund, which is invested for growth and used to purchase an annuity from an insurance company when the pension is finally taken. They are, therefore, variously referred to as defined contribution schemes or money purchase schemes. The value of a person's fund at the time an annuity is purchased will depend upon the level of contributions made thus far - minus the plan provider's fees and commission - plus the investment income earned and any capital gains/losses made. Since annuity rates vary in line with long-term interest rates, the actual income obtained from a defined contribution scheme will depend upon the size of the accumulated fund and the prevailing capital market conditions at the time the pension is taken. Defined contribution schemes are always front-loaded because, due to compounding, contributions made early on will have a greater pay-off than those made later. Time is, therefore, another important factor in determining the final pension income.

The tax treatment of personal pension plans is very similar to that of occupational schemes. Tax relief on contributions is received at the individual's highest marginal rate, subject to an upper contributions limit. The funds themselves are exempt from all tax liability on both investment income and capital gains and the pensions received from these new plans are taxed at the recipient's appropriate marginal rate. Although there is an upper limit on any tax-free lump sum payable on retirement from a personal pension plan, individuals can circumvent this limit by simultaneously contributing to more than one plan.

To stimulate the take-up of personal pensions, the government offered individuals a generous financial incentive. For a limited period only, employees opting out of SERPS and into a personal pension plan were entitled to have a proportion of their NICs for the two previous tax years transferred into their new fund. This national insurance rebate was equal to the current contracting out rebate for occupational schemes, calculated as 2 per cent of the individual's own national insurance contributions between the lower and upper earnings limits plus 3.8 per cent of the contributions made by their employer. Moreover, those individuals who had not already contracted-out of SERPS into an occupational scheme, or who had been members for less than two years, were offered an additional contribution to their fund from the government equal to 2 per cent of relevant earnings. Since that part of the rebate applicable to the individual's own contributions was grossed up to take account of the income tax relief on pension contributions, the final net contribution was actually equal to 8.46 per cent of relevant earnings.

The working assumption used by the Department for Social Security was that about half a million individuals would opt for a personal pension during the period that the 2 per cent incentive was available. By 1990, however, some four million people had actually done so by contracting out of either SERPS, their former occupational scheme, or both. By the time the incentive was withdrawn at the end of the 1992-93 fiscal year, the number of optants was believed to have reached five million. According to a report from the National Audit Office (1991) the long-term saving resulting from reduced SERPS liabilities will amount to £3.4 billion. The reduction in national insurance revenues, on the other hand, is put at £9.3 billion for the period that the 2 per cent incentive was in operation. The implied cost to the tax-payer of introducing personal pensions is thus £5.9 billion.

By 1992, it was becoming increasingly apparent that large numbers of individuals had been wrongly sold personal pensions. It is reckoned that of over eight million personal pensions sold to date, at least one million were mis-sold. The worst affected were those employees who, as a result of appalling advice, offered by a poorly trained and commission hungry sales force, were duped into opting out of perfectly good occupational schemes. Opting out of a company pension scheme can be worthwhile when workers change jobs and where the new employer does not provide an occupational scheme. The alternative would be for these individuals to see their accrued pension entitlements frozen and eroded by inflation. For most workers, however, especially members of high quality public sector schemes such as health service employees, teachers, etc., opting out makes no sense at all. Personal pensions are almost always inferior to occupational schemes, because the high administration costs associated with money purchase schemes means that a much higher level of contributions is required in order to achieve an equivalent pension.

The Securities and Investments Board, the lead regulator of the pensions industry, has given pension providers until the end of 1997 to sort out arrangements for compensating the victims of mis-selling. The final cost of compensating all those individuals wrongly sold a personal pension plan is likely to be in the order of £3 billion, and the industry is currently debating the thorny question of who should foot the bill. A report in the *Investors Chronicle* (Eaglesham, 1995) highlighted the lack of agreement among the pension providers. For example, United Friendly was reported to have decided that its shareholders should pay the compensation bill in full. Legal & General and Prudential, on the other hand, were said to be planning to split the bill between their shareholders and policyholders. In the case of Legal & General, it was expected that policyholders would pick up the largest portion of the bill. Refuge is reportedly adamant that its policyholders will foot the bill in full.

The wholesale mis-selling of personal pensions clearly represents a major failure in the implementation of the 1986 reforms. Were it not for the obvious distress caused to those people who were inappropriately sold a personal pension, parallels might easily be drawn with similar failures in other areas of the privatization programme. For example, the failure to set a realistic offer price for shares in some of the privatized utilities, which led to the government foregoing billions of pounds in lost revenue and at the same time permitted large numbers of individuals, and financial institutions, to make spectacular capital gains. If events such as these are not to muddy the analytical waters, however, it is important to distinguish between the process and the principle of privatization. Whilst the fiasco of mis-sold personal pensions represents an obvious failure in the process of privatization, it has no bearing on the soundness, or otherwise, of the underlying principle.

In fact, personal pensions have a number of potential advantages over other forms of supplementary pension provision. For example, following the downgrading of SERPS in 1986, a personal pension plan can, subject to two important qualifications, offer the prospect of a superior retirement income to that made available through the state scheme. The first qualification is that the plan must be started early. The second is that there should be no significant interruptions in the flow of contributions. Personal pensions can also enhance job mobility by providing workers with a means by which they can extract accrued pension entitlements that would otherwise remain frozen in a previous employer's occupational scheme. In addition, personal pensions make early retirement easier, since they can be taken at any time between an individual's fiftieth and seventy-fifth birthdays. Because the level of contributions to a personal pension plan can be varied from time to time, to take account of an individual's changing financial circumstances, personal pensions offer a very flexible way to accumulate future pension entitlements. They are, therefore, potentially well suited to those whose income fluctuates over time, such as actors, writers, etc.

Despite their advantages, however, there are a number of significant disadvantages associated with personal pensions. These disadvantages mainly stem from the prime importance of starting a personal pension plan early and maintaining an uninterrupted flow of contributions. The need to start contributing to a personal pension plan early on in an individual's working life, means that they are an inappropriate way for workers in mid-career to begin accruing additional pension entitlements. Therefore, as Table 7.7 shows, take-up of personal pensions to date is heavily skewed towards younger workers.

Since a regular and stable flow of contributions, combined with an early start, is required in order to generate a large enough fund to purchase an adequate annuity on retirement, personal pensions are also inappropriate for people who experience frequent or extended periods of unemployment. Although the pension that is ultimately derived from a money purchase scheme is not linked to an individual's length of employment - as is the case with SERPS and occupational schemes - during periods of unemployment individuals might need to reduce or suspend their pension contributions, leading to a commensurate reduction in their future pension entitlement. These individuals could, in theory, make up the lost ground when in employment by making additional contributions to their fund.

In practice, however, catching up in this way would almost certainly require a prohibitively high level of additional contributions. In fact, the level of contributions made to a money purchase scheme is a crucially important determinant of the ultimate size of an individual's fund. Low-paid and part-time workers, therefore, constitute another important group for whom personal pensions have little to offer. This is because these workers will only be able to afford to make comparatively small contributions to their pension plans.

Table 7.7

Take up of personal pensions by age in 1991

Age group	Per cent of total
16 - 24	26.8
25 - 34	42.9
35 - 44	23.8
45 - 54	6.3
55 +	0.1

Source: National Association of Pension Funds.

Even where such plans are started early, and where contributions are maintained over an entire working life, the final fund is unlikely to be sufficient to purchase an adequate pension on retirement.

Like SERPS and occupational schemes, personal pensions are likely to give rise to less favourable outcomes for women compared to men. One reason for this is that women are typically much more likely than men to be in receipt of low pay and to be employed in part-time or temporary occupations. The need to take time out of paid work to care for young children or dependent relatives - still a predominantly female activity - means that women are also far more likely than men to have interrupted employment patterns. In addition, annuity rates are lower for women than men, to compensate for the difference in life expectancy. As a result, a given amount of contributions to a personal pension plan will usually purchase a lower level of pension income for a woman than it would for a man.[10] It is not surprising, therefore, that of the 4.1 million individuals who had opted for a personal pension by 1990, males outnumbered females by more than three to one.

In the event of a divorce, women can also lose out as a result of their former spouse having opted for a personal pension. This situation is most likely to arise where a married woman has, prior to a divorce, relied either wholly, or in part, on her husband's future pension entitlement for her own financial security in retirement. Following her divorce, it might well be too late for a woman to build up an adequate pension of her own. With around one in three marriages in the UK currently ending in divorce, this aspect of pensions privatization is likely to represent a major problem for large numbers of women. A useful analysis of the treatment of women by different pension schemes is provided in Johnson et al. (1992).

Conclusion

The fact that personal pension plans are an entirely inappropriate way for a sizeable portion of the workforce to accrue future pension entitlements casts serious doubt upon their usefulness as instruments for reducing long-term state expenditure on the elderly. What savings are achieved as a result of their introduction, and the associated downgrading of SERPS, will be largely at the expense of women, the low-paid and those with unstable employment patterns. Nevertheless, if future state pension expenditures are to be kept to acceptable levels, the redistributive element in the existing UK pension arrangements must be substantially reduced and replaced by higher levels of personal saving. The solution to this dilemma lies in extending the coverage of personal pensions to include the whole workforce, by making defined contribution schemes perform equally well for all employees, regardless of their individual circumstances.

Field and Owen (1993) suggest that personal pensions could be made to perform well for all workers if the state was to stand as guarantor for individuals' pension contributions. Their proposal is for SERPS to be phased out and replaced by a compulsory personal pension scheme. Individuals would be required, by law, to contribute 4 per cent of their gross earnings to a personal pension plan of their choice. In addition, employers would be required to make a contribution to their employees' pension fund equal to 6 per cent of earnings. In the event of redundancy, unemployed workers would have their contributions maintained by the state, subject to their satisfying the usual availability for work criteria. Women who temporarily left the workforce to bring up children, or care for dependent relatives, would have their pension contributions protected in a similar way. The state would also make contributions on behalf of individuals who were unable to work as a result of sickness or disability.

The idea that SERPS should be abolished and saving for retirement made compulsory is also favoured by the National Association of Pension Funds. The NAPF has proposed a scheme whereby all employees not covered by an occupational pension would be obliged to contribute 5 per cent of their earnings to a personal pension plan, with a further 5 per cent being contributed by their employer. Low-paid workers would have their contributions topped-up by the state, and the unemployed would have their contributions paid in full. Support for the NAPF scheme, or something very much like it, can now be found right across the political spectrum.[11]

One idea currently under discussion is for the establishment of a state-managed personal pension scheme. The necessary administrative machinery for such a scheme already exists, in the form of the Contributions Agency, which is currently responsible for collecting national insurance contributions. Contributions to such a scheme could be invested in low risk securities, for example government bonds. Although low risk investments offer lower rates of return than equity investments, they would provide pension plan holders with greater security, albeit at a price. Because a state-administered scheme would not need to make a profit, but simply be required to cover its operating costs, management charges could be kept to a minimum. A low cost state-administered scheme would thus act as an industry benchmark against which commercial pension providers could be compared. A pension system based on compulsory saving would, of course, need to be phased in gradually, since older workers would not benefit from the change. Over a period of perhaps fifty years, therefore, the new scheme would gradually be increasing its coverage as the old one was phased out.

There is nothing at all radical in the idea that people should be compelled to save for their old age. Indeed, there is a large measure of compulsion in the existing pension system. All employees with an income above the lower earnings limit are compelled to make national insurance contributions towards their basic old age pension. In so far as they have the choice of contributing to SERPs or contracting out in favour of an occupational scheme or a personal pension plan, employees are still obliged to contribute to some form of supplementary pension provision. Although personal pension plans offer retirement benefits, the value of which it is difficult to accurately predict in advance, the future value of the current state pension is also uncertain. If price indexation continues to be used to uprate the basic pension, its value, relative to incomes from employment, is likely to fall from around 15 per cent now, to 7 per cent 50 years hence.

Notes

1. Population projections should always be regarded with caution, given the potential for unanticipated changes to occur in birth and death rates and in the rate and direction of migration.

2. A pension scheme is said to be mature when all or most of its members are entitled to receive the maximum level of benefit on retirement.

3. Single men and women and married couples.

4. In fact, the principle was really one of quasi-insurance, since, as Mailer and Shafto (1992, p. 34) point out, 'there has never been any separate pension fund and any actuarial calculations have always been subordinate to political management'.

5. One reason for this change seems to have been the typical five year age difference between married couples at the time, which had hitherto made joint retirement impossible. It has also been suggested that the female retirement age was reduced in recognition of the vital war work being performed by women.

6.　　The assumption, in 1975, was that real earnings growth of 3 per cent per annum and unemployment of no more than 2.5 per cent would make the scheme affordable after twenty years.
7.　　The so-called early leaver problem.
8.　　The economic activity rate is a measure of the number of individuals in the workforce or in a particular cohort of the workforce, who are either in work or seeking employment, expressed as a proportion of the entire workforce or cohort.
9.　　The Government's original intention had been to abolish SERPS altogether.
10.　　That part of a woman's fund derived from the contracting out rebate, however, must be used to purchase a sex-neutral annuity.
11.　　Both the Institute of Directors and the TUC have recently expressed support for compulsory personal pensions.

References

Atkinson, A. and Rein, M. (eds) (1993), *Age, Work and Social Security*, Macmillan Press, Basingstoke.

Beveridge, W. (1942), *Social Insurance and Allied Services*, Cmnd 6404, HMSO, London.

Central Statistical Office (1995), *Social Trends*, HMSO, London.

Creedy, J. (1982), *State Pensions In Britain*, Cambridge University Press, Cambridge.

Dilnot, A. *et al.* (1994), *Pensions Policy in the UK: An Economic Analysis*, Institute for Fiscal Studies, London.

Dilnot, A. and Johnson, P. (1992), 'What Pension Should the State Provide?', *Fiscal Studies*, vol. 13, no. 4.

Disney, R. and Whitehouse, E. (1992a), *The Personal Pensions Stampede*, Institute for Fiscal Studies, London.

Disney, R. and Whitehouse, E. (1992b), 'Personal Pensions and the Review of the Contracting-Out Terms', *Fiscal Studies*, vol. 13, no. 1, February.

Eaglesham, Jean (1995), 'Surplus Aids Pensions Bill', Investors Chronicle, April 7, p. 10.

Field, F. and Owen, M. (1993), *Private Pensions for All: Squaring the Circle*, Fabian Society.

Fry, V., Smith, S. and White, S. (1990), *Pensioners and the Public Purse*,

Institute for Fiscal Studies, London.

Hannah, L. (1986), *Inventing Retirement: The Development of Occupational Pensions in Britain*, Cambridge University Press, Cambridge.

Hills, J. (1993), *The Future of Welfare: A Guide to the Debate*, Joseph Rowntree Foundation, York.

Hutton, S., Kennedy, S. and Whiteford, P. (1995), *Equalisation of State Pension Ages: The Gender Impact*, Equal Opportunities Commission, Manchester.

Johnson, P. *et al.* (1992), *Income: Pensions, Earnings and Savings in the Third Age*, The Carnegie United Kingdom Trust, Dunfermline.

Mailer, T. and Shafto, T. (1992), 'Options for Retirement: Mandatory or Flexible?', *National Westminster Bank Quarterly Review*, November.

Napier, C. (1983), *Accounting for the Cost of Pensions*, Institute of Chartered Accountants in England and Wales, London.

National Audit Office (1991), *The Elderly: Information Requirements for Supporting the Elderly and Implications of Personal Pensions for the National Insurance Fund*, HMSO, London.

Organization for Economic Cooperation and Development (1988), *Ageing Populations: The Social Policy Implications*, OECD, Paris.

Secretary of State for Social Services (1985), *Reform of Social Security*, Cmnd 9517, HMSO, London.

8 OFWAT and the Regulation of Change

GRAHAM TAYLOR

Introduction

The privatization of state industries and agencies developed as a central component of 'Thatcherism'. The debate within social science on the origins and implications of Thatcherism and the privatization programme has been somewhat one-sided and contributions have tended to focus on either the 'political' (Bullpitt, 1986; Jessop, Bonnett, Bromley and Ling, 1988; Jessop, Bonnett and Bromley 1990), 'economic' (Nairn, 1981) or 'ideological' (Hall, 1983, 1988) level of analysis. The one-sidedness of these analyzes has prevented a consideration of the extent to which the privatization programme represents the culmination of a process which has transformed the whole range of social relations underpinning British state and society. The transformation has been particularly marked in respect of the ideology and practice of 'public service'. Within social institutions the political rights of citizens, the economic rights of consumers and the ideological representation of what constitutes the 'public good' have all been fundamentally transformed. The totality of the transformation and its increasingly global implications implies that the privatization programme cannot be understood as a simplistic 'strategy' by either the British Conservative Party or the City of London to regain and maintain their hegemony in response to threats posed by social democratic politics and trade union struggle. The issues that need to be addressed are why social democratic and trade union conceptions of 'public service' and the 'common good' were so vulnerable to attack by the New Right, how the New Right programme has fundamentally transformed 'public service' as a state ideology and practice, and the implications of this for social and political struggle in the decades to come.

In this chapter the privatization of the UK water industry is explored in order to develop the argument that privatization of the industry and the resulting 'neo-liberal' regulation of the industry through the Office of Water Services (OFWAT) is an attempt to resolve the contradictions inherent in the 'public service' industry as it developed in the post-war period. I develop the argument that this restructuring has involved a fundamental redefinition of the notion of 'public' on the basis of the individualistic postulates of neo-liberal social theory. I highlight the importance of analysing the privatization programme of the post-1979 Conservative governments in a historical and global context and the complex pattern of continuity and change in respect of state administration and regulation throughout the 20th century. The privatization programme of the 1980s had the effect of re-drawing the boundaries between public and private and has increasingly resulted in the disengagement of the state from the direct administration of public services and the development of new regulatory state agencies premised on the protection of 'individual' consumer interests in regulated markets. These developments have resulted in a fundamental restructuring of the discourse and practice of public service.

The central argument developed in this chapter is that the crisis of public service in the water industry was determined through a crisis in Keynesian forms of state regulation and planning in the context of a wider crisis of global capital accumulation. The 'neo-liberal' restructuring of the state is an attempt to realign the state and international capital through a process of 'monetarization' in which decisions concerning service allocation and provision are de-politicized and increasingly subordinated to the abstract and indifferent power of money. This has involved a fundamental redefinition of the concept of public service, and I explore the way in which New Right conceptualizations of the 'common good' have played a central role in challenging traditional social democratic conceptions of the 'common good', providing the basis for the articulation of an emergent 'neo-liberal' conceptualization of 'public service'. I conclude by arguing that the analysis of the crisis and contradictions of public service and the privatization of state agencies provides important political lessons for the left and illustrates the need to challenge and question the political and ideological assumptions on which social democratic politics has rested throughout the 20th century.

Fabian socialism and the origins of public service

Throughout the 20th century the concept of 'public service' has played a central role in defining the organizational and ideological forms of state enterprise in the UK. Ideologically, the concept of public service articulated the notion of the state as an agency of the 'common good' overarching and mediating the sectional and competing interests of civil society. The material underpinning of this discourse was the abject failure of private enterprises to maintain an adequate provision of 'public goods' through the market. The state increasingly undertook the direct administration of goods and services in the 'public interest', which simultaneously overcame the limitations of the market and provided the basis for the development of an empowering social citizenship (Marshall, 1991). In Britain the domination of social democratic 'labourism' by Fabian socialism (Miliband, 1983; Nairn, 1965; Saville, 1973) has transcribed the form of the public service state and the ways in which this state form articulated notions of the 'common good' (see Taylor, 1996, chs. 2-3).

The main problem in assessing the development of Fabian state theory arises from the absence of a coherent or systematic Fabian paradigm. The conceptual premises of Fabianism are eclectic and essentially pragmatic: Utilitarian Liberalism, Hegelian Idealism, Christianity and Marxism-Leninism have all contributed towards the construction of a nebulous and logically inconsistent Fabian paradigm. There are a number of unifying elements that give an external coherence to Fabianism as a conceptual paradigm: total commitment to parliamentary democracy, unequivocal support for the welfare state, and an idealist interpretation of history by which socialism is seen as advancing and surpassing capitalism owing to the moral superiority of the socialist values of equality, freedom and fellowship (George and Wilding, 1985, pp. 69-70).[1] Fabian Socialism is further unified by a total commitment to the notion of the state as public servant. The Fabian conception of the state is essentially liberal democratic in its acceptance of the state as a neutral embodiment of the 'general will'

185

(see Cole, 1943; Melitz, 1959, pp. 554-560). Combined with the moral collectivism outlined above, this had important implications with respect to the legitimation of the centralized and bureaucratic state agencies such as the water industry as progressive and inherently socialistic. The crisis of public service developed through the way in which the above ideological appearance of the state was constantly ruptured by the concrete and substantive regulatory activities of the public service state.

The crisis of the public service water industry

The problem of maintaining the ideological appearance of the state as an embodiment of the common good and the emergent crisis of public service can be explored through an examination of the development of the post-war water industry. This grew out of concerns over the way in which the fragmented and uncoordinated water sector could provide an effective delivery of water services particularly in rural areas and at times of drought. The 1945 Water Act was concerned to establish a 'national water policy' and was premised firmly on Fabian conceptions of public service. The Act articulated three central principles: central control to prevent haphazard and wasteful development; democratic control through ministers responsible to parliament at the centre and elected local authorities at the periphery; and the common good to facilitate the subordination of sectional interests to national interests (HM Government, 1944). The Act established the Central Advisory Water Committee (CAWC) on a statutory basis which gave political and technical interests within the sector a forum within the national state. As a result, the post-war period was marked by an increasingly technocratic and systematic approach to the augmentation and conservation of water resources.

The reforms, however, produced an increasingly serious 'fiscal crisis':[2] the failure to rationalize the operations of the industry in the context of a squeeze on public spending heightened the conflicts of interest between both organizations operating at different stages of the water cycle and between the central and local state over the allocation of capital grants. The resolution of the crisis was perceived as a technical problem of overcoming the fragmentation of interests in the water sector. The Water Resources Act, 1963, created 29 new hydrologically-based river authorities and the 'Water Resources Board' as a national agency for planning, research and the collection of data. The 1963 reforms, however, failed to resolve the conflict between organizations and agencies at different stages of the water cycle: in particular, the divergence of interest between agencies concerned with the cheap disposal of sewage and agencies concerned with procuring water for drinking or land drainage. The new river authorities had responsibility for land drainage, fisheries, the control of pollution and water conservation. However, representatives from local government constituted the majority on the new river boards and as local authorities were also interested in the cheap and efficient disposal of sewage effluent the reforms produced an administrative paralysis in the water sector. In the context of an increasingly tight control of the Public Sector Borrowing Requirement (PSBR) by the central state, local authorities were unwilling to commit resources to capital projects which would primarily benefit the ratepayers of other local authorities located downstream in the river basin.

The perceived failure of the 1963 reforms resulted in the de facto nationalization of the water industry by the 1973 Water Act. The problems of uncoordination and conflict between agencies were presented as matters for managerial, technical and administrative resolution (Jordon, Richardson and Kimber, 1977; Jordon and Richardson, 1977). The 1973 Water Act provided the scientific and technical justification for the development of 'managerialism' within the water industry and resulted in the removal of water and sewage services from direct democratic control and the reorganization of the industry on the basis of 'integrated river basin management'. The managerialization of the water industry appeared as the technical and scientific way to resolve the fiscal crisis of the water industry but given the contradictions of the managerial state resulted in its intensification. The 1973 Water Act was primarily concerned with the mechanisms of financial regulation and operational planning that would be required to manage the capital investment programme anticipated to meet projected increases in the demand for water services. The regional water authorities (RWAs) were constituted as 'public utilities' that would operate to 'commercial criteria' with 'investment appraisal' mechanisms to prevent the over-investment of capital (Department of the Environment, 1971, 1973).

The removal of the water industry from democratic control, however, also removed what had been the rational (democratic) basis for the determination of financial investment and control strategies. In the context of a global crisis of capital accumulation, the 1973 reforms heightened the level of fiscal inflation and produced state regulatory strategies concerned to reduce levels of spending and investment. These developments resulted in RWAs becoming inefficient, ineffective and unable to proceed with the planned capital investment programmes. The need to improve efficiency was imposed through restrictions on outside finance (external finance limits), performance aims and target rates of return on capital (O'Connell-Davidson, 1993, pp. 26-31; National Water Council, 1983). The failure of technocratic Fabianism therefore resulted in the fiscal crisis of the water industry being resolved through the (re)imposition of a politically mediated 'law of money' onto the regulatory and administrative structures of the industry.

The managerialization of the water industry developed in response to a serious fiscal crisis of the state. While managerialization intensified the crisis it also allowed a fundamental commercialization of social relations both within water companies and between water companies and their consumers. In this sense managerialization provided a transitional form between technocratic Fabianism and the reintegration of the water sector into the global capitalist economy. Managerialism facilitated the realignment of state and capital through the way in which it produced large efficient entities capable of operating as capital. The privatization of the water industry can therefore be examined in the context of the wider development and crisis tendencies of the global capitalist system. In the context of a global crisis of over-accumulation, managerialization produced large efficient organizations capable of operating as capital in a context of surplus capital looking for investment (Clarke, 1988, pp. 341-351).

The privatization of the water industry by the 1989 Water Act and the development of the regulatory framework constituted by OFWAT has provided a rational basis for the development of a major capital investment programme projected to exceed £28 billion between 1990 and 2000: a two-fold increase in capital spending for all water companies following privatization (OFWAT 1991, p. 15). Indeed, the utilities sector is becoming an increasingly important sector in the UK and global capitalization (Buchanan and Clapham, 1988). This reconvergence of state and capital has been facilitated by the imposition of forms of regulation and management on the operational activities of the water industry that subordinate the operational activities of water companies to the dynamics and constraints of the global capitalist system. This can be illustrated through a detailed examination of the form and function of OFWAT and the role of OFWAT in the neo-liberal transformation of the water industry.

OFWAT and the regulation of change

OFWAT was created by the 1989 Water Act as the stage agency responsible for the economic regulation of the water industry. The Act privatized the existing ten RWAs and enforced a separation between the 'core' monopoly functions of supplying water and disposing of sewage and other 'enterprise' functions. The 'core' business operations of the former RWAs and the existing SWCs were taken over by 'Water Supply Plcs' (WSPLCs) and were licensed to supply water and dispose of sewage by OFWAT. The licence established charging limits and performance standards and managers were left free within this framework to make profits while meeting quality standards. The function of the regulator was to establish a framework that safeguarded the 'public interest' whilst providing incentives to efficient management (HM Government, 1986, pp. 16-17). OFWAT provides a proxy for the competitive market. The market proxy was constituted by the development of measurements of comparative competition and the threat of mergers and takeovers. OFWAT has the function of establishing the licence conditions of the 39 WSPLCs and 'regulating' compliance with the licence conditions through the collection and application of data on operating and capital costs, levels of service and customer care. The data was to form the basis of the conditions laid out in licence agreements and would form the basis of the comparative competition through which 'the market' would assess the efficiency of water undertakers. In the following two sections I outline the way in which OFWAT regulates the prices charged by water companies and the quality of service water companies provide to their customers. The central point to note is that in both these functions the operation of OFWAT has been to de-politicize, individualize and monetarize the provision of water services in a way that corresponds to the neo-liberal form of the OFWAT regulatory regime.

OFWAT and the regulation of prices

In the water industry price increases are regulated by a (RPI + K) formula. The value of 'K' is a function of what a company needs to

189

finance the provision of service to customers whilst taking into account the amount needed for capital expenditure and operating costs, offset by improvements in productivity and proceeds from the sale of land. In order to finance a proposed £25 billion investment programme in improved drinking water quality and reduced pollution in the 10 years following privatization all water companies were initially awarded positive 'K' values (an average of 5.5 per cent for the first 5 years and 4 per cent for the second 5 years). The levels of 'K' were reassessed in 1994 and the reductions in 'K' have resulted in a situation in which the resources for improved standards will have to be found from increases in operating efficiency (*The Guardian*, 29 June 1994).

The regulation of prices is the responsibility of the 'Charges Control Division' of OFWAT. The Division is responsible for advising on adjustments to 'K' either on an interim basis or via a periodic review. The Division undertakes the collection and analysis of financial information, encourages comparative competition, and undertakes periodic efficiency studies. The Division monitors the performance of companies and the costs and benefits of changes in service standards; limiting 'charges to those that would be charged by companies competing directly with each other' (OFWAT, 1990a, p.13).

The Charges Control Division is also responsible for developing policy on tariff structures and charging methods. OFWAT launched a consultation document in 1990 in order to promote a debate on alternative charging methods. OFWAT was concerned to promote the advantageous, though economically prohibitive, method of metering which would provide customers with 'a sensible price message to enable them to affect their consumption pattern' (*ibid*. p. 16). The context of the exercise was a situation in which, owing to the need to finance improved quality standards, water charges are set to rise by between 22 per cent and 122 per cent by 2000. The situation was compounded by the 1989 Water Act which prohibited charges based on rateable value on new properties immediately and on all properties after 2000. The determination of individual charges needed to be considered within the (RPI + 'K') formula. The 1989 Act gave each WSPLC the power to fix charges for its services within (RPI + K) although there are constraints set by 'Licence Condition E' by which WSPLCs are required to ensure that no undue preference is shown to, and that there is no undue discrimination against, any class of customer or potential customer (OFWAT, 1990b, Annex 1, p. 1).

The above legal framework highlighted the importance of developing a series of 'objectives' that charging policies should meet, viz, fairness, incentives for economy, and simplicity. The 1989 Water Act prohibited the calculation of water charges on the basis of 'ability to pay'. The balance between 'standing' and 'variable' elements of water bills was to follow consumption, as standing charges weighed heavily upon small properties with low consumption, and households that 'chose' to use large amounts of water should to have this reflected in their water charges. The customer should to be able 'to control his (sic) consumption and expenditure in the light of his needs and resources' (OFWAT, 1990b, pp. 9-10). The 'objective' of providing 'simple incentives' to customers and companies was to help ensure that the right level of service is provided at the right price to achieve improved economy and efficiency and to ensure that resources are well allocated. Tariff structures needed to 'provide clear price messages which encourage companies to meet customers' demands, subject to achieving statutory environmental and health objectives, at the lowest price' (*ibid*. pp. 9-11). In order to provide incentives the tariff structure needed to be organized on the basis that if a customer changes the volume of water or sewage services demanded, the change in his (sic) bill would broadly reflect changes in both capital and environmental costs.

The vast capital expenditure programmes required to meet increasingly rigorous environmental standards highlighted the relationship between the economic and environmental aspects of regulation (*ibid*. Annex 2, pp. 1-5). Environmental considerations were central to decisions on future investment programmes and the nature and implementation of charging systems. 'Economic efficiency' required that both the costs and benefits of environmental decisions should be a concern of the regulator. Customers both benefited from, and shared the costs of, environmental programmes, and it was important that the costs of initiatives were presented in a way which indicated their implications for individual water bills. It was important to allow customers of water services to make judgements about the value they place on environmental benefits. Regulation needed to be premised upon an articulation between economic and environmental operations of the water industry. Decisions on new (environmental) obligations needed to be translated into investment programmes and prices, and implementation needed to be structured within a medium-term framework that gave customers certainty on their charges and the industry space to manage.

The establishment of distinct roles for the National Rivers Authority, OFWAT and WSPLCs made it important that prices reflected the environmental costs attributable to distinct stages in the use cycle (abstraction, treatment, discharge). Increasingly tight environmental standards necessarily implied higher charges for customers. The 'Municipal Waste Water Directive' (MWWD) required an end to the dumping of sludge at sea by 1998, and the expansion of treatment to the sewage outflows that flow into estuaries or the sea. Between 1991 and 1994 around £2.5 billion per year was projected for water industry capital investment, and of this between £0.8 billion and £1.25 billion was required to meet existing and future environmental improvements. The costs spread unevenly across the ten WSPLCs.[3] Improvements were to be financed through the bills paid by customers as determined by (RPI + K), and this needed to be reflected in the process of environmental planning and decision making. OFWAT has argued that customers would not welcome further price rises unless they were confident 'that (price increases) are justified and provided good value for money' (OFWAT, 1990b, p. 15).

The objective of OFWAT was the development of a rational framework within which costs and benefits of environmental programmes could be evaluated in order to ensure that ministers' decisions were translated into investment programmes with known consequences for prices. The action of quality regulators on new environmental initiatives and the costs of the differential impact upon the investment programmes of individual companies needed to be analysed in the context of the likely impact upon the bills of individual customers. The final decisions on proposals would fall on ministers who would need to balance the cost of making the improvements and the consequences for customers' bills against the environmental benefits. The main concern was the development of tariff structures that adequately reflected the subjectively defined values placed on utility services by abstract individuals and thereby resolve the fiscal crisis of the Fabian water industry.

Technocratic Fabianism attempted to meet the politically-defined needs of consumers through the planning of large-scale capital investment projects. The neo-liberal regulation of the water industry is an attempt to resolve the fiscal crisis which resulted from this form of Keynesian planning and to de-politicize the provision of water services. The development of improvement programmes with respect to drinking water and sewage disposal has to be equated with the prices paid by individual consumers. Hence, the operation of OFWAT in respect of pricing policy has attempted to de-politicize the provision of services and decisions on capital investment programmes and subordinate service provision to individuated money relations. The regulation of price by OFWAT highlights the way in which the substantive political and democratic content has been emptied out of public service as a form of state practice. Decisions on capital projects and environmental improvements are no longer the result of democratic and technical assessments of need and are increasingly premised on the prices paid by the abstract marginal-maximizing individual of neo-liberal social theory.

OFWAT and the regulation of quality

The 1989 Water Act placed a duty on OFWAT to promote competition and encourage efficiency and effectiveness through the mechanisms of 'inset' appointments by which companies supply customers within the areas covered by other companies, comparative competition and mergers. The licences of water companies lay down the detailed accounting information that is to be made available to OFWAT in its function of encouraging comparative competition. Comparative competition allows OFWAT to 'form useful conclusions on the benefits to consumers' and allows the financial markets to make judgements about the different quoted companies. The technical, engineering and scientific aspects of water company performance are monitored by the 'Engineering Intelligence Division'. The Division reports on, and certifies information submitted by, WSPLCs. The Division is intended to establish a mechanism that ensures the development of the necessary reporting arrangements to enable OFWAT to 'monitor and compare a company operating performance, levels of service, and investment expenditure..... (and) to support planning for periodic reviews and the efficient and economic integration of new obligations' (OFWAT, 1990b, p. 21). The 1989 Act required WSPLCs to develop detailed, long-term 'Asset Management Plans' outlining the way in which companies plan to manage, maintain and improve fixed assets. These reports together with investment and levels of service projections form the basis of the 'K' setting. The projections were designed to improve the service provided to water customers, and it is the function of OFWAT to ensure that projected developments are achieved on time and at the lowest acceptable cost to customers.

193

In order to balance arm's length regulation with an assurance that water customers' monies are being effectively and economically managed, OFWAT requires companies to submit an annual report. The Report provides 'a framework for the submission of the majority of information required to enable OFWAT to monitor progress and compare performance.... (enabling) the generation of time-series information and facilitating non-financial comparisons' (OFWAT, 1990b, p. 22). Companies report on their medium term progress regarding the 'Asset Management Plan'; investment procurement strategy; quantitative data on service 'outputs'; progress in meeting drinking water and sewage compliance programmes; an outline of the methodology and procedures adopted to enable the accurate representation of levels of service indicators. Outputs are measured and monitored by a series of quantitatively defined quality standards that are laid down by the operating licences.

The regulatory auditing developed by OFWAT has had a fundamental impact on the managerial structure of water companies. The collection and auditing of performance data has resulted in a massive investment in new management information systems and provided a major dynamic in the development of 'total quality management' and 'constant improvement programmes'. The output measures have been central in the recent organizational and management restructuring of water companies. The measures have been incorporated into management control strategies forming the basis of the appraisal and performance-related-pay of senior managers and have been central to the development of new 'quality systems'. The quality systems have centralized and intensified management control within water companies. Performance against the indicators is constantly monitored by senior managers and specialized 'customer service' departments that have been established within water companies following privatization. The regulatory activities of OFWAT have thus played a central role in increasing the intensification of labour within the water industry and has facilitated a range of regulatory indicators which have embedded the dynamic of 'constant improvement' within the organizational structure of water companies. The regulation of quality by OFWAT has played a central role in the development of 'total quality management' (TQM) and highlights the central function of TQM in reducing the porocity of the working day and increasing the intensification of labour (see Dawson and Webb, 1989; Taylor, 1996, chs. 5-6).

The regulation of quality by OFWAT provides a further illustration of the neo-liberal alignment between state and capital in the privatized water industry. The OFWAT quality audits institutionalize the dynamic of constant efficiency improvements within the organizational form of the water industry and ensure that the organization of both the labour process and the systems of service provision are subordinated to the abstract and indifferent power of money. The social function of OFWAT is to provide the institutional context for the successful production and realization of surplus value. The concrete rights of producers and consumers of water services have both been subordinated to the valorization imperatives of capital. Public service has been redefined, as the 'common good' is increasingly premised on the negative and abstract rights of the marginal-maximizer of neo-liberal social theory. Human needs have thus been (re)subordinated to the valorization of capital in contrast to the democratically or substantively defined conceptions of human need which marked the Fabian water industry. The crisis of the Keynesian water industry has been resolved through the incorporation of the industry within the post-Keynesian global capitalist system.

The development of the OFWAT quality audits are part of a process through which the water industry has been subordinated to the power of international financial institutions and the institutional form of the water subordinated to the power of money through the development of devolved management accounting systems and the commercialization of social relations within water companies. The OFWAT regime therefore not only provides the major dynamic in the adoption of constant improvement programmes but determines the indicators around which constant improvement is structured. These processes developed in the context of a wider crisis of the global economy and the mechanisms of Keynesian planning which had provided stable economic growth in the post-war period. The resulting fiscal crisis of the state has been resolved through the monetarization of UK state and society and the increasing replacement of concrete and substantive citizenship rights within the democratic state by the negative and abstract rights of consumers within markets and state-defined market proxies.

Neo-liberal theory, citizenship and the crisis of public service

The Fabian public service water industry was part of a wider Keynesian settlement which institutionalized the rising expectations of the working class within the institutions of the state. The Fabian water industry attempted to resolve the problem of under investment through the planning of investment and resources according to technocratic and democratic conceptions of concrete needs. The state, however, is embedded in a global capitalist system and the autonomy of the state is strictly by the circumscribed logic and dynamics of the global capitalist system. The operation of Keynesian planning ultimately resulted in an increasingly severe fiscal crisis of the state, and governments were forced to abandon Keynesianism owing to the way in which persistent inflation, rising public expenditure and a weak balance of payments put (them) under financial pressure in domestic and international financial markets. Keynesianism collapsed into 'stagflation', with both prices and unemployment rising, real wages stagnating, and public expenditure falling at the expense of both services and public sector pay (Clarke, 1988, p. 302).

The democratic pretensions of the Keynesian state as an embodiment of the 'common good' were increasingly undermined by the oppressive and restrictive restructuring of state agencies that attempted to overcome this crisis. The neo-liberal theories of the New Right have played an important role in providing the legitimation to a process through which state agencies have been subordinated to the disinterested and abstract power of money in order to overcome the fiscal crisis of the Keynesian welfare state. In order to understand this proposition it is necessary to understand the nature of money in capitalist societies (see Neary and Taylor, 1995). Money is the most abstract form of capitalist power and the social form through which labour is subordinated to the dynamics of capital accumulation. Money is not simply an economic category but simultaneously economic, political and ideological. The subordination of state and civil society to the power of money therefore implies a restructuring of the whole gamut of relations between capital, labour and the state. Money embodies the domination of concrete by abstract labour. The subordination of the state by money (i.e. monetarism) therefore implies that the concrete and substantive rights of individual citizens are made increasingly abstract and mediated by monetary relations. This process has resulted in a fundamental redefinition of public service or the common good which has been redefined in increasingly abstract and liberal terms.

The development of monetarism shifted the theoretical premises of 'public service' from Fabian Socialism to neo-liberal economic and social theory. Liberalism has provided a refined conception of the 'common good' and citizenship that is essentially abstract. Hence, the liberal revival has been concerned to demonstrate the extent to which (abstract) social rights emanate from the operation of property rights in regulated markets rather than from (concrete) entitlements to welfare state services. This has important implications with respect to the regulation of 'public goods' such as water. In 1989 the National Consumer Council produced a report entitled *In the Absence of Competition: A Consumer View on Utilities Regulation*. The report played a central role in determining the regulatory form of OFWAT. The report is suffused with conceptual categories derived from neo-liberal social theory, and the central argument developed was that the regulatory regime needed to be premised on the interests of the marginal maximizing individual of neo-liberal economic theory.

Neo-liberal economics is premised upon a conception of the individual as a rational utility-maximizing consumer. The action of calculating utility-maximisers spontaneously and impersonally interacting in the market results in both individual liberty and economic efficiency. The market allows individuals to incorporate all their consumption behaviour into a personal consumption plan that spontaneously produces the optimum allocation of social resources (Barry, 1987, pp. 52-53). The economic freedom of individuals in the sphere of consumption constitutes the direct and most immediate form of freedom. Freedom is defined as freedom from coercion - freedom in the abstract. Neo-liberal theory has been concerned to develop a social theory on the individualist postulates of micro-economic theory and the postulates of micro-economic theory have provided the modus operandi of neo-liberal state regulation. The 'market' is central to this project as a result of its individualistic premises. The market has no ends or purposes and consequently resources are allocated on the basis of subjectively determined values through the competitive dynamic of supply and demand.

The public benefit is maximized unintentionally through the actions of individual marginal-maximizers pursuing their own self-interest. The imperfections of real markets heighten the importance of 'property rights', which provide incentives for entrepreneurs to create profits through the location of price differences in real markets. The state lacks the knowledge that is available to decentralized entrepreneurs, and planned systems of provision therefore fail to deliver the optimum allocation of resources. Liberal social theory is thus premised on the utilitarian notion of

197

'unanimity' and is critical of tendencies towards the politicization of economic life. The 'public interest' or 'common good' is derived from the interests of autonomous and anonymous (abstract) individuals, and (abstract) economic freedom constitutes the fundamental basis of social power. The power conferred on consumers within the neo-liberal water industry is essentially abstract and negative. The concrete and substantive rights of consumers within the Fabian public service state have been fundamentally transformed into essentially abstract and negative rights. Public service has been fundamentally depoliticized and the regulation and management of the industry has been restructured through the introduction of state-mediated processes which ensure that infrastructural and operational decisions are subordinated to the abstract imperatives of money capital.

The development of abstract public service implies that the need[4] for water services is subordinated to the abstract imperatives of the valorization of international finance capital. The OFWAT audit, for example, provides a range of indicators to allow international capital markets to make comparative judgements with respect to quoted UK water companies and together with the RPI + K pricing formula provides a stable medium term framework for managers to pursue improvements in efficiency and thereby make profits. Between 1989, when the water industry was privatized, and 1993 average profitability in the water industry increased by 20 per cent a year from a combined profitability of £1.1 billion to £2 billion. In the same period total share value increased from £5.2 billion to £13 billion (*The Guardian*, 28 July 1994). The privatization of the water industry has thus provided the regulatory mechanism which has facilitated the total subordination of human need to the valorization of capital and the production of profit. This represents an attempt to contain the demands and aspirations of human beings for pure and wholesome drinking water and clean and unpolluted rivers within the abstract and stultifying world of capital. The domination of labour by capital can never be total and cracks are inevitably beginning to appear in the pristine edifice of popular capitalism.

Public service, privatization and the crisis of the state

The regulation of service by OFWAT forms the basis of the new abstract citizenship. Public service is redefined on the basis of the micro-economic postulates of neo-liberal economics, the function of regulation being to ensure that individual customers receive 'value' for money. There are, however, fundamental problems with the 'marginalist' conception of value articulated by neo-classical economics and the conception of the individual on which both modern economics and modern sociology are premised (Clarke, 1991b). The 'subjectivist' conceptualization of value posits the individual as an essentially 'abstract' being owing to the separation of the formal rationality and substantive irrationality of capitalist society. The neo-liberal restructuring of the state is thus an attempt to subordinate the institutional form of the state to the formal rationality of capital. The resolution of the Keynesian crisis of the state has therefore to be partial and incomplete and across water, education, health and other public services there is increasing public opposition focused on the enduring substantive irrationalities of a system of service allocation subordinated to the accumulation of capital.

It is perhaps ironic that the discourse of abstract citizenship has been accepted by both the Right and the post-Marxist and Fabian left. The recent acceptance of neo-liberal regulatory agencies by the Labour Party highlights the failure of the left to learn from past mistakes. In a 'policy review' document entitled *Meet the Challenge - Make the Change* published in 1989 the Labour Party laid out the idea, which has recently been developed by Tony Blair, that ownership of public utilities is no longer relevant and that the interests of consumers can be protected by strengthening the regulatory frameworks developed during the privatization programme of the 1980s and 1990s. Hence the blind commitment by the Labour Party to forms of state regulation which embody and articulate the repressive and alienating logic of capital accumulation. There is a real need to recognize and learn from the weaknesses and contradictions of public service provision as it has existed throughout this century. The Fabian technocratic state failed to resolve the contradictions of capitalism through planning and imploded under the weight of an increasingly serious fiscal crisis of the state. The managerialist state imposed a politically mediated law of money onto state agencies in an extremely vicious and oppressive way and destroyed the last vestiges of social democratic conceptions of public service. The neo-liberal state is an attempt to realign state and capital through the subordination of service provision to the dynamics of international finance capital.

The privatization programme has illustrated the important point that nationalization in itself was a partial and contradictory response to the stultifying contradictions of capitalism. The state is contradictory: it delivers things that we need, but in an oppressive and alienating way (London Edinburgh Weekend Return Group, 1979). The state developed through, and articulates the fundamental contradictions of, capital and is logically unable to unproblematically represent the 'common good'. In the increasingly globalized capitalist system nationalization is increasingly neither an option nor particularly desirable given the alienating form of the neo-liberal state. There is a real sense in which the privatization programme of the past fifteen years provides the basis for a renewed and reinvigorated politics of the left that goes beyond the sterile and outmoded categories such as nationalization and privatization to explore in more detail the alienating and oppressive form of the political and economic institutions of capitalist societies. This form was veiled beneath social democratic ideologies of public service and the 'common good'. The regulation of public services through money renders the alienating form of these agencies more transparent and an easier focus for struggle. In the long term it may yet turn out that the left may have rather a lot to thank Mrs Thatcher and the British Conservative Party for!

Notes

1. There are useful expositions of the Fabian conceptualization of the state in the work of G.D.H. Cole (1943) and Anthony Crosland (1952). See also Taylor (1996, chs. 2-3) for a lengthy and detailed consideration of the importance of Fabian Socialism to the development of public service ideology and practice in the UK.

2. I am aware of the essential ambiguity surrounding this concept and would distance my approach from the structuralist accounts of writers such as Offe (1984) and O'Connor (1973). The fiscal crisis of the state does not emerge from contradictions between the 'accumulation' and 'legitimation' functions of the state but articulates the contradictory social determination of the state within capitalist societies. The state is logically and historically premised on the subordination of social production to money capital but exists in a concrete 'political' form which allows the

state partial autonomy from capital. The state cannot escape the 'law of money' and this is manifested in a constant 'fiscal crisis' of the state (see Clarke, 1988, pp.120-54; Holloway and Picciotto, 1991).

3.	Costs have fallen most heavily on WSPLCs with long tracts of coastline. The percentage increase in investment required to meet the MWWD is: South West - over 35%; Southern, Welsh, North West, Northumbrian - 15-20%; Yorkshire, Anglian - 10-15%; and Severn Trent, Thames, Wessex - less than 10% (OFWAT, 1991, p. 16). The overall impact on water prices has been far more marked. The average increase in domestic water charges in the area covered by South West Water between 1989 and 1994 was 74 per cent. This has led to heightening protests from consumers in counties such as Devon and Cornwall where pressures from the EU and tourists for cleaner beaches have placed onerous increases in water charges (*The Guardian*, 28 July 1995).

4.	See Heller (1974) for a discussion on the way in which the capitalist system subordinates human needs to the valorization of capital. Doyal and Gough (1991) present an excellent discussion on the universality of human needs and an incisive critique of the recent relativistic approach to this question by postmodernist writers.

References

Barry, N.P. (1987), *The New Right*, Croom Helm, London.
Buchanan, A. and Clapham, S. (1988), *Utilities: Preview of the Privatization of the Water and Electricity Industries*, Hoare and Government Investment Research Ltd., Broadgate, London.
Bullpitt, J. (1986), 'The Discipline of the New Democracy: Mrs Thatcher's Domestic Statecraft', *Political Studies*, vol. 34.
Clarke, S. (1988), *Keynesianism, Monetarism and the Crisis of the State*, Edward Elgar, London.
Clarke, S. (ed.) (1991a), *The State Debate*, Macmillan, London.
Clarke, S. (1991b), *Marx, Marginalism and Modern Sociology: From Adam Smith to Max Weber*, Second Edition. Macmillan, London.
Cole, G.D.H. (1943), *Fabian Socialism*, Frank Cass, London.

Crosland, C.A.R. (1952), 'The Transition from Capitalism', in Crossman, R.H.S. (ed.), *New Fabian Essays*, Turnstyle Press, London.

Dawson, P. and Webb, J. (1989), 'New Production Arrangements: The Totally Flexible Cage?', *Work, Employment and Society*, vol. 3, no. 2.

Department of the Environment (1971), *The Future Management of Water in England and Wales: A Report by the Central Advisory Water Committee*, HMSO, London.

Department of the Environment (1973), *A Background to Water Reorganization in England and Wales*, HMSO, London.

Doyal, L. and Gough, I. (1991), *A Theory of Human Need*, Macmillan, London.

George, V. and Wilding, P. (1985), *Ideology and Social Welfare*, RKP, London.

Hall, S. (1983), 'The Great Moving Right Show', in Hall, S. and Jacques, M. (eds), *The Politics of Thatcherism*, Lawrence and Wishart, London.

Hall, S. (1988), *The Hard Road to Renewal: Thatcherism and the Crisis of the Left*, Verso, London.

Heller, A. (1973), *The Theory of Need in Marx*, Allison and Busby, London.

HM Government (1944), *A National Water Policy*, HMSO, Cmnd. 6515. London.

HM Government (1986), *Privatization of the Water Authorities in England and Wales*, HMSO, Cmnd 9734. London.

Holloway, J. and Picciotto, S. (1991), 'Capital, Crisis and the State', in Clarke, S. (ed.), *The State Debate*, Macmillan, London.

Jessop, B., Bonnett, K., Bromley, S. and Ling, T. (1988), *Thatcherism: A Tale of Two Nations*, Polity Press, Oxford.

Jessop, B., Bonnett, K. and Bromley, S. (1990), 'Farewell to Thatcherism? Neo-Liberalism and "New Times"', *New Left Review*, no. 179.

Jordon, A.G., Richardson, J.J. and Kimber, R.H. (1977), 'The Origins of the Water Act 1973', *Public Administration*, vol. 55, no. 3.

Jordon, A.G. and Richardson, J.J. (1977), 'Outside Committees and Policy-Making: The Central Advisory Water Committee', *Public Administration Bulletin,* no. 24, August.

London Edinburgh Weekend Return Group (1979), *In and Against the State*, Pluto Press, London.

Marshall, T.H. (1991), *Citizenship and Social Class and Other Essays*, London, Pluto Press.

Melitz, J. (1959), 'The Trade Unions and Fabian Socialism', *Industrial and Labor Review*, vol. 12, July.

Miliband (1983), 'Socialist Advance in Britain', *Socialist Register, 1983* Merlin, London.

Nairn, T. (1965), 'The Nature of the Labour Party', *New Left Review*, no. 27.

Nairn, T. (1981), 'The Crisis of the British State', *New Left Review*, no. 130.

National Consumer Council (1989), *In the Absence of Competition: A Consumer View of Public Utilities Regulation*, HMSO, London.

National Water Council (1983), *Annual Report and Accounts 1982/3*, HMSO, London.

Neary, M. and Taylor, G. (1995), *Money Changes Everything*, University of the West of England Occasional Papers in Sociology no. 12., Bristol.

O'Connell-Davidson, J. (1993), *Privatization and Employment Relations: The Case of The Water Industry*, Mansell, London.

O'Connor, J. (1973), *The Fiscal Crisis of the State*, St Martin's Press, New York.

Offe, C. (1984), *Contradictions of the Welfare State*, Hutchinson, London.

OFWAT (1990a), *Annual Report 1989*, HMSO, London.

OFWAT (1990b), *Paying for Water: A Time for Decisions*, OFWAT, Birmingham.

OFWAT (1991), *Annual Report 1990*, HMSO, London.

Saville, J. (1973), 'The Ideology of Labourism', in Benwick, R. *et al.* (eds), *Knowledge and Belief in Politics*, London, Allen and Unwin.

Taylor, G. (1996), *Safe in Their Hands? Public Service and the State Regulation of the UK Water Industry*, Mansell, London.

9 Nuclear Power and the Commanding Heights of Energy Privatization

IAN WELSH

Introduction

This chapter considers the privatization of the erstwhile commanding heights of the British economy represented by the electricity supply industry (ESI). The government's announcement that it is to privatize nuclear power severs the final link between electricity supply and 'high' state policy, passing the associated responsibilities to the market. This fundamental transfer of responsibility will form the central analytical theme of this chapter which takes nuclear energy as its primary focus whilst arguing that all the energy privatizations must be considered as an integrated government agenda.

This analytical theme and empirical foci allow us to examine the boundaries of state responsibility in a decade of accelerating globalization (Featherstone, 1990; Albrow, 1990; Lash, 1995). By embracing global energy markets the government displaces its capacity to secure energy supplies to international fora which are determined by multilateral interests. The international arena cannot be relied upon to ensure British energy interests, as emergent global regulatory regimes - such as climate change conventions, the GATT (Purdue, 1995) and others - demonstrate, producing unforeseen stress in domestic political agendas and creating the political frameworks for new global industries such as biotechnology (Beck, 1995; Welsh, 1995).

Whilst privatization remained limited to domestic issues, the consequences upon the productive sectors of the economy remained indirect. The privatization of energy supply begun in the early 1980s provides an opportunity to assess the more direct economic implications and their global ramifications. The global rhetoric of the privatized utilities is revealed in the depiction of British Gas as a 'world class company' requiring world class salaries. What is obscured in this process, however, is the fact that the market, most notably the oil market in 1957, 1973 and 1990, is no guarantor of security of supply (Waters, 1995, pp. 74-75).

Successive UK energy privatizations have been driven by an ideological commitment to the market steered by political expediency. In their haste to abolish all vestiges of the post world war two corporatist energy sector the original reasons for nationalization have been forgotten. The idea that the state has a crucial role in the strategic development of science and technology policy has been substantially weakened and technical discourses of legitimation have been replaced by market discourses. The ascendancy of this rhetoric is amply demonstrated by the leader of the Labour Party's ready embrace of globalization as part of his modernizing agenda.

In championing the market as the best means of effecting energy policy (HM Govt., 1989, 1995; House of Commons Trade and Industry Committee, 1993) government policy has turned full circle in just fifty years. Then, state sponsorship of nuclear power was seen as the means of reinvigorating the British economy, securing a cheap source of domestic electricity and building an industry which would dominate a world market in nuclear reactors (HM Govt., 1955). Had nuclear power lived up to its promise what should have gone on sale would have been a formidable business offering a potentially endless supply of competitively priced electricity from 'fast breeder reactors' (FBRs).

In reality, the rather bleak market dawn for nuclear power sees a mere eight nuclear power stations being offered for sale at a price regarded by some as 'realistic', whilst others see it as a 'give away'. The full story of the nuclear dream turned share shop scheme is beyond the scope of a short chapter (see Welsh, 1996). By concentrating here on the way in which the political desire to protect nuclear power has distorted the privatization of the ESI, I will demonstrate several things. These include: the extent to which the 'free market' in energy has been a direct product of government intervention, the limits of market-based approaches which treat all

206

commodities as if they are the same, the need to reassert the importance of non-market political considerations in policy making and finally the extraordinary nature of the financial gamble faced by investors in the nuclear dream.

In this sense privatization in the electricity supply sector, and elsewhere, is part of an interlocking state strategy to intervene to reconstitute the structure of market relations within Britain. This has reinvigorated what Lash and Urry (1989) term the Makler economy, by weakening the direct regulation of the British economy, leaving it to be driven by world trends and international pressures (Hutton, 1995a). Two main strategies can be identified here. A reduction in labour costs accompanied by more flexible working hours and the attempted use of global spot markets to drive down the cost of domestically produced energy.

The Energy Sector in the UK

It is important to recognize that the public visage of electricity supply has always been harnessed to ideological forces. During the inter-war years electricity was perceived as a force which would unite the country, physically through the construction of a national grid and symbolically by universal access to the 'all electric society' (Luckin, 1990, p. 12). The decentralized municipal and private generating network became subject to a progressively centralized control. Centralization made the ESI the backbone of the constituent energy industries by determining domestic markets, particularly for coal. Consequently the operation of the ESI became the focus of persistent debates between technocrats eschewing all political interference (Hinton, 1976) and more humanist commentators seeking a degree of social control over technological developments (Wynne, 1982).

Against this background the analysis of energy privatizations, like the analysis of Thatcherism, depends upon the perception of what went before it. The dominance of technocracy, noted above, has been one persistent theme (Roberts, 1992; Touraine, 1983), which has been complemented by a focus on the importance of scientific and technical expertise (Jasanoff, (ed.) 1995). The Conservatives' assertion of market discourses must be seen as one means of overcoming the impasse resulting from the politicization of expert debates over nuclear energy in the 1970s and

1980s. A nuclear future for electricity supply has been firmly embedded in government policy since 1955 (HM Govt., 1955). This White Paper presented nuclear power as a technology embodying the essence of British scientific and technical achievement, evoking a brave new world where scientists would keep Britain at the very frontiers of progress. The language of discovery, progress and scientific heroism was interwoven with a view of the future where no more coal-fired power stations would be built by the 1970s. Britain's nuclear scientists were valorized as heroes and the sentiment expressed that if 'Britannia no longer ruled the waves then she certainly ruled the reactors and the isotopes' in this 'second age of Elizabethan splendour' (see Welsh, 1993, p. 21).

The 1957 Electricity Act creating the Central Electricity Generating Board (CEGB) closely followed the first nuclear power programme (HM Govt., 1957). Together these pieces of legislation set the structure of the ESI for the next thirty years, enshrining the CEGB as king maker in the domestic fuel market. As the organization with statutory responsibility for the security of electricity supplies the CEGB had the power to determine, subject to government capital expenditure agreements, the mix of power stations to be built, and the merit order in which these were to be connected to the grid. The area electricity boards were statutorily obliged to purchase power from the CEGB.

The intention behind the creation of the CEGB was made quite clear in the accompanying debates in the House of Commons. The CEGB was to have responsibility for the advanced nuclear stations, leaving the area boards to run conventional coal-fired stations. The CEGB's purpose was 'to promote and distribute atomic electricity. It might very well be called an atomic energy Bill' (Hansard, 942-967).

Despite strong state backing, the transfer of eminent scientists and engineers from the United Kingdom Atomic Energy Authority (UKAEA) to the CEGB and Foreign Office support in seeking overseas markets, the development of nuclear power for electricity generation was a disaster. British research and development quickly became locked into a gas-cooled line of reactor development which other nuclear powers abandoned. The result was domestic Magnox reactors that initially produced expensive electricity (Welsh, 1994a; Burn, 1978; Williams, 1980).

The electricity supply industry also became dominated by a number of structural conflicts. The CEGB became steadily more committed to nuclear power, leaving the area boards obliged to buy a product they perceived as expensive and inflexible. Under considerable pressure to demonstrate accountability the UKAEA and CEGB developed a complex set of conventions to determine the profitability of competing generating stations known as the Net Effect Cost (Welsh, 1994a).

Applied with absolute secrecy, this claimed to show that nuclear power stations produced the cheapest electricity provided that they were operated continuously. This view was controversial with large-scale industrial users, with the area boards, which remained sceptical about the cost advantages of nuclear power, and the coal industry, which was heavily reliant on the CEGB for sales. Meanwhile, tariff barriers made independent electricity generation by large industrial users unviable due to the penalties attached to selling surplus supplies to the national grid. Instead the CEGB entered into special bulk purchase contracts with customers like Alcan and ICI.

After years of pressure the CEGB's 'Net Effective Cost' was investigated by two powerful House of Commons Committees. The findings of both inquiries were damning (House of Commons Selelect Committee on Energy (HCSCE), 1981; Monopolies and Mergers Commission, 1981). It became clear that the CEGB had been 'cavalier in their approach to investment decisions', had exaggerated the performance of nuclear stations and had failed to make adequate provision for the final disposal of nuclear wastes and decommissioning costs. The energy sector was thus beset with a number of long-running tensions arising from past legislative structures, and with their embodiment in organizational cultures and operational practices, by the time privatization agendas began to be considered by the Conservatives.

Early days: Conservative market incentives

In 1979 the incoming Conservative adminstration was quick to embrace the nuclear industry. The nuclear industry looked forward to a period of favourable tutelage from the State after the tribulations of Tony Benn's obstruction of the pressurized water reactor (PWR) and insistence on enhanced public scrutiny (Benn, 1989). Private industry wanted more freedom to generate electricity directly, the area boards wanted freedom from CEGB domination, the coal industry wanted a clear statement on the costs of nuclear energy and a policy commitment to a secure level of coal burn. The nuclear power lobby was initially rewarded by orders for advanced gas-cooled reactors (AGRs) at Heysham and Torness. These orders represented a stopgap to keep the nuclear industry in work until policy could be clarified.

In December 1979 the Cabinet's Economic Sub-Committee approved an ambitious programme of ten PWRs. The widely leaked minutes revealed the political agenda behind this policy decision. Nuclear power had 'the advantage of removing a substantial portion of electricity production from the danger of disruption by industrial action by coal miners or transport workers'.[1] Against this had to be balanced the risk that nuclear power would become a sphere of entrenched expert dissent, acting as a focus for a vociferous anti-nuclear movement. It was considered that the 'government may make more rapid progress towards its objective by adopting a low profile approach' (ibid).

The sensitive legitimation issues raised were considered in the context of the Government's commitment to a wide-ranging and lengthy public inquiry into the first PWR at Sizewell, which effectively put an end to the prospect of a rapid nuclear expansion. Throughout the miners strike of 1984-1985 the government's commitment to the nuclear industry was repaid as nuclear base load kept the lights on.

The other major initiative in the electricity supply sector during this period was a shift in the legislative balance intended to encourage the private generators to enter the supply side (HM Govt., 1983). By offering more favourable terms for the sale of privately generated electricity to the national grid the government hoped to kick start a private supply sector. Private capital associated with the power station construction industry expressed some interest in the purchase of ex-CEGB power station sites but this never translated into firm commitment. An important aspect of this legislation was the removal of any barriers preventing private capital moving into electricity generation, including nuclear power.

Despite this inducement, ministers remained disappointed that there was no organic market growth as a result. As time passed this necessitated further legislation if the privatization of the energy sector as a whole was to be accomplished. The interlocking nature of the energy supply sector and the centrality of the electricity supply industry within this, however, made privatization an immensely complex task.

Parallel privatizations: gas and coal

The privatizations of British Gas and the National Coal Board were already accomplished or in train by the time the ESI was privatized. It was clear that the structure of the new ESI would have important consequences for each of these industries. In particular it was difficult to envisage a truly free market continuing to favour nuclear power. The fate of British Gas and British Coal were to be definitively sealed by the arrangements for privatizing electricity supply.

British Gas had embarked upon an aggressive overseas policy, developing interests in gas-field developments throughout the world whilst continuing to enjoy a monopoly supply position in its domestic market. In terms of UK gas supplies the most important overseas development was the exploitation of huge reserves in the former USSR. Changes in European legislation, pricing structures, and short term surplus supplies, enabled gas to compete for electricity generating contracts. From being a marginal player confined to supplying emergency spinning reserves, British Gas developed an aggressive drive to expand its share of the electricity generating market.

The preparation of the National Coal Board for privatization was a long and protracted process requiring the neutralization of the National Union of Mineworkers (NUM) under the leadership of Arthur Scargill. The scale of the cuts envisaged in the coal industry were so dramatic that Scargill's denunciations of government intentions were met with incredulity. The resultant 'Battle for Coal' waged at pit heads throughout the country obscured to some extent the length of the modernizing hand played by government and senior management within the industry (Beynon, 1985).

The abandonment of the 1970s 'Plan for Coal', which depicted Britain as an island of coal in a sea of oil, marked the beginning of this process. The long term capital investment strategy of British Coal foreshadowed a dramatic cut in the number of working mines. The Wintertons have persuasively argued that the capital logic of this programme resulted in a commitment to only mining thick seams of coal. The necessary deep face mining technology simultaneously increased management control over the labour process underground, whilst making pits with shallow, less favourable seams, uneconomic (Winterton and Winterton, 1989; Winterton, 1993). The failure to recognize this resulted in some influential analysts arguing that one of the real issues uncovered by the coal crisis was the

211

short life span of indigenous coal reserves (Parker and Surrey, 1993). In reality what was revealed was that investment decisions had prioritized certain types of mines that coincided closely with those which the government subsequently privatized. These investment decisions were sanctioned by successive Conservative administrations pursuing twin political strategies of privatization and defeat of the NUM. The privatization of the electricity supply industry was only attempted once these 'long hands' were well in train (Welsh, 1994b).

The privatization agenda

In February 1988 the government published its White Paper on the privatization of the electricity supply industry (HM Govt., 1988). The framing principles of the paper were a clear statement of New Right 'laissez faire' policy applied to the monopoly power of the CEGB. As suppliers of 95 per cent of the nation's power requirements, owners of all power stations, and the distribution system, the CEGB were seen as exerting 'too much influence in power station investment decisions' (*ibid.*, p. 4), an important determinant of the price paid by consumers.

Despite previous legislation, less than half of one per cent of total public supplies of electricity was privately generated by 1986. As encouragement had failed it now became necessary to legislate. State intervention would have to create the necessary legal and legislative framework for a 'free market'. The structure of the electricity supply industry was thus to be of the government's making (HM Govt., 1988, p. 13).

In place of corporatist planning and investment programmes a market-driven framework was sought. The White Paper declared that, 'Every part of the industry will become properly accountable to its shareholders.' (*ibid.*, pp. 2-3). The original intention was to end the monopoly position of the CEGB by creating two new utilities: one entirely conventional, the other larger and including the nuclear stations. Ownership of the national grid would fall to the twelve distribution companies which, significantly, were also given the freedom to generate electricity from independently owned stations (*ibid.*, p. 7).

In effect the regional electricity companies became the holders of monopolies to supply and became statutorily responsible for security of supply (*ibid.*, p. 9). Contracts were to govern the 'commercial

212

relationship' between generators and distributors. Distributors could elect to generate their own electricity and became free to obtain 'coal and other fuels from the most competitive sources.' (*ibid.*, p. 10). The government clearly envisaged that through a contract pricing mechanism an equivalent of the old merit order system would be maintained. The White Paper made clear pronouncements on the future of nuclear power. The government was 'determined that public confidence in the nuclear programme should be maintained.' (*ibid.*, p. 12). As existing nuclear safety legislation made 'no distinction between public and private ownership' (*ibid.*) there was no legislative barrier to the nuclear stations passing into private hands. In the government's view there remained 'a vital strategic need for the significant non-fossil-fuelled contribution that can only be made by nuclear power' (*ibid.*, p. 12). As we shall see, this led the government to intervene in ways inimical to the operation of a free market that it sought to create.

The proposed privatization was seen as producing major benefits. Investment decisions would be driven by the needs of customers, competition would drive down prices, managers would be free to manage, investment plans would be subject to the commercial rigour of the capital markets, and employees would become shareholders in the component concerns. The success of this operation was ultimately dependent upon the legislative detail and its successful translation into practice.

The White Paper recognized some of the complexities involved, such as identifying 'the nature of the price to be controlled', and the difficulty involved at arriving at a pricing formula sufficiently sensitive to achieve the desired range of outcomes (*ibid.*, p. 13). The doubts expressed over the formula reflect bitter disagreements between New Right theorists over whether statistical averaging produces any useful information in relation to market systems (Hayek, 1944, 1960; Friedman, 1962). Balancing individual energy use, diversity of supply and the collective good through a pricing mechanism would be a very difficult task. Other equally difficult issues remained poorly formalized.

Old state responsibilities such as the determination of overall demand forecasts and the requirements for reserve generating capacity, seemed 'likely' to be 'agreed on a national basis' (HM Govt., 1988, p. 8). How these issues were to be agreed, between whom they were to be agreed, and how the responsibility for maintaining spinning reserves were to be dealt with, were areas where the White Paper remained silent.

In a free market there would have to be some incentive for a generator to maintain excess capacity in a state of constant readiness to meet unanticipated demand, or the sudden removal of a large station from the grid. In the end no national view on this issue emerged and the distribution companies decided to follow their own routes towards ensuring security of supply. The consequence of this has been the emasculation of the national interest within security of supply arguments and its subordination to short-term profit taking.

Whilst determining the nature of the ESI the then Secretary of State for Energy, Cecil Parkinson, expressed some caution about 'what the market could stand' but held the view that commercial contracts would be the subject of a normal business discourse. Questioned on the future of such negotiations between British Coal and the new generators he asserted that 'the two industries have every reason to get this sorted out. I believe that very realistic talks are going to start between them very shortly' (HCSCE, 1989, p. 11).

A Little Local Difficulty: The Energy Select Committee

The Energy Committee's report on the proposed privatization produced unusually strong expressions of cross-party disquiet. The Committee was 'strongly of the view that the nuclear preoccupations of the government' had dominated their thinking 'so that the nuclear tail seems to be wagging the ESI dog' (HCSCE, 1988, para. 41). Concerns were expressed over the 'imbalance of market power', the 'duopolistic structures chosen for generation' and 'placing too much faith in a price control formula acting on one side of the ESI' (ibid., paras. 53, 56, 71). The Committee expressed recurrent concerns about the 'real' costs of nuclear power, noting the potential for further hidden increases in nuclear liabilities (ibid., para. 150). The potential for a regulatory quagmire, given the multitude of factors which the single regulator had to monitor, has proved all too real. Whilst the Select Committee endorsed government proposals that there be a single regulator, it was naive to expect this office to deliver the bewildering range of regulatory functions without a considerable full-time staff. The need to ensure something resembling an even playing field between coal and nuclear was a major case in point. The Committee considered that: 'One of the most disturbing aspects of the government's privatization proposals is the uneven treatment it has given to the coal and nuclear industries' (*ibid.*, para. 155). The government had offered only 'two factors to justify its decision - security of supply and a party manifesto commitment to a continuing nuclear power programme' (*ibid.*, para. 156).

The Committee warned that: 'If this situation is handled clumsily or with indifference, unnecessary and costly damage could be done to the country's economic performance, balance of payments and employment prospects in the 1990s' (*ibid.*, para. 157). The government was cautioned against letting the 1984-85 miners strike 'prejudice their judgement' and urged to 'make a full statement on the strategic role ... of coal.' (*ibid.*, para. 159). It was hoped that the government would respond to these serious issues with a White Paper; 'a mere declaration of faith does not provide answers' (*ibid.* para. 178). As Select Committee reports go, this represented the savaging of government proposals.

I term this a little local difficulty because the government's response was the abolition of the Energy Select Committee. Its final report was treated with absolute contempt. The government's response consisted of 'one memorandum of three and a half pages from the Secretary of State' which addressed nine of the 50 conclusions' and a further memo from the 'Director of Electricity Supply to the other 41' (Hansard, 1992, col. 235). These documents had been deposited in the House of Commons Library where they 'are not normally available to the media' (*ibid.*). As we shall see, the resulting privatization failed to address many of the issues raised.

The anatomy of the privatized industry

In 1989 the Conservatives' resolve to privatize the entire ESI collapsed at the eleventh hour when first the ageing Magnox reactors and then the AGRs were withdrawn. A four-year moratorium on further nuclear constructions was announced with the promise of a nuclear review to consider the future of the industry.

The resultant structure of the ESI thus included the two main privatized generators, Power Gen and National Power; two state-owned nuclear generators, Nuclear Electric and Scottish Nuclear; and the Scottish Hydro Electricity Board. In England and Wales the old area boards became twelve regional electricity companies (RECs). The national grid became constituted as a separate company owned by the RECs and the Government. At the centre of the Government's scheme was the pool. This took the form of an half hourly spot market in electricity with the cheapest generators being connected to the grid. The pool was the heart of the market, designed to drive the cost of electricity down as close as possible to the marginal cost of production. There are, however, several crucial caveats which have to be highlighted in relation to this arrangement.

Government concerns over global warming combined with the desire to ring fence the nuclear power industry resulted in the introduction of a non-fossil fuel obligation. This obliged the RECs to purchase a pre-determined quantity of electricity from nuclear stations and renewable sources such as wind farms.[2] The bulk of the non-fossil fuel obligation was ring fenced for nuclear power.

In addition a fossil fuel levy was imposed on conventional stations, representing a cross subsidy to the nuclear generators. The levy was intended to fund the disposal of nuclear waste and the decommissioning of nuclear power stations. The subsidy, which was expected to amount to £12 billion by 1998, became the subject of intense political debate when it became clear that Nuclear Electric was using money from the levy to finance the construction of Sizewell 'B'. The structuring of the market for electricity effectively ring fenced nuclear power at the expense of coal.

The responsibility for security of supply was now vested in the RECs, which had also been given the freedom to generate electricity in their own right. The RECs' predecessors, Area Electricity Boards, had a long history of subordination to the CEGB, which had controlled investment decisions determining the type of generating sets built. The organizational frustrations born of this subordination produced an accelerated dash for freedom. The RECs embarked upon the construction of combined gas turbine power stations. These were quick to construct, clean in operation and infinitely flexible. By 1991 the so-called 'dash for gas' was far advanced. In an audacious act of market-making, British Gas entered into very attractive contracts to supply fuel for these sets. It was estimated that gas would contribute 16GW[3] of generating capacity by the year 2000.

Consent to proceed with these stations were all subject to the regulatory procedures laid down in the government's legislation. Between 1990 and 1994 electricity supply from gas-fired stations rose from zero to 9.1 per cent of national demand. Outstanding consents will see this figure rise steadily throughout the rest of this century, further diminishing the internal market for coal.

The generators had also been given powers to seek the cheapest supplies of fuel available, thus breaking the monopoly of domestic fuel suppliers such as British Coal. The world spot market was flooded with coal from Eastern Europe and Columbia, providing a ready weapon for the generators to drive down British Coal prices. When the Labour-controlled Bristol City Council sold the municipally owned docks, Power Gen entered into a partnership with private capital to construct a coal import facility to exploit this spot market. In the utilities' view every penny of this investment was worthwhile even if no coal was ever imported, provided it had the desired effect on domestic coal prices.

The 1992 coal crisis

The consequences of the government's market making in the energy sector came to a head in October 1992 when it was summarily announced that 31 of British Coal's 50 deep mines would close over the course of six months (Hansard, 1992, col. 205). The announcement produced a storm of protest which resulted in a stay of execution whilst detailed reports were prepared. The House of Commons Trade and Industry Committee's (1993) first report was dedicated to the coal crisis, being closely followed by a Department of Trade and Industry White Paper (DTI, 1993b).

These are long and detailed documents but broadly confirm the view of the abolished Select Committee on Energy that the government's privatization had been dominated by nuclear interests at the expense of coal. It emerged that under EC legislation the government, unlike its German counterpart, could not preserve the deep-mined coal industry by direct subsidy as the nuclear industry was receiving the permissible levels of subsidy. Domestically the fossil fuel levy could not be abolished without jeopardizing the future privatization of the nuclear industry. The 'dash for gas' had turned into firm contracts which could not be broken without incurring penalties. To have forced cancellation would have demonstrated that no free market existed. Similarly, Ministers refused to intervene in 'negotiations' between British Coal and the generators, which were commercial matters unsuited to political intervention. Identical arguments were used to reject the option of limiting coal imports.

The most significant factor precipitating the crisis for coal was the pricing mechanism operating through the pool (see above). Instead of operating as an effective spot market the Trade and Industry Committee revealed that the price of only 5 per cent of the electricity available to the pool was actually determined in this manner. The remaining 95 per cent was determined by binding financial contracts between generators and purchasers of electricity (House of Commons Trade and Industry Committee, 1993, p. 26). The DTI's (1993, p. 73) own White Paper subsequently concluded that National Power and Power Gen were acting as a duopoly to drive up pool prices, a view also shared by academic analysts (Green and Newbery, 1992). In keeping with dominant market discourse this price fixing was described as an 'exercise of market power' rather than a return to monopoly pricing through a cartel of two. Contract determined supply resulted in many stations being bid at prices below marginal cost to avoid expensive penalties. The consequence of this was that coal-fired stations could fail to be selected despite low costs (House of Commons Trade and Industry Committee, 1993, pp. 99-100). Adherence to a 'free market' was in effect being bound by pre-existing contractual obligations reflecting neither 'customer interests' nor market prices (Sutherland, 1993, p. 1199).

By 1992 the Government's energy privatizations had accelerated the displacement of coal, which was now squeezed between a resurgent British Gas, a confident Nuclear Electric, and world spot markets. The government successfully presented this situation as arising from the operation of 'normal' market forces. After delaying the closure of any of the threatened pits, Michael Hesletine, the then President of the Board of Trade, announced a government subsidy to make good the difference between pit head price and world spot market prices. The subsidy would only be available for new firm contracts during a limited period intended to allow British Coal to establish a realistic market position (DTI, 1993, p. 7). The subsidy was set to decline in line with expected efficiency improvements and it was made quite clear that: 'The number of pits which survive will depend on the amount of coal sold' and the delivery of the expected reductions in cost (*ibid.*, p. 8). As the only significant source of further contracts remained electricity generators, who already had seven months coal reserves, there was in fact no immediate prospect of any additional market for coal whatsoever.

Heseltine's declaration that this was a matter for political determination meant in effect that there had been a decision to sterilize the majority of Britain's coal reserves. This was recognized by the in-house journal of the United Kingdom Atomic Energy Authority where the coal review was described as 'little more than a political fix' which had extricated the 'government from a tight corner with some embarrassment but no real concession'.

The energy sector was one where there was 'a public interest' which could not be assumed to be 'congruent with the interests of the market'. The article concluded by hoping that the nuclear review would be an examination of the 'broad needs of energy strategy'. If it were not, then the nuclear industry would be 'the next victim of a short term and narrow political fix' (Lucas 1993, p. 12).

The nuclear review

After months of Whitehall power struggles for control of the review process between the DTI and the Department of the Environment (DoE), the terms of reference were announced in the House of Commons in May 1994. The DTI emerged ascendant with its agenda of achieving a privatization intact. The DoE would hold a separate review of waste disposal policy which the DTI would 'take into account' when reaching their conclusions.

The separation of the two issues meant that the DTI's terms of reference could concentrate on a narrower privatizing agenda which emphasized: the commercial viability of new nuclear stations, the role of nuclear energy in meeting environmental and strategic targets and the potential for privatizing the industry (HM Govt., 1995, p. 75). The review process was conducted over the summer when the absence of lobby correspondents ensured it a 'low profile'.

The nuclear industry's case had been in preparation from the announcement of the review in 1989. By 1994 significant headway had already been made towards removing obvious barriers to privatization. The immediate costs of decommissioning reactors had been reduced by abandoning the previous policy of prompt restoration to greenfield site status. The operation of the AGRs had shown significant improvement. Sizewell 'B' had been completed on time and within tender. Within the nuclear sector British Nuclear Fuels Ltd (BNFL) alone wanted to remain within the state sector whilst Nuclear Electric and Scottish Nuclear both embraced privatization but remained divided on how this should be achieved.

Nuclear Electric's case can be taken as representative of the general argument for a further commitment to nuclear energy in the UK (Nuclear Electric, 1994, para.I-IV). Put concisely, their case was that a new nuclear power station, Sizewell 'C', should be given the go ahead, that this would require some element of underwriting by the government and that nuclear power stations were capable of privatization. The economies to be gained from building a second PWR at Sizewell and the strategic export capacity embodied in the Sizewell design were all emphasized.

The economic case for nuclear power was based on the anticipated performance of Sizewell 'B' and the projected performance of Sizewell 'C'. The technicalities of the economic case are considerable but some of the more startling elements are worthy of further elaboration. Perhaps most notable was Nuclear Electric's view that it would be uneconomic to reprocess the spent fuel from Sizewell 'B'.

Less than a year prior to this the whole nuclear industry had argued that the case for BNFL's oxide reprocessing plant was economically robust. In the cold light of market acceptability Nuclear Electric had obviously rethought its position. Pessimism about BNFL's performance contrasted starkly with optimism over the performance of the new PWR design, which was thought to be capable of a load factor of 85 per cent.

Decommissioning and waste disposal costs were discounted far into the future. In the case of Sizewell 'B' it was argued that decommissioning would occur over a period of 135 years at an overall cost of 1 per cent of the value of the electricity generated. The basis for this estimate was not made clear. In Nuclear Electric's eyes there was no immediate hurry to move towards a deep engineered waste repository.

The environmental and strategic importance of further nuclear build were also emphasized. Here it was argued that reductions in the UK's carbon dioxide emissions in line with greenhouse gas conventions could be achieved by nuclear power. A strong domestic reactor vending capacity was also regarded as a strategic resource likely to result in lucrative export orders.

220

Capital at risk

Each nuclear power station represents an enormous amount of fixed capital investment - Sizewell 'B' alone cost £3 billion. The potential for such a large investment to be lost in an accident acts as a strong disincentive to investors. Nuclear Electric attempted to minimize the perception of investment risk by a number of devices. These included the 'state of the art' design of Sizewell 'B', the rigorous regulatory standards operated within the UK and the record of the nuclear industry over a considerable period of time. The possibility that a multi-million pound investment could be sterilized by one serious accident, however, continued to haunt these sections and a government commitment to underwrite private investment was sought.

Scottish Nuclear

The risk to fixed capital investment was a critical factor in Scottish Nuclear's case as, following the closure of the Magnox station at Hunterston, the company owned only two twin AGR stations. The company argued that the need to diversify its asset base could be met by transferring some of Nuclear Electric's AGRs to Scottish Nuclear (Scottish Nuclear, 1993). By transferring the northern AGRs to Scottish Nuclear the two nuclear generators would be in a position to compete effectively with one another.

The prospects for nuclear power

The government's White Paper in response to the review (HM Govt.,1995), whilst supporting nuclear privatization, rejected key elements of the industry's case. In particular, no new nuclear power stations were foreseen within the immediate future. The industry's case for more nuclear power based on environmental considerations, the strategic industrial base, and diversity of energy supply were all firmly rejected.

The fossil fuel levy which had provided a rich source of cross subsidy to the nuclear industry would be ended immediately privatization occurred. The government opted for a single nuclear holding company run by BNFL, which would preside over the operations of the former Nuclear Electric and Scottish Nuclear. BNFL would also formally own and run the ageing Magnox reactors. The location of the new generating company's headquarters in Edinburgh was widely seen as a sop to Scottish interests (Smith, 1995, p.8). The timetable for the privatization was tight, with a sale being envisaged in the summer of 1996. Any slippage in this date would place the sensitive sale too near a general election for it to be politically credible.

Immediate press comment focused upon the structure of the new companies and a range of financial issues related to investment potential. Calls for the industry to be sold under a 'realistic' price tag began immediately (*ibid*.) in an attempt to talk down the projected sale figure of £3 billion. The technical bases of the privatization were not, however, questioned, reflecting the extent to which market discourses had displaced technical discourses.

The technical bases for economic scepticism

Historically, ministerial statements on nuclear power in the UK are notoriously unreliable. The reintroduction of nuclear privatization towards the end of the Conservative's fourth term of office is perhaps best regarded as no more than a statement of intent and not something which would be delayed until after the next general election. The decision to resurrect the idea reflects a range of pragmatic political objectives including the introduction of more cuts in direct taxation and the resumption of the privatization offensive after months of defending huge pay rises for senior executives (*ibid*.). By ending the levy, electricity prices would fall by around 8 per cent, thus making good the imposition of VAT on domestic fuel, which had been electorally disastrous.[4] Whether any surplus would remain once decommissioning costs were met remained unclear.

Market doubts

Privatization will only be possible if the modern nuclear stations and the associated organizational structures win the confidence of the city. There remains much scope for scepticism about this and the intervening months will be ones of hard bargaining and strenuous politics. My own reading of the White Paper suggest several areas where financial institutions and brokers will be demanding reassurances.

Decommissioning

The White Paper argues extensively that 'back end costs are both lower and more certain than was the case in 1989' (*ibid.*, 1995, p. 16). This claim is particularly important as it was decommissioning and waste disposal which frightened the City away in 1989. At more than one point the government states that the experience of decommissioning the Magnox reactor at Berkeley reveals the extent to which the industry's previous forecast of costs had been 'pessimistic' by as much as 30 per cent (*ibid.*, p. 65). Technically, this is an interesting claim as the station at Berkeley was amongst the first to be built and was unique amongst the 'commercial' stations in that its boiler assemblies were external to the reactor's concrete biological shield. Decommissioning Berkeley is a poor basis for a general argument as this experience simply does not translate directly to any other station in the UK. The failure to compare like with like within the nuclear industry has been the basis of numerous past false confidences - caution in relation to this one would be exceedingly wise.

The White Paper is primarily suggesting that further savings in decommissioning can be achieved by an appropriately 'incentivised' approach to 'liabilities management' that is 'clearly focused on driving down costs' whilst simultaneously meeting 'rigorous safety and regulatory requirements' (*ibid.* p. 58). The language of the privatization gazette does not conceal the fact, however, that this will be a moveable feast. Regulatory standards can go up as well as down and in the nuclear case an ever-tightening regulatory regime has historically prevailed and can be expected to continue in key respects for the foreseeable future. The envisaged savings could easily be illusory.

Load factors and profit streams

The government's economic case for Sizewell 'B' is another area where illusion continues to operate. The Nuclear Utilities Chairmen's Group (1994) argued that Sizewell would achieve an 85 per cent load factor over its lifetime operation. The profit streams arising from Sizewell 'B' and the proportion of this thought sufficient to meet decommissioning costs are thus both contingent upon meeting this target.

Critics of the figure argued for a more realistic load factor of between 70 and 80 per cent. Nuclear Electric's figure was justified on grounds of 'the recent good performance by the UK's other nuclear stations' and figures derived from other PWRs in America. To link the performance of existing AGR stations to the PWR is disingenuous as the two designs are completely different. The AGR was specifically designed to refuel whilst on load, unlike the PWR, suggesting that it should be capable of a higher load factor. The 'state of the art' design of Sizewell 'B' means that direct comparisons with other PWRs can not be made.

A load factor of, for example, 75 per cent at Sizewell would significantly reduce the total amount of electricity generated during the station's life, making each unit more expensive and reducing the amount of 'segregated funds' available for decommissioning. Historically, the nuclear industry has been consistently over-optimistic about the performance of new plant, and members of the Chairmen's Group include key figures like John Collier, Chairman of Nuclear Electric, whose career dates from the heady days of the 1950s when optimism such as this was endemic. In 1993 Collier was arguing that given the global energy scene 'today's imperatives' included the construction of more PWRs and 'will require the introduction of fast reactors' (Collier 1993). To place an argument from this group at the heart of the government's case should set alarm bells ringing in every financial institution.

To BNFL fall the spoils?

Within the Government's proposed scheme BNFL will assume responsibility for the Magnox stations, the decommissioning of which will fall on the public purse. BNFL stand to profit handsomely by running these reactors during their twilight years, producing around 8 per cent of the nation's electricity (Hansard, 1995, cols. 406-407).

The basis of my argument lies in the government's statement that the historic costs of Magnox decommissioning will be met by a combination of monies raised by the levy up to 1996 plus monies from the sale of the nuclear generators (HM Govt., 1995, pp. 57, 63). According to this point of view, 'most of the income from' Magnox has 'already accrued to the public sector' (*ibid.*, p. 57).

There is broad agreement that in the twilight years the profit stream from the Magnox reactors is at its height and indeed the Magnox bonus has been a significant part in Nuclear Electric's improving financial performance since 1989. If the government is correct in believing the nuclear industry's argument that past income, plus sale price, equals Magnox decommissioning and disposal costs then the thick profits from their final years will accrue to BNFL's new Magnox division. The resultant earnings explains BNFL's eagerness to acquire these assets and Nuclear Electric's regret at losing them (Smith, 1995, p. 8).

The argument for keeping Magnox running is based on the fact that the fixed capital assets have been completely amortized, leaving only running costs to cover. The DTI's White Paper on the future of coal argued that Magnox continued to be viable on the basis of their avoidable costs. Put crudely, this is the cost incurred by either closing the station down immediately or committing limited further investment to keep the station running balanced against the predicted profit stream. Magnox avoidable costs are contentious and highly disputed, as the government's merchant bankers never published their calculations in full. Thus, whilst there is room for some caution over the profits still to accrue from Magnox stations, it appears that BNFL stands to gain considerable revenue.[5] Magnox thus stands to play an important role in making the balance sheets of BNFL appear ripe for future privatization.

A further factor for investors to consider here is the implication of having a publicly owned nuclear generating company comprised entirely of fixed assets which carry no capital costs. The unit price of electricity from this source should easily undercut all other nuclear and conventional generators. The output from the AGRs and the PWR may require some ring fencing to ensure them access to the pool. If access is not guaranteed then the Magnox stations could displace some of the other nuclear stations.

The truth, the whole truth and nothing but the truth?

The Conservatives' commitment to privatization and the free market remain tied to a naive conception of the role of information in market systems. This is part of a standard critique of neo-classical economics where perfect competition is crucially underpinned by equal access to perfect information. The 1995 White Paper marks something of a watershed in this respect, as for the first time there is a clear acknowledgement by the government that its interventions in the energy sector have not produced a market situation and that it will take some time, perhaps more than ten years, for a proper market to become established (HM Govt., 1995, para. 3.41, p. 16).

In this sense the government acknowledges its role as market maker, recognizing that this places certain responsibilities at the government's door. Amongst these the government acknowledges that it must do what it ideologically claims to be impossible, namely, to act in the same way as the 'private sector' would (*ibid.*).

The earlier DTI report also acknowledged the government's responsibility to provide certain forms of information which it alone had access to. The government has already failed to live up to these responsibilities by refusing to reveal figures used to calculate the avoidable costs of Magnox stations. Its trustworthiness with other market-sensitive information has also been called into question within the City, casting a long shadow over nuclear privatization.

Inside insider dealing

The fall-out from the sale of the government's 40 per cent stake in Power Gen and National Power quickly removed any return to an aggressive pro-privatization stance. The sale of the shares coincided with the announcement of the electricity regulator, Professor Stephen Littlechild, that he was mounting an inquiry into the pricing regimes of the RECs. The expectation of aggressive price cuts to consumers combined with the prospect of a referral to the Monopolies and Mergers Commission wiped £3.7 billion off the value of the two generators (Brummer, 1995, p. 17).

The ensuing furore between the Stock Exchange and the government revealed that the Treasury had knowledge of Littlechild's decision 'late' on the day before the flotation. As the government enjoys immunity from the City's regulatory frameworks and bodies of inquiry the Stock Exchange first demanded a Treasury Inquiry (Beavis, *et al.*, 1995, p. 1) then refused to sign a Treasury document indicating that it welcomed such an inquiry (Wintour, 1995, p. 1). It thus became clear that the London Stock Exchange was not prepared to jeopardize its standing as a reputable trader by sanctioning an internal inquiry prior to the publication of its findings.

Given the range of sensitive information affecting any nuclear privatization that resides exclusively with the government, the incident has proved extremely damaging to nuclear privatization prospects. As one of the merchant bankers involved in preparations for the nuclear privatization commented: 'The City was already nervous about the nuclear sale. Now it is downright terrified' (Donovan, 1995, p. 35).

Political considerations

The market preoccupations of the government in making this last privatization of the commanding heights can be expected to lead them into other troublesome areas. To the right wing of the Conservative party the proposed privatization has reduced the amount of competition in the generating sector by subsuming Scottish Nuclear and Nuclear Electric beneath a single holding company.

There is an emergent consensus that the privatization is aimed at securing the future dividends of shareholders. By aiming to produce ready profits at a bid price which is competitively placed to overcome the risk averse tendency of investors, the prospect of another undervalued sale of a public asset looms large. In the House of Commons a price tag for nuclear privatization of just £2 billion is in circulation. This is less than the cost of building Sizewell 'B' and amounts to giving away 'the other seven reactors for free' (Hansard, 1995, col. 399).

Can the shareholder be god?

Other political considerations relating to the stake of consumers and shareholders in Britain's energy future remain to be played out. The government argues that energy security and economic competitiveness are dependent upon the market preference of consumers working through into appropriate investment decisions (HM Govt., 1995, p. 37). The question of whether today's price structure can be an incentive to act against tomorrow's unforeseen risk is a difficult one. In a market system the answer can only be yes if all the affected companies in a particular sector accept higher prices in today's market to safeguard against the future risk. If only some follow this option then their short-term market position is negatively affected unless they have sufficient capital assets to protect their market share. Companies with a weak capital base cannot incur extra short-term costs unnecessarily and are least able to embark on innovation. The concentration of market power in fewer and fewer companies thus leads to monopolies and cartels. This reduces rather than expands customer choice. If you want to buy a nuclear reactor there are relatively few companies one can turn to and their price structures are very similar. The factor which divides them is the availability of attractive deals to finance construction. Such deals frequently rely on state backing and historically the British state has limited such backing to arms-related transactions. How this resembles anything that can be described as a market, let alone a free market, is an open question.

Conclusion: privatization the victim of success?

Throughout this chapter I have argued that government privatization of nuclear power stations arises from a mixture of ideological commitment and political expediency. The argument I have presented here suggests that there are no substantive grounds for this privatization. The supposed benefits of placing nuclear power in the private sector are not worth the cost of the privatization process. The fossil fuel levy could have been ended by the government at any time without privatization. The nuclear generators have already produced significant productivity gains, are operating efficiently and show the potential for further optimization. Privatization is similar to Thatcherism in that it constitutes itself as its own worst enemy. By this I mean that the project either succeeds in rendering itself unnecessary, or fails, rendering itself a disaster. Either way the phenomenon ends, as Mrs Thatcher found out in person. In this respect the Post Office and nuclear power represent examples where the efficiency gains supposedly only possible under privatization have been delivered without flotation on the Stock Market.

The argument that consumers and shareholders are the best means of determining Britain's energy policy leaves too much power vested in sectors with short-term interests. These groups are structurally incapable of taking strategic decisions that cannot be taken on market considerations alone. Such decisions include long-term product innovation with long lead times requiring long-term stability and some market intervention in pursuit of clearly enunciated policy objectives. Hostile take-over bids by private conglomerates and foreign interests mean that control over some RECs will pass to non-specialist or foreign companies (Barrie, 1995; Hutton, 1995b).

The sale of RECs would make decisions relevant to security of electricity supply subject to board rooms outwith the ESI or even outside this country.   External interests then assume responsibility for capital investment programmes vital to the national interest. In terms of electricity distribution and fuel supply energy security has been displaced into the global arena with scant attention to environmental security debates. One

228

example of this is the government's reliance on Russian gas supplies, ignoring the possibility that increasingly these will be consumed internally (Boyle, 1992; Radetzki, 1991; Scanlan, 1991). To declare that the free market is one's energy policy is to have no policy at all.

Notes

1. The minutes of the meeting were leaked to *Time Out* and *The Guardian*. Quotes here are from the original document (E79 13th Meeting, 23.10.79). For press accounts see *The Guardian*, 6.12.79, p.1.
2. The rate of return required from wind generation was set at a level necessitating the use of high visual impact sites. In the House of Commons well-known supporters of nuclear power dubbed them 'toilet brushes in the sky', a theme readily picked up by the press.
3. By 1995 this figure had been revised downwards, with 4GW under construction and a further 10GW in the planning stages (HM Govt., 1995).
4. The government presented the introduction of VAT on domestic fuel as part of its commitments under the Rio Earth Summit. The issue became central in the 1994 Christchurch by-election with a safe Conservative seat being lost to the Liberal Democrats.
5. Assuming an 8 per cent share of the electricity market, Magnox will yield a turnover of £500 million p.a. In 1995 BNFL's annual pre-tax profits declined from £81 million to £74 million and the company threatened not to accept the transfer of Magnox reactors without binding financial assurances from the Government over decommissioning costs (Fagan, 1995).

References

Albrow, M. (1990), *Globalization, Knowledge and Society*, Sage, London.
Barrie, C. *et.al.* (1995), 'Fury at Hanson power swoop', *The Guardian*, 1 August, p. 1.

Beavis, S. *et.al.* (1995), 'Insider deal inquiry into power sale', *The Guardian*, 9 June, p. 1.

Beck, U. (1995), *Ecological Politics in an age of Risk*, Transl. A. Weisz, Polity, Cambridge.

Benn, T. (1989), *Against The Tide: Diaries 1973-76*, Hutchinson, London.

Beynon, H.(1985), *Digging Deeper*, Verso, London.

Brummer, A. (1995) 'Power politics at the Stock Exchange', *The Guardian*, 9 June, p. 17.

Burn, D. (1978), *Nuclear Power and the Energy Crisis*, MacMillan, London.

Collier, J.G. (1993), *The Role of Nuclear Power in a Changing World*, The 1993 Newitt Lecture, Nuclear Electric.

Department of Trade and Industry (1993). *The Prospects for Coal: Conclusions of the Government's Coal Review*, Cmnd 2235, HMSO, London.

Donovan, P. (1995), 'Fall-out from power furore may delay sale of nuclear stations', *The Guardian*, 10 June, p.35.

Fagan, M. (1995), 'BNFL warns on nuclear plants', *The Independent*, 24 March, p. 25.

Featherstone, M. (1990), *Global Culture*, Sage, London.

Friedman, M. (1962), *Capitalism and Freedom*, Chicago University Press.

Green R.J. and Newbery D.M. (1992), 'Competition in the British Electricity Spot Market', *Journal of Political Economy*, pp. 100, 51, 933-953.

Hansard (1957), *House of Commons Parliamentary Debates*, vol. 562, HMSO, London.

Hansard (1992), *House of Commons Parliamentary Debates*, vol. 212, HMSO, London.

Hansard (1995), *House of Commons Parliamentary Debates*, vol. 260, HMSO, London.

Hayek, F. (1944), *The Road to Serfdom*, Routledge, London.

Hayek, F. (1960), *The Constitution of Liberty*, Routledge, London.

Her Majesty's Government (1955), *A Programme of Nuclear Power*, Cmnd 9389, HMSO, London.

Her Majesty's Government (1957), *Electricity Bill*, HMSO, London.

Her Majesty's Government (1983), *Energy Act*, HMSO, London.

Her Majesty's Government (1988), *Privatizing Electricity: The Government's proposals for privatization of the electricity supply industry in England and Wales*, Cmnd 322, HMSO, London.

Her Majesty's Government (1989), *Energy Act*, HMSO, London.

Her Majesty's Government (1995), *The Prospects for Nuclear Power in the UK*, Cmnd 2860, HMSO, London.

House of Commons Select Committee on Energy (1981), *The Government's Statement on the Nuclear Power Programme*, HC 114, vols. I-IV, HMSO, London.

House of Commons Select Committee on Energy (1988), *The Energy Committee Third Report, The Structure, Regulation and Economic Consequences of Electricity Supply in the Private Sector*, HCP 307, vol. 1, HMSO, London.

House of Commons Select Committee on Energy (1989). *Energy Committee: Minutes of Evidence*, 25 January, HMSO, London.

House of Commons Trade and Industry Committee, (1993). *British Energy Policy and the Market for Coal*, HC 237, First Report, HMSO, London.

Hutton, W. (1995a), *The State We're In*, Jonathan Cape, London.

Hutton, W. (1995b), 'Plug in to profit flow', *The Guardian*, 1 August, p.13.

Lash, S. and Urry, J. (1989), *The End of Organised Capitalism*, Polity, Oxford.

Lash, S. and Urry, J. (1995), *Economies of Signs and Space*, Sage, London.

Lucas, N. (1993), 'Cold Comfort for Coal', *ATOM*, no. 428, p. 12.

Luckin, B. (1990), *Question of Power: Electricity and the Environment in Inter-war Britain*, Manchester University Press, Manchester.

Monopolies and Mergers Commission (1981), *The CEGB - Report on the Operation by the Board of its system for the Generation and Supply of Electricity in Bulk*, HC. 315, HMSO, London.

Nuclear Electric (1994), *The Government's Review of Nuclear Energy: Submission from Nuclear Electric*, vols. I-IV, Nuclear Electric, Gloucester.

Nuclear Utilities Chairmans Group (1994), *The Future Role of Nuclear Power in the UK*, Scottish Nuclear, East Kilbride.

Parker M. and Surrey J. (1993), 'The 1992 Coal Crisis and UK Energy Policy', *The Political Quarterly*, vol. 64, no. 4.

Roberts, J. *et al.* (1992), *Privatizing the Electricity Supply Industry*, Belhaven, London.

Scottish Nuclear (1994), *Securing Our Energy Future*, Scottish Nuclear, East Kilbride.

Smith, M. (1995), 'A hard sell for high risks', *Financial Times*, 10 May, p. 8.

Sutherland, B.J. (1993), 'Natural gas contracts in an emerging competitive market', *Energy Policy*, vol. 21, no. 7, pp. 1191-1204.

Touraine, A. (1983), *Anti-Nuclear Protest*, Cambridge University Press, Cambridge.

Waters, M. (1995), *Globalization*, Routledge, London.

Welsh, I. (1993), 'The NIMBY Syndrome: Its significance in the nuclear debate in Britain', *British Journal for the History of Science*, vol. 26, pp. 15-32.

Welsh, I. (1994a), 'Letting the Research Tail Wag the end User's Dog', *Science and Public Policy*, vol. 21, no. 1, pp. 43-53.

Welsh, I. (1994b), 'When is Non-intervention an Intervention?', *The Political Quarterly*, vol. 65, no. 3, pp. 348-351.

Welsh, I. (1995), Risk, reflexivity and the globalisation of environmental politics, SEPEG Working Paper No. 1, CESER, UWE, Bristol.

Welsh, I. (1996), *Mobilising Modernity: The Nuclear Moment*, Routledge, London.

Williams, R. (1980), *The Nuclear Power Decisions*, Croom Helm, London.

Winterton, J. and Winterton, R. (1989), *Coal, Crisis and Conflict: The 1984-85 Miners Strike in Yorkshire*, Manchester University Press, Manchester.

Winterton J. (1993), 'The 1984-85 miners strike and technological change', *British Journal for the History of Science*, vol. 26, pp. 5-14.

Wintour P. *et.al.* (1995), 'City snubs Treasury on sell-off', *The Guardian*, 10 June, p. 1.

Wynne, B. (1982), *Rationality and Ritual: The Windscale Inquiry and British Nuclear Power Policy*, BSHS, Chalfont St Giles.

10 The Political Economy of Privatization in Southern Europe

KOSTAS LAVDAS

Introduction

As processes which entail shifts in the balances and the boundaries between the public and the private, privatizations in different national contexts share a number of common features. Differences between national privatization experiences, however, can be just as significant. To begin with, despite the near-universal rhetoric of privatization in the 1980s, only a limited number of countries implemented privatization programmes of substantial proportions (cf. Pitelis and Clarke, 1993). Furthermore, significant differences in the scope, forms and goals of privatization exist even among countries implementing substantial privatization programmes. Differences may be attributable in part to different priorities and objectives (cf. Vickers and Yarrow, 1988). Differences also emerge from national political and institutional factors, which mediate preferences and affect outcome selection. Because privatization programmes can have a profound impact on established patterns of public-private relations, they become areas of political contestation. But the extent and content of that contestation will depend on national political and institutional arrangements.

The political economy of privatization in Italy, Greece, Spain and Portugal concerns privatizations of fairly substantial proportions, set against a background of politicized economies with complex linkages between state institutions and private interests. These states share a number of common characteristics, which sustain Southern Europe as an area concept in comparative politics and political economy. Because of similarities in twentieth century development trajectories, the dynamics of Greek, Portuguese and Spanish regime transitions in the 1970s, and aspects of their relation to European integration, Southern European states appear to constitute a distinct grouping. But it is a grouping which consists of political systems whose patterns of government formation and duration, party competition and electoral behaviour are variably situated in the broader West European picture. In the case of privatization, the Southern European members of the European Union (EU) have demonstrated a number of common traits, as well as distinct national characteristics. With the partial exception of Italy, privatization in Southern Europe has not been associated with the lively theoretical and policy debate on state failure and the supposed efficiency of market resource allocation which prefaced and accompanied efforts to roll back the state in West Europe and North America.

This chapter examines privatization in Southern Europe as a process with significant political dimensions, which are illustrated with case studies of the Italian, Greek, Spanish and Portuguese experiences. Privatization processes have to come to terms with policy-opposing interest coalitions (Lavdas, 1995), which use a variety of formal and informal veto points in the political system (Immergut, 1992) in order to shift the content, forms or direction of privatization plans. The politics of these processes, mediated by national institutional arrangements, help define the particular responses to a set of largely similar stimuli and challenges. Southern European privatizations owe less to neo-liberal policy ideas or party platforms and more to the need to tackle deficits and public indebtedness. At the same time, and in contrast to the situation in Eastern Europe, privatizations in Italy, Greece and the Iberia owe less to systemic transformation and more to subtle shifts in public-private balances. Southern European privatizations have evolved against a background of private capitals with often conflicting interests in different aspects of the privatization process and its implications in areas such as public

234

procurement, the removal of constraints on competition and market entry, and the incentives for other firms' restructuring.

In addition, since the early 1990s privatization in Southern Europe has become part of the larger effort to meet the convergence criteria for full participation in economic and monetary union (EMU) and the future development of the EU. The concern with deficits and public indebtedness has been associated with an underlying shift from privatization as an instrument of restructuring to privatization as an instrument of European convergence. The ensuing two basic dimensions of Southern European privatizations (states in fiscal crisis struggling to balance the books; relatively weak members of the EU striving to adjust to its development) have defined much of the debate about how best to use privatization receipts. The receipts could be used to reduce the deficit, or they could be used to invest in infrastructure and industry modernization.

The politics of difficult adjustment

Processes of privatization and of what has conventionally come to be known as 'deregulation' do not actually weaken the significance of the state's role in advanced industrial societies.[1] Rather, the state's role becomes more complicated and its parameters change. Despite considerable shifts from the public-private mix characteristic of the consensus underlying post-war European political economy (Shonfield, 1965), the state's role in regulatory processes is crucial. And because European societies have lacked the regulatory tradition of the US, they have had to go through processes of policy and institutional experimentation. These processes evolve at two levels: the national and the European.

European states, most of which engaged in privatization programmes in the 1980s, were faced with international competitive pressures. In EC member states, international pressures were usually mediated by the European institutional and regulatory system, which aims to coordinate and help shape national responses. Apart from international pressures, national privatization policies often resulted from domestic economic stalemates with the advent of the slow growth years in the early 1980s. The financial resources for the public sector dried up, while national electorates appeared to be opting for solutions that would avoid increasing tax burdens to finance public enterprises (Vernon, 1988). Against a background of considerable theoretical groundwork, forms of privatization appeared desirable as solutions to political forces of the right and centre-right, which calculated also that rolling back the state would weaken organized interests in the public sector.

The weight of public enterprises has been especially significant in Southern Europe (cf. Bermeo, 1990).

Southern European economies have been marked by heavy politicization, exemplified in the extensive state presence in economic life, in complex and often particularistic links between public authorities and private interests, in politicized regimes of credit allocation, subsidization and procurement, and in elaborate price controls. OECD data on public enterprises in the non-agricultural business sector in terms of percentage shares for 1990 (a year which, as we will see, represents a turning point for most Southern European privatizations) suggest that, with the exception of Spain, Southern Europe leads the twelve EC member states when it comes to the weight of public enterprises in value added, employment and gross fixed investment.

The politicization of the economies also encourages prompt politicization of issues of economic management and adaptation. The public debt has emerged as a significant problem area in economic management, and also, at various degrees and at various stages in the different states, as a political issue.

In terms of public debt as a percentage of national GDPs in the early 1990s, Italy, Greece, Portugal and Spain display significant public debt/GDP ratios, with Italy and Greece having by far the most serious problems (124 and 117 per cent for 1994 respectively). Furthermore, for both Italy and Greece the other crucial economic policy problem remains the public sector deficit. In 1994, Italian public sector deficit as a percentage of GDP was at 11 per cent, while the Greek equivalent had reached 12 per cent.

Politicization of the economy and of economic policy has resulted in 'soft budgets' (Kornai, 1979, pp. 801-819), in which the links between expenditures and receipts have been relaxed. Such economies are faced with considerable political and economic difficulties when it comes to responding to the challenges of international competition and of full participation in the EU. In particular, the inflation control requirements for participation in the EMU along with the Maastricht Treaty's limit of a budget deficit that does not exceed 3 per cent of GDP have imposed strict criteria for the formation and implementation of European convergence plans. Apart from the historical factors involved, the states of Southern Europe suffered from certain more recent problems in their adjustment efforts.

Despite their successes as high growth newly industrialized countries (NICs) in the 1960s, Spain, Portugal and Greece encountered similar problems in the mid-1970s, when faced with a deteriorating international economic climate (Diamandouros, 1986). The exigencies of regime change and democratic consolidation took precedence over the need to adapt to the economic situation following the first oil shock in 1973. Adjustment measures were postponed, and expansionary economic policies were instead promoted to help consolidate the new regimes.

While all three economies had been growing at a very fast pace in the 1960s, their failure to adjust to the first oil shock had serious destabilizing consequences, which were even more harmful in view of the openness of these economies. With the partial exception of Spain, and the obvious addition of Italy, these have been fairly open economies at least since the 1960s in the sense of a high share of trade to the GDP. With EC membership since the 1980s for the three Southern European NICs, dependence on export expansion to Europe has meant that convergence is dependent also on European growth.

Finally, difficulties in Southern European adjustment efforts emanate from the state itself and its features. Differences in state structures and the rules of the game can be significant. In interaction with national models of economic governance, such state and political characteristics constitute different national policy patterns.

For example, elements in Spain's economic performance can be attributed in part to structural features of the Spanish state system post-1977, such as the relative strength of the executive (Heywood, 1991). On the other hand, if one feature of state power is the ability, through historically formed capacities, to develop and implement strategic objectives, even in opposition to the demands of powerful groups (Evans *et al.*, 1985), then the state in Southern Europe combines organizational expansiveness and strategic weakness.

Privatization processes can be analysed as the responses of that state to stimuli, in part international in part domestic, which challenge the public-private power balance.

Strategic weakness should lead us to expect significant waverings over the goals, methods and desired effects of privatizations. Furthermore, despite the need for investment in modernization, the political conditioning of the process will imply that if privatization receipts are used directly to reduce the deficit, governments may anticipate political benefits resulting from their ability to afford tax reductions (cf. Katsoulacos, 1993, p. 368).

Europeanization and domestic change

European Community membership has been both a factor influencing domestic change and an issue that has been used in domestic political debate. We need to distinguish between European constraints and opportunities, on the one hand, and the domestic use of anticipated effects of Europeanization in attempts to bring about desired outcomes, on the other. To begin with the use of EC membership in domestic politics, we find that the Portuguese case, with its socialist features inherited from the particular mode of regime change in 1974, presents a characteristic example.

The right has pointed to the apparent incompatibility of extensive state ownership and EC membership almost continually since the late 1970s, in an attempt to expedite constitutional revision[2] and to roll back the expansion of the state. The link between EC membership and domestic reform became established in the run-up to the 1979 elections, when the centre-right (PSD) and the right (CDS) focused their attack on the legacy of the 1974-75 nationalizations. In the context of such domestic political uses of the issue of EC membership, the European Commission has on some occasions felt obliged to stress that the Rome Treaty had no bearing on the size of the public sector, provided that competition rules are observed (Tsoukalis, 1981, p. 119).

At the same time, the EC system functions as a set of rules and institutions which represent constraints as well as opportunities for national political economies. For the political economies of Southern Europe, a critical area in the context of an emergent European regulatory regime has been the European policy on competition (Lavdas and Mendrinou, forthcoming).

European competition policy has a bearing both on economic policy and, indirectly, on the issue of public ownership, by intervening in the regulation of mergers and monopolies while at the same time limiting the use of subsidization of national industry, an economic policy instrument much in use in Southern Europe. Italy, Greece and Portugal give state aid to manufacturing (expressed as a percentage of GDP) at levels well above the EC average (see Commission of the EC, 1992a, pp. 11, 39). A more active European enforcement regime (Mendrinou, forthcoming) has meant that states become increasingly unable to support companies in crisis, while the extension of market principles to the operation of public enterprises requires greater transparency in relations between states and public firms (McGowan, 1993). In addition, as these economies are dominated by small and medium-sized enterprises (SMEs), the negotiation of exemption regimes for SMEs from the European control of state aid has been crucial for the Southern EU members and for the survival of small firms (Lavdas and Mendrinou, 1995).

The emergent European-level regulatory system has another, more subtle impact on national policy patterns. The Italian case is particularly interesting in this regard. Along with the rest of the Southern European states, Italy lacked any effective national instruments for the control of mergers.[3] Between 1988 and 1990 legislative activity, culminating in Law 287/1990, created Italy's first anti-trust statutes.

What accounts for the timing of the creation of an Italian competition policy? Two different but related factors have been at work. First, privatization had put on the agenda the issue of the potential for collusive behaviour of previously state-owned enterprises. Against the background of a state with little if any regulatory experience, there was concern that, in the absence of an anti-trust regime, the situation might get out of hand. Second, the Italian competition debate in the late 1980s was prompted by the European debate on the adoption of an EEC Merger Regulation (which was eventually adopted in December 1989).

The first Italian anti-trust bills were tabled in the wake of the EEC measures, and Law 287/1990 was adopted by the Italian Parliament in September 1990, the month when the EEC Merger Regulation came into effect. In view of imminent EC regulation, the Italian Government took the initiative in filling gaps in the Italian legal system with new provisions modelled on EC competition law, while at the same time inviting the European institutions to take part in a division of tasks between the Community and national levels (Siragusa and Scassellati, 1992).

The resulting Italian Anti-trust Authority has since acquired considerable powers, and has often used them against state-controlled groups. The emergence of an Italian competition policy on merger control was therefore the result of a response to privatization and European regulatory development. That response had to address a number of problems, not least attributable to the particularities of the national legal culture (see Siragusa and Scassellati, 1992).

Country profiles

Variation as well as similarities between the national privatization experiences in Southern Europe can be gauged from brief country profiles. While the main aim is to present general country profiles of privatization processes, I will also be looking at particular cases of privatization which present points of special interest.

Italy: from individual privatizations to privatization programmes

Italian privatization has been an exercise in the reproduction through adjustment of the Italian public policy pattern.[4] Privatization emerged in the mid-1980s as the sale by the state holding companies (IRI, ENI and EFIM) of parts or the whole of their stakes in ventures. The privatization debates have their source in the context of industrial restructuring of the early 1980s, when the problem to be addressed was that of state-owned firms being in decline as well as becoming uncontrollable in their financial and management situation (Segnana, 1993, p. 277). The actual privatization process consists of two distinct phases (see Cassese, 1994). The first phase, between the mid-1980s and 1989, was distinguished by the selling off of individual ventures by the state holding groups to the private sector. It developed on the basis of close relationships between the state holding companies, which selected the ventures to be privatized and acquired the privatization receipts, and private groups. For example, Alfa Romeo was sold to Fiat, the Lanerossi textile group to the Marzoto textile group. In view of widespread corruption apparently deciding the direction of a number of programmes, it appears that the first phase of privatization was less politicized than the second one but certainly not immune to the operation of informal networks linking business and government.

The second phase, initiated by the Andreotti government in 1989, has been both more structured and more politicized. The government included in its programme the intention to privatize, 'so as to contribute to a significant reduction of public debt' while introducing to the market 'assets previously unavailable thus releasing new entrepreneurial initiative' (quoted in Cassese, 1994, p. 53). The next, seventh, Andreotti government in 1991 adopted a privatization law which involved the transformation of public enterprises into joint stock companies, in order to sell shares more widely. By that time, the need to tackle the public debt had emerged as the main problem (cf. Segnana, 1993, p. 277). Privatization programmes, providing frameworks for privatization processes, have increased the government's role while also specifying that privatization receipts should go to the Treasury. This provoked opposition from the state holding companies and their allies in the governing parties, which insisted that privatization receipts should continue going to them (Cassese, 1994, p. 53). The public enterprises have resisted the transition from the individual privatizations to privatization programmes, while at the same time, politicization has increased as a result of the greater public exposure of privatization as an issue in government programmes.

The Amato government promised a more effective privatization programme in July 1992, and passed a new law that aimed to transform compulsorily IRI, ENI and other public holding groups into joint stock companies. Privatization was then implemented vigorously by the Ciampi government. The emphasis on sequential privatization (the profitable companies being sold off first) through the stock exchange, with the aim of widespread shareholdings, was confirmed by the governments in 1992-93. Despite some difficulties early in 1993 (EIU, *Country Report*, 2nd quarter 1993), which were partly due to the relative weakness of the Milanese bourse, the privatization programme soon took off with the privatization of the Credito Italiano bank, a major project widely regarded as a test case.

Privatization was in effect slowed down by the Berlusconi government in 1994, despite Berlusconi's introduction of a new privatization timetable in September. The difficulties of privatization in 1994 are in part due to apparent differences of opinion within the government over the method of privatization (EIU, *Country Report*, 4th quarter 1994, p. 21). Following the downfall of the Berlusconi government, Dini and his 'government of experts' sought to revive the privatization process in 1995, concentrating on large-scale privatizations, especially in the banking sector, with telecommunications and energy appearing next on the list (EIU, *Country Report*, 1st quarter 1995, p. 23).

The banking sector, which was state-controlled to a considerable extent, had shown signs of deregulation in the early 1980s, before the privatization wave.[5] Privatization has resulted in more straightforward shifts in public-private relations, although the public presence in banking remains heavy in mid-1995. Since it was privatized in late 1993, Credito Italiano has become a major player in the sector, purchasing the Credito Romagnolo of Bologna in a bid battle that has been described as 'the biggest takeover battle in Italian stock market history'. More generally, the Credito has been seeking to play a role in the restructuring of the economy by proposing jointly with three other banks to take over the Italian state's 61 per cent stake in STET, the telecommunications holding company (see *Financial Times*, 13 April 1995).

Telecommunications is the next major area to be affected by privatization, with STET due for full privatization later in 1995. In view of the European agreement for the liberalization of telephony services after 1998, Telecom Italia (controlled by STET) is already facing competition from international operator alliances targeting Italian business users in areas such as mobile phones and the linking of phones and computers (*Financial Times*, 13 April 1995). STET and Telecom Italia have responded actively by exploring international markets while striving to retain their up-to-now loyal clientele of major Italian companies such as Fiat and Pirelli. With a view to eventual privatization, STET had been coordinating rationalization and merger processes since the early 1990s. In addition, the state telecoms groups spent heavily in the early 1990s in an attempt to modernize the network, leading to a string of rights issues (*Financial Times*, 30 September 1993).

Despite party-political discontinuities, a number of long-term economic and political developments favouring economic liberalization appear to have acquired a relatively secure status. The problems of the public debt and the public deficit will remain pressing for the government to succeed Dini, and despite differences at the level of party rhetoric the commitment to European convergence is strong enough to help define as well as constrain political priorities and economic policy. In 1992, a series of formal measures were taken to increase the autonomy of the Bank of Italy (EIU, *Country Report*, 1st quarter 1993, p. 16). At the same time, however, it is significant that the ineffectiveness of the Berlusconi government in the privatization field has been partly the result of disagreements over privatization methods and the implications of different methods for public-private relations. While the early stages of the Italian privatization process have not favoured 'popular capitalism', some of the more recent attempts by the Ciampi and Dini governments have been shifting the balance towards the promotion of more widespread shareholding.

Greece: early politicization

Privatization in Greece was set in motion by the fall of the socialist (PASOK) government in the June 1989 elections. The PASOK government in the 1980s pursued expansionary economic policies and redistribution, in an approach that appears to have miscalculated the constraints imposed by international developments and by the inefficiency of the Greek public sector (cf. Tsoukalis, 1993, p. 254). The inefficient and swollen public sector reproduces long-established clientelist practices that constrain the state's ability to pursue consistent programmes of public investment and industrial development (Katseli, 1990). Greek 'disjointed corporatism' (Lavdas, 1995) has been static and incoherent, constraining the liberal elements in the Greek economic system while at the same time being incapable of brokering social pacts.

Greek privatizations encompass a number of sectors and range from textile companies that were taken over to avoid unemployment to oil refineries and major utilities. Approximately 200 companies were listed for privatization by the government in 1990-91 (for the lists see *To Vima*, 4 August, 1991). The selling of public enterprises got a difficult start in the late 1980s with a number of government announcements of intention to privatize but without any agreed plan as to the pace or sequence of privatization: the possibility of sequential selling, beginning with the most profitable firms and then restructuring the less efficient ones which can be sold at a later stage (Katsoulacos, 1993, pp. 365-369) was seriously considered but not followed as a clear policy line. As a result, privatization of major utilities and strategic firms emerged as an issue very early, even if actual privatization plans were unclear.

Privatization of smaller companies has attracted criticisms that these were offered to pro-conservative businesses on favourable terms; larger privatizations have been more complicated. A single large privatization in the early 1990s, that of the cement company AGET, one of Europe's biggest cement exporting companies, accounted for Dr130 billion of the Dr160 billion of general privatization receipts by 1992 (OECD, *Economic Surveys*, Greece, 1993, p. 43).

Despite initial oscillations concerning both the scope of privatization and the necessary regulatory measures that would have to be introduced in a country with poor regulatory experience, considerable progress was made between 1990-94. Predictably, one targeted area was the banking sector, in which state presence has always been considerable. Privatization was extended to energy companies, the manufacturing industry and construction firms. Although privatization was initiated by the conservative (ND) government in 1990, forms of privatization were accepted, in principle, by the incoming socialist government in 1993. In some cases the socialists' preference was for partial privatization, but the PASOK government has been committed to achieving substantial receipts (Dr700 billion for the 1994-97 period) from privatizations (EIU, *Country Report*, 3rd quarter 1994, p. 23). Internal PASOK splits and infighting, rather than any generally accepted government line, have been responsible for confining PASOK's selling of major enterprises to partial privatization.

The initiation of privatization programmes above all reflected the need to close gaps in public finances, reduce the deficit and tackle the debt. Not only did the size of the public sector deficit call for urgent attention, but, more specifically, several utilities had accumulated high levels of debt (*Financial Times*, 7 May 1993). Furthermore, the conservative party (ND) was undergoing a process of change, with neo-liberalism acquiring real as well as symbolic significance in the party's shift from economic paternalism to economic liberalism as a result of an internal change of guard.

Last but not least, all of the public finance-related aspects of EU membership impact (loans, convergence criteria and convergence plan) were linked to privatization efforts in two ways. Obviously there was need for receipts that would help balance the books, but a second link was in the sense of international and European confidence-building means, aiming to persuade both prospective investors and European institutions.

The politics of large-scale privatization is particularly interesting in the case of telecommunications. In Europe, telecommunications as a policy area has witnessed a strong mediating role played by EU institutions in their attempts, first, to coordinate a European response to international pressures and, second, to participate in national telecoms liberalization processes (see Dang-Nguyen, Schneider and Werle, 1993).

In Greece, telecommunications is at once a critical area, an area in respect to which a major privatization programme was launched, and one which has presented considerable resistance to privatization efforts. It makes interesting coalition politics; it is also having difficulties in adapting to the EU framework. Along with Italy and Ireland, Greece has been a member state with a consistently low record (below 70 per cent) of incorporation of directives on telecommunications in the recent, crucial years (see Commission of the EC, 1992b, 1993, 1994).

The development of OTE, the state telecoms group, has witnessed a succession of networks linking politicians, civil servants, trade unionists and telecoms-related companies. Most of the aforementioned frictions with the EU have involved issues of public procurement. The 1989-1993 conservative government decided the sale of a 35 per cent stake to an international telecoms operator and a stock market flotation of another 14 per cent. As OTE was profit-making, the government was hoping for substantial receipts. In 1992, Law 2075 prepared the ground for privatization by limiting OTE monopoly and by establishing a regulatory body (National Telecoms Commission - EET) which would also be responsible for licensing (Ministry of National Economy, *OTE - Partial Privatization*, Athens, 6 August 1993). Trade unions (including conservative unions) opposed the programme, initially arguing against any form of privatization for telecoms. Opposition came also from several backbenchers and even cabinet members. Last but not least, Intracom, the Greek telecoms equipment and software manufacturer, has been querying a number of aspects of the privatization programme.

OTE has been Intracom's biggest client, while the company's dynamic growth and considerable successes in East European markets in the early 1990s have given it increased weight in negotiations with the government (*Financial Times*, 21 May 1993). Intracom, along with Siemens of Greece, have been the major beneficiaries of OTE procurement policy. Relations between Intracom and the ND government turned sour not only because of the government's efforts to privatize OTE by giving 35 per cent and the management to one 'strategic investor' (Law 2167/1993), which would have long-term implications for procurement, but also due to short-term disputes about the fate of a major procurement contract for digital lines.

245

In 1993 the incoming PASOK government aimed to construct a privatization package that would be more acceptable to a number of groups. In an era of telecoms alliances, the control of the privatized OTE's management is a crucial issue and the PASOK government's pledge to keep OTE control 'in public hands' has satisfied both unionists and procurement beneficiaries. The new government decided the flotation of a total of 25 per cent, of which 18 per cent to foreign operators through a book building procedure and 7 per cent to domestic small investors.

OTE privatization was temporarily suspended in November 1994 (see *Financial Times*, 9 November 1994). The government cited as a reason for the temporary suspension of the privatization the relatively disappointing offers of the international bidders. But this, in itself an apparent vote of no confidence by international investors, requires explanation. The socialist government's insistence on OTE management remaining in the hands of the state (with its implications also for the group's procurement practices), on the one hand, and the oscillations with regard to the eventual stake to be floated, on the other, created uncertainty. Although the government has insisted that OTE privatization will eventually go ahead, within PASOK the opposition to privatization spread to the parliamentary party, with a small number of socialist MPs openly against even the new government's telecoms partial privatization bill.

Procurement practices typical of government-business relations in the Greek policy pattern have been at the centre of the difficulties encountered by the telecoms privatization. The opposing coalitions have used various veto points, including the parliament, and the main defence line has mobilized a number of networks connecting private interests, banks, unions, and factions within both main parties. In view of the nature of the problems and the adjustment challenges involved, the government has insisted that it remains committed to partial privatization of major state groups, such as the Public Petroleum Corporation (DEP) which is due to be part privatized in autumn 1995 (EIU, *Country Report*, 1st quarter 1995, p. 30).

As with the other Southern European cases, it would be wrong to underestimate the potential significance of the changes that are taking place. As a result of economic liberalization since the late 1980s, Greece is becoming a much more market-driven economy, while persisting traditional elements such as the underground economy (which is significant but notoriously difficult to measure) will continue to play roles mostly as social buffers (Jacquemin and Wright, 1993, pp. 282-283). The public sector borrowing requirement declined by more than one-third in the early 1990s, and inflationary pressures appear to be under control by the mid-1990s. Still, the volume of the public debt remains very significant, while the Greek economy suffers structurally from a slow and incomplete transition to high value-added production (a transition undertaken more successfully by Spain and to some extent Portugal in the 1980s).

Spain: supply-side socialism

In Spain, efforts to roll back the state presence in the economy have been one aspect of a relatively consistent policy of supply-side economic management since the early 1980s. Despite oscillations, the overall strategy of the socialist (PSOE) governments has been to improve international competitiveness, contain the public sector deficit, tighten monetary policy and increase labour market flexibility. This strategy appeared vindicated between 1986 and the early 1990s when Spain returned to the track of high growth rates that had been a feature of the Spanish economy back in the 1960s. However, and despite the high growth rates, the restrictive government policies along with the decline of employment in agriculture have pushed unemployment levels up to 20 per cent in the mid-1980s, 17 per cent in the early 1990s. Since the early 1990s growth rates have been lower, and the trade deficit has widened. Economic policy has presented signs of relaxation[6] against a background of relative political instability, as the government was implicated in a number of corruption cases and managed to survive the 1993 elections only with substantial losses.

The Spanish policy pattern owes much to the lack of abrupt change and the prevalence of negotiated gradualism in the course of democratic transition and consolidation (Maravall and Santamaria, 1986; Perez-Diaz, 1993). The PSOE economic record can be regarded moderately successful in terms of growth, international business confidence and inward investment, banking rationalization and liberalization. The promotion of labour market deregulation, along with policies which maintained light corporate taxation and a general pro-business outlook have alienated large segments of the socialists' support, while linking the peseta to the European monetary system necessitated tight inflation controls. Although the PSOE economic management record is distinguished by an adherence to a neo-liberal policy line even in view of very high unemployment levels,[7] the Spanish policy mix retains a number of different elements which point to the roles of policy traditions, on the one hand, and the results of the consensus phase referred to above, on the other. For example, employers' social security contributions are the third heaviest among the OECD states, following France and Sweden (OECD, *Economic Surveys*, Spain, 1988/1989, p. 67), while the socialists introduced a number of social security policies, such as a national pension scheme for elderly citizens.

As in Italy, privatization has its roots in attempts to tackle industrial decline and implement restructuring. The 1980s concentrated attention on industrial decline and the need for restructuring of a number of firms, many being public enterprises (cf. Myro Sanchez, 1993, pp. 613-640). The first effort was made in 1981 by the centre-right (UCD) government with an industrial reconversion law which targeted sectors that were either in decline or in need of restructuring. Not many concrete measures were taken under the 1981 law (OECD, *Economic Surveys*, Spain, May 1984, pp. 46-47), and the PSOE government introduced a new law on industrial restructuring in 1984. The new law also sought to modernize the viable industries while reducing capacity in others (e.g., shipbuilding), using a variety of financial and other instruments. In the context of this process, which was managed by INI, the state holding group, it was decided first in 1986 to increase private shareholding in order to widen the capital base of public enterprises (OECD, *Economic Surveys*, Spain, 1988/1989, p. 39). The first substantial transactions took place in 1988, when shares for ENDESA (electricity supply) and other firms were placed in the capital market, the state retaining a majority holding (EIU, *Country Report*, No. 1-1988, p. 18).

Despite its overall emphasis on economic liberalization, the Spanish government has maintained a moderate and even cautious approach to full privatization. In part, this has been due to the politically explosive problem of the regional concentration of certain declining industrial sectors. It has become clear in policy debates, for example concerning the plans to split the INI group into two parts,[8] that the government favoured selling to the private sector mainly structural loss-making firms. Partial privatization was considered to be the most appropriate strategy regarding profitable enterprises. When it comes to partial privatization of strategic enterprises, which are considered to be of public interest, the state can maintain various forms of control over specified areas of such firms' activities. In 1995 the government proposed a law that would allow the definition of activities over which the state should maintain control by the implementation of individual decrees regulating each privatization (EIU, *Country Report*, 1st quarter 1995, p. 14).

Privatization receipts are meant primarily to reduce public debt (e.g., OECD, *Economic Surveys*, Spain, 1991/1992, p. 53), but a number of other objectives have been considered. The inefficiency of the Spanish public sector should not be allowed to obscure the fact that this has been also a weak public sector. This weakness has been reflected in a relatively low level of public spending and an emphasis on transfers as against public investment. In the early 1990s, the government considered it a greater priority to reduce the deficit in order to facilitate EU convergence than to work systematically towards a more efficient public sector, with the implication that the main efforts towards rationalization are concentrated in activities with the higher costs, such as welfare benefits and health provision (Jacquemin and Wright, 1993, pp. 405-407).

Spain's relatively modest privatizations have been a largely ad hoc process, depending on a number of different configurations. Rather than leading the efforts of economic liberalization, privatization in Spain has been just one aspect of a comprehensive but often uneven and tortuous process of shifting the balance of economic power while establishing the institutional parameters of a Europeanized economy. Along with other aspects of that process, privatization has been supported by the business confederation (CEOE) which has developed a consistently pro-European image since the 1980s. The tradition of pacts between the government, the business associations and the unions has weakened in view of the constraints imposed by the government's intention to adhere to its European convergence plans. At the same time, the newly independent Bank of Spain commenced its new phase by setting an inflation target of under 3 per cent in 1997 and criticizing the government for tolerating an excessive deficit (EIU, *Country Report*, 1st quarter 1995, pp. 6, 12-13).

Portugal: ambitious gradualism

A country with extensive state involvement in economic affairs and with a dramatic experience of regime transition in the mid-1970s that increased further the state's presence in the economy, Portugal is the third largest privatizer in the OECD, after the United Kingdom and New Zealand, in terms of the percentage of privatization receipts to the country's GDP (OECD, *Economic Surveys, Portugal*, 1994, p. 64). The public sector had been extended considerably as a result of the nationalizations which accompanied the regime transition (Maxwell, 1986; Bermeo, 1986). In 1972, two years before the regime change, the public sector accounted for approximately 9 per cent of total value added. In 1976, it accounted for 24.4 per cent. The emphasis on public ownership accruing from developments in 1974-76 was superimposed over a tradition of a strong role for the state in the economy. Relative closure and attempts to industrialize with import substitution rested on a system which controlled and stifled both external and internal competition (cf. Pintado, 1964). Membership of EFTA since 1960 marked the turn to an export-oriented growth policy. Within a decade, foreign investment rose from 1 per cent of gross fixed capital formation in 1960 to 27 per cent in 1970.

In the decade between the regime change in the mid-1970s and EC accession, the Portuguese political economy was characterized by fiscal instability leading to two IMF stabilization programmes in 1979 and 1983-84.[9] Accession to the EC in 1986 marked a turning point in the direction of economic policy, in the sense that a more serious adjustment effort was undertaken. EC membership stimulated long-term attempts at structural adjustment. It coincided with the dominance, since 1986, of the centre-right Social Democratic Party (PSD) which has promoted pro-Europe and pro-market policy lines. Since 1987 the government has produced successive medium-term adjustment programmes with various macro-economic goals.

The most persistent problems have been the inflationary pressures and the large public deficits. In view of the Maastricht timetable, the government has been producing convergence programmes since 1991, aiming to meet the requirements for full participation in EMU. Privatization started as partial privatization in 1989. Although very soon (by 1990) it included cases of full privatization, the policy was only extended to major utilities in the mid-1990s. The legal basis for privatization was laid down by a Constitutional Amendment of June 1989, limiting public majority ownership to strategic firms. The privatization law of 1990 that followed specified four goals for privatizations: raising Portugal's competitiveness; strengthening entrepreneurship; stimulating capital markets; and broadening share-ownership (OECD, *Economic Surveys, Portugal*, 1994, p. 62). The 1990 privatization law had two interesting features that were later modified or abolished. First, it earmarked 80 per cent of privatization receipts for public debt redemption. That portion was reduced in 1993. Second, the law put a 25 per cent limit on foreign ownership of privatized firms. This provision was of course challenged by the EC and was abolished in 1994. The fear that control of strategic enterprises would pass to foreign capital has been expressed by those in the government, such as Finance Minister Catroga, who have been more generally against relinquishing state control of firms considered to be of strategic importance to the Portuguese economy (EIU, *Country Report*, 2nd quarter 1994, p. 18).

Whatever the actual standing of the aforementioned four declared goals of privatization, the programme has been explicitly used in order to tackle the deficit. Because privatization receipts are earmarked for retiring government debt, privatization has influenced debt accumulation directly, reducing future interest payments (OECD, *Economic Surveys, Portugal*, 1993, p. 38). But despite the use being made of receipts to reduce public debt, results were less impressive than anticipated by the government, to some extent because the state often had to absorb public enterprise debts in preparing the firms for privatization. By early 1993 sales of public assets had slowed partly due to the deepening recession, partly because of factors such as the aforementioned limit on foreign ownership of privatized firms. The result was bids which the government was unwilling to accept because it considered them too low. At the same time, public enterprise losses mounted in 1993. IPE, the state industrial shareholding company, TAP, the national airline, and other groups announced losses substantially higher than their earlier forecasts (EIU, *Country Report*, 2nd quarter 1993, pp. 23-24). Against this background, the government sought to revive the privatization programme. A bank, a shipping firm, and a radio station were sold off later in 1993, and more determined efforts in 1994 concentrated on a major banking group, steel and cement firms, the state coach operators, and other ventures. Despite a strong emphasis put by some in the government on the need for encouraging small investors (*Financial Times*, 14 April 1994), shares in most privatized companies have ended up under the control of long-term investors (see EIU, *Country Report*, 2nd quarter 1994, pp. 18-19). In many cases, firms were re-acquired by Portuguese groups (e.g., Champalimaud, Espirito Santo, Mello) which owned them prior to the nationalizations of the mid-1970s (OECD, *Economic Surveys, Portugal*, 1994, p. 64).

Privatization plans for 1995-96 included a number of ambitious targets as regards both receipts from sales and particular areas of economic activity to be affected. Expected receipts from the 1995 privatization plans are estimated at Esc250 billion, against Esc122 billion raised in 1994 (EIU, *Country Report*, 4th quarter 1994, pp. 22-23). Telecommunications enter the privatization scene with plans for the partial flotation of Portugal Telecom. Portugal Telecom was formed in 1994 from the merger of three state-owned companies, and the government's plans to sell 25 per cent of the group simultaneously on the Lisbon, London and New York stock markets is expected to raise an amount that comes close to meeting, by itself, the target of Esc250 billion for 1995 (EIU, *Country Report*, 1st quarter 1995, p. 25). In addition, the government plans to sell 20-25 per cent of CPPE, the power production division of the state electricity utility (EDP). These privatizations are significant also as indications of the gradual extension of the Portuguese privatization programme into areas which would have initially appeared politically sensitive in view of the country's particular experience of the 1970s. The politicization and mobilization which accompanied the abrupt regime change in 1974 created the conditions which made necessary a cautious privatization policy.

The ambitious gradualism of the Portuguese privatization programme is partly the result of political conditions associated with the dominance of the PSD. Polls, however, indicate a steady decline of PSD popularity. What will be the impact of the possible weakening of the PSD on the Portuguese privatization programme? The socialists are committed to European convergence and to a degree of privatization, with the exception of major utilities. Even if the shift of the PSD and of the country towards neo-liberalism under Cavaco Silva is halted, the other main parties' European commitments are likely to caution against any significant alteration of general policy lines.

Conclusion: privatization, politicization and relative convergence

Privatization is a complex process in Southern Europe, involving shifts in public-private relations that have been marked by long-established patterns of close and often particularistic exchanges between political power and private interests. In what follows, I will outline a number of tentative conclusions about the ongoing process of privatization in Southern Europe, concentrating in particular on comparative aspects and broad development lines.

Although clearer in the cases of Italy and Spain, the broad lines of the development of privatization in Southern Europe more generally involve the shift from concerns of industrial decline to the requirements of European convergence. Because of that shift, the states acquire more central roles in structuring processes of privatization and determining the use of privatization receipts. The centrality of the state's role in privatization processes, and the extent to which privatizations become government programmes, influence the politicization of the issue of privatization.

A further factor determining politicization is recent economic and institutional history. In Portugal and to a much lesser extent in Greece, a persistent business demand for denationalization of the ventures taken over by the state following regime change in the mid-1970s provided support for the privatization programmes of the late 1980s. Business opinion was of course highly critical of the nationalizations of the mid-1970s, but the timing of the privatization programmes is a clear indication that conflicts generated by the legacy of the regime change provided a background against which the main shaping factors of privatization (international environment, debt pressures) played their roles.

The extent and nature of politicization will also depend on the enterprises to be privatized (whether they are SMEs, banking groups, major utilities, etc.), on the particular process of privatization followed and on the timing of the different steps of privatization processes. For example, the process followed in the Greek case was bound to create tensions and politicization at an early stage. The contrast between Greece and Portugal is interesting in this respect: while major utility privatizations were included in privatization programmes at a relatively early stage in the Greek case, the result being that plans had to follow the particular path determined by the intense politicization of the issues, equivalent privatizations were introduced gradually in the Portuguese case, and even in an electoral year (1995) did not become as politicized as in Greece.

If the aforementioned point to the central role of the state in structuring privatization processes, other factors appear to be eroding the state's capacity in economic policy while underlining its supervisory function. Privatization programmes increasingly need to be seen as aspects of policy packages broadly related to the requirements of European convergence -

for example, movement towards greater independence of central banks (consider the newly acquired independence of the Bank of Spain and the increased autonomy of the Bank of Italy). Economic liberalization and Europeanization have been the twin processes gradually reshaping the political economies of the European South since the 1980s. On the one hand, pressures of international competition as mediated by EU institutional arrangements often result in state retreat from areas of activity. For example, the Southern European states have been engaged since the early 1990s in negotiations with the European Commission on rescue packages for national airlines. These negotiations largely determine the future ownership of the carriers, because the states' future capability to subsidize them is limited (the packages agreed usually concern one-off rescue efforts).

On the other hand, capital markets have been revitalized. For example, in part due to the privatization programmes, the traditionally weak Athens Stock Exchange has been strengthened in the 1990s, with a great number of companies waiting for listings and whole sectors being represented for the first time. Equally significant, of course, have been the funds from EU structural policy which have been directed to infrastructural modernization, thereby reinvigorating construction, which used to be the motor behind Greek growth since the 1950s (*Financial Times*, 10 November 1993). But although construction companies were setting the pace, a number of other businesses (software, textiles, shipping, electrical appliances) were very active and, despite oscillations, the general picture remains positive (*Financial Times*, 20 April 1994).

While EU-level redistributive policies have hitherto been important in securing that poorer states acquiesce to the single market project, economic liberalization may prove a more critical area in deciding processes of relative convergence in the future. The requirement of 'additionality', built into the principles of structural policy, makes it difficult for the states concerned to rein in public finances (as funds for projects need to be matched by equivalent national monies): the mobilization of the resources necessary to meet the 'additionality' requirement may jeopardize efforts to meet the Maastricht economic convergence criteria. In addition, as the payment of convergence funds becomes linked from 1995 to deficit targets, it appears likely that there will be cases in which fiscal difficulties lead to reduced EU transfers. And yet structural funds are still necessary for the much needed growth of public investment in Southern Europe.

The economic convergence criteria of the Maastricht Treaty constitute one aspect of the more general phenomenon of relative convergence in policies and institutional arrangements. An interesting research question is the extent to which a degree of European convergence in policy goals and policy contents is also leading to convergence in policy instruments and policy style (cf. Bennett, 1991). Policy stimuli in the 1980s and the 1990s call attention to the implications of different state institutional traditions and political cultures for policy responses: domestic changes are mediated by forms and sequences of politicization and by policy coalitions forming in and around state structures.

It is in relation to such factors that privatization processes can be approached and assessed. While the inflation differentials between the Southern European states and Germany have indeed shown signs of narrowing, the overstretched state sector has been curbed somewhat and the capital markets have been revitalized, a comprehensive assessment of the ongoing process of privatization will have to take into account two problem areas in particular. First, it will have to evaluate the interactions of different policy patterns and policy responses. Aspects of policy traditions and state institutions reassert themselves in the process of articulating responses to the stimuli of economic liberalization and Europeanization, thereby mediating and possibly limiting the development from the convergence in policy goals and policy contents to the convergence in policy instruments and policy style. Second, an assessment of these ongoing processes will also need to consider their political and social repercussions in societies which relatively recently went through difficult but apparently successful transitions to, and consolidations of, democratic government.

Notes

1.   On the political economy of deregulation and reregulation see Cerny (1991); on the European dimension see especially Majone (1989). On the deregulation and reregulation experiences in Southern Europe see Lavdas (forthcoming).

2.   The 1976 Constitution (amended in 1982, 1989 and 1992) had endorsed the nationalizations and land expropriations which followed the regime change. As a result of a turbulent process of

regime transition and democratization, the original constitutional document had included a number of socialist formulations (e.g. Articles 86, 91-94).

3. By the late 1980s, when the EC started developing a tighter anti-trust regime, only Germany, France and the UK possessed elaborate national systems of merger control (cf. Tsoukalis, 1993, p. 109).

4. For overviews of Italian politics, political economy and EC participation see Furlong (1994), Hine (1993) and Bardi (1993).

5. Mainly through the implementation of deregulation and the changes in the relationship between the Bank of Italy and the Treasury, often referred to as the 'divorce'. See Epstein and Schor, 1989, pp. 147-163. As we will see, the tendency towards a more independent central bank has been strengthened in the 1990s.

6. The Spanish government's fiscal policy has in fact been criticized as excessively expansionary by the IMF, the EU finance ministers and the newly independent Bank of Spain (see EIU, Country Report, 1st quarter 1995, p. 9).

7. For a negative assessment of PSOE's record of economic management since 1982 see Petras (1993, pp. 95-127).

8. Viable firms would be regrouped under INISA (INI company limited), and INISA companies would eventually have to operate as a private holding group. Structural loss-making firms would be regrouped under INISE (INI state company). Some INISE companies would be sold, others liquidated, and still others would be restructured while receiving diminishing state aid. Some of the aid-receivers have activities concentrated in declining or underdeveloped regions, and the government sought to 'proceed gradually in order to minimize the employment effects on the region'. See OECD, Economic Surveys, Spain, 1991/1992, p. 52.

9. For different accounts of the development of economic policy see Dauderstaedt (1988) and Chilcote (1993).

References

Bardi, L. *et al.* (1993), 'Italy: The Dominance of Domestic Politics', in

Van Schendelen, M. (ed.), *National Public and Private EC Lobbying*, Dartmouth, Aldershot.

Bennett, C. (1991), 'What is policy convergence and what causes it?', *British Journal of Political Science*, vol. 21.

Bermeo, N. (1986), *The Revolution within the Revolution: Workers Control in Rural Portugal*, Princeton University Press, Princeton.

Bermeo, N. (1990), 'The Politics of Public Enterprise in Portugal, Spain and Greece', in Suleiman, E. and Waterbury, J. (eds.), *The Political Economy of Public Sector Reform and Privatization*, Westview Press, Boulder.

Cassese, S. (1994), 'Deregulation and Privatization in Italy', in Moran, M. and Prosser, T. (eds), *Privatization and Regulatory Change in Europe*, Open University Press, Buckingham.

Cerny, P. (ed.) (1991), The Politics of Transnational Regulation: Deregulation or Reregulation, Special Issue, *European Journal of Political Research* vol. 19.; nos. 2/3.

Chilcote, R. (1993), 'Portugal: From Popular Power to Bourgeois Democracy', in Kurth, J. *et al.*, *Mediterranean Paradoxes*, Berg, Oxford.

Commission of the EC (1992a), *Third Survey on State Aids in the European Community*, Office for Official Publications of the European Communities, Luxembourg.

Commission of the EC (1992b), *Ninth Annual Report of the Commission on the Application of Community Law*, COM(92)136 final, Office for Official Publications of the European Communities, Luxembourg.

Commission of the EC (1993), *Tenth Annual Report of the Commission on the Application of Community Law*, COM(93)320 final, Office for Official Publications of the European Communities, Luxembourg.

Commission of the EC (1994), *Eleventh Annual Report on Commission Monitoring of the Application of Community Law*, COM(94)500 final, Office for Official Publications of the European Communities, Luxembourg.

Dang-Nguyen, G. *et al.* (1993), 'Networks in European Policy-Making: Europeification of Telecommunications Policy', in Andersen, S. and Eliassen, K. (eds), *Making Policy in Europe*, Sage, London.

Dauderstaedt, M. (1988), 'Schwacher Staat und schwacher Markt: Portugals Wirtschaftspolitik zwischen Abhaengigkeit und Modernisierung', *PVS*, vol. 29.

Diamandouros, N. (1986), 'The southern European NICs', *International Organization*, vol. 40.

EIU, *Country Reports, Country Profiles*.

Epstein, G. and Schor, J. (1989), 'The divorce of the Banca d'Italia and the Italian Treasury: a case study of central bank independence', in Lange, P. and Regini, M. (eds), *State, Market and Social Regulation: New Perspectives on Italy*, Cambridge University Press, Cambridge.

Evans, P. *et al.* (eds) (1985), *Bringing the State Back In*, Cambridge University Press, Cambridge.

Financial Times, various dates.

Furlong, P. (1994), *Modern Italy: Representation and Reform*, Routledge, London.

Heywood, P. (1991). 'Governing a New Democracy: The Power of the Prime Minister in Spain', *West European Politics*, vol. 14.

Hine, D. (1993), *Governing Italy: The Politics of Bargained Pluralism*, Oxford University Press, Oxford.

Immergut, E. (1992), *Health Politics*, Cambridge University Press, Cambridge.

Jacquemin, A. and Wright, D. (eds) (1993), *The European Challenges Post-1992: Shaping Factors, Shaping Actors*, Edward Elgar, Cheltenham.

Katseli, L. (1990), 'Economic integration in the enlarged Community: structural adjustment of the Greek economy', in Bliss, C. and Braga de Macedo, J. (eds), *Unity with Diversity in the European Community*, Cambridge University Press, Cambridge.

Katsoulacos, Y. (1993), 'Rationale and Optimal Implementation of Privatization Policies: The Case of Greece', in Clarke, T. and Pitelis, C. (eds), *The Political Economy of Privatization*, Routledge, London.

Kornai, J. (1979), 'Resource-constrained versus demand-constrained systems', *Econometrica*, vol. 47.

Lavdas, K. (1995), 'Policy Coalitions and Disjointed Corporatism: State Structures in Greece', in Lovenduski, J. and Stanyer, J. (eds), *Contemporary Political Studies 1995*, Political Studies Association of the United Kingdom, Exeter.

Lavdas, K. (forthcoming), *Junctures of Stateness: Political Boundaries and Regulatory Change in Southern Europe*, Dartmouth, Aldershot.

Lavdas, K. and Mendrinou, M. (1995), 'Competition Policy and Institutional Politics in the European Community: State Aid Control and

Small Business Promotion' *European Journal of Political Research*, 28, 2.

Lavdas, K. and Mendrinou, M. (forthcoming), *Politics, Subsidies and Competition: The New Politics of State Intervention in the European Union*, Edward Elgar, Cheltenham.

Majone, G. (1989), 'Regulating Europe: Problems and Prospects', *Jahrbuch zur Staats- und Verwaltungswissenschaft*, vol. 3.

Maravall, J.M. and Santamaria, J. (1986), 'Political Change in Spain and the Prospects for Democracy', in O'Donnell, G. *et al.* (eds), *Transitions from Authoritarian Rule: Southern Europe*, Johns Hopkins University Press, Baltimore.

Maxwell, K. (1986), 'Regime Overthrow and the Prospects for Democratic Transition in Portugal', in O'Donnell, G. *et al.* (eds), *Transitions from Authoritarian Rule: Southern Europe*, Johns Hopkins University Press, Baltimore.

McGowan, F. (1993), 'Ownership and Competition in Community Markets', in Clarke, T. and Pitelis, C. (eds), *The Political Economy of Privatization*, Routledge, London.

Mendrinou, M. (forthcoming), 'Non-Compliance and the European Commission's Role in Integration', *Journal of European Public Policy*.

Ministry of National Economy, Greece (1993), *OTE - Partial Privatization*, 6 August, Athens.

Myro Sanchez, R. (1993), 'Las empresas publicas', in Garcia Delgado, J.L. (ed.), *Espana, Economia*, Espasa Calpe, Madrid, OECD, *Economic Surveys*.

Perez-Diaz, V. (1993), *The Return of Civil Society*, Harvard University Press, Cambridge, MA.

Petras, J. (1993), 'Spanish Socialism: The Politics of Neoliberalism', in Kurth, J. *et al.*, *Mediterranean Paradoxes*, Berg, Oxford.

Pintado, V. (1964), *Structure and Growth of the Portuguese Economy*, EFTA, Geneva.

Pitelis, C. and Clarke, T. (1993), 'Introduction: The Political Economy of Privatization', in Clarke, T. and Pitelis, C. (eds), *The Political Economy of Privatization*, Routledge, London.

Segnana, L. (1993), 'Public-Private Relations in Italy: The Experience of the 1980s', in Clarke, T. and Pitelis, C. (eds), *The Political Economy of Privatization,* , Routledge, London.

Shonfield, A. (1965), *Modern Capitalism: The Changing Balance of Public and Private Power*, Oxford University Press, Oxford.

Siragusa, M. and Scassellati-Sforzolini, G. (1992), 'Italian and EC Competition Law: A New Relationship - Reciprocal Exclusivity and Common Principles', *Common Market Law Review*, vol. 29. *To Vima*, various dates.

Tsoukalis, L. (1981), *The European Community and its Mediterranean Enlargement*, Allen & Unwin, London.

Tsoukalis, L. (1993), *The New European Economy: The Politics and Economics of Integration*, 2nd ed., Oxford University Press, Oxford.

Vernon, R. (1988), 'Introduction: The Promise and the Challenge', in Vernon, R. (ed.), *The Promise of Privatization*, Council on Foreign Relations, New York.

Vickers, J. and Yarrow, G. (1988), *Privatization: An Economic Analysis*, MIT Press, Cambridge, MA.

11 Privatization in Central and Eastern Europe: Models and Ideologies

JONATHAN BRADLEY

Introduction

The purpose of this chapter is to analyze and compare the various justifications which have been offered for privatization in the so-called Economies in Transition (henceforth EITs) of Central and Eastern Europe. In keeping with the inter-disciplinary nature of this book the analysis takes account of the inseparability of politics and economics in EIT privatization. The starting point is a brief definitional section and this is followed by a review of alternative views in the literature. The author finds that Western-derived models of privatization are neither useful descriptively nor appropriate normatively in the context of EITs. A notable flaw in the drive for rapid privatization has been the inherent incapability of many command economy 'enterprises' to function in a commercial fashion without fundamental changes that may take some time to achieve. The chapter concludes by identifying new meanings for privatization implicit in the practice of economic reform in those countries.

Privatization is a favourite tool of those engaged in the great experiment to create capitalist out of command economies, some of whom are indigenous policy-makers, and many of whom are visiting academics who will not be obliged to live with the consequences of their own advice. All of the European EITs claim to have privatization programmes and some of them have already implemented major changes. Moreover, it is difficult to identify any EIT government or relevant academic work which does not place privatization at the centre of the process of economic reform.[1] It is generally acknowledged to be vitally integral to the fashioning of market-based economic systems with a large measure of private ownership.

Central and Eastern European privatization: a brief history

The course of events so far in Central and Eastern Europe has revealed new ideas and innovative instruments of policy which have themselves broadened the significance of privatization. Hungary was the first of the EITs to take measures which were recognizably 'privatizing' in nature, having been engaged in a gradual reform for some years under the old regime. It had a rudimentary stock exchange even in Communist days and the 1990 public flotation of Ibusz attracted enthusiastic if misplaced support from Western investment institutions. These developments of private commerce and finance were, however, essentially derived from Western experience. More radical solutions appeared in some of the countries in which the pre-1990 economic command system had most notably deviated from a conventional market economy, such as Russia and the Czech Republic. Poland toyed with sweeping alterations and then stood back from them, only in 1995 finally implementing a scheme first adumbrated some years previously by Lipton and Sachs (1990). All of the above countries have ostensibly transferred many of their industrial and commercial assets out of the public sector. It remains to be seen whether their destination has been a 'private' sector in the common understanding of that term. Other states, such as Romania and Bulgaria, have been slower to introduce privatization policies.

Defining 'privatization'

This chapter will seek to justify one of its main observations - that there does not exist one simple definition of 'privatization' that is adequate in the present context of EITs.

As explained in Chapter 1, definitions of privatization vary on the one hand from the most narrow interpretation based on asset disposals in countries such as France, to a meaning on the other hand which is construed so widely that it could apply to the whole practice of economic transformation. In the privatization literature examples of the former are evident in some of the plans proposed soon after the revolutions of 1989/1990, especially by EIT commentators. The Shatalin/Yavlinsky Plan of August 1990, for instance, conceived of privatization in terms of the sale of joint-stock companies, perhaps through a stock market - apparently an Easternized version of an OECD country public flotation (Baldassarri, 1993, ch.2). An instance of a very broad definition of privatization appears in a somewhat later piece of work by Western commentators (Bim *et al.*, 1990, p. 252).

The coming of momentous change to Central and Eastern Europe has added impetus to the continuing evolution of the meaning of 'privatization'. Its scope, methods and purposes have been diversified and it has been invested with nuances peculiar to the unique recent events in EITs. An example is 'spontaneous' privatization. The two main forms of this are 'commercialization', in which businesses become joint stock companies and gain supposed autonomy from ministerial intervention. This is sometimes in EITs described as privatization but clearly is not. The other variant was tantamount to organized theft, when members of the Communist nomenclature in the early days of reform took control and de facto ownership of undertakings. Some writers are reluctant to describe the latter as privatization, although if the companies concerned eventually act independently of the state, subject to the rigours of the market, this writer would argue that a form of privatization has indeed occurred.

The experiences of EITs are likely in any case to change conceptions of what privatization is. Two of the leading theoreticians of transitional privatization, Frydman and Rapaczynski (1994), point out that the historical process in which economic institutions tend to develop is gradual, incremental, and contingent. The present author would suggest that this is also true of the broad economic ideas, such as privatization, which inform the process.

Privatization justifications

Pre-transitional

This section discusses arguments advanced in favour of private rather than public enterprise *before* transition began. It is traditional to trace the origins of such arguments back to the classical economists such as Adam Smith (1776). More recently neo-Austrian economists such as Mises and Hayek wrote their pro-capitalist tracts in response to what they saw as the evils of command economies. *Socialism*, published by Mises in Nazi Germany in 1936, was an attack on socialism in all its manifestations, including nationalization specifically. In *The Constitution of Liberty* Hayek favoured nurturing a multiplicity of private enterprises, providing sufficient alternatives to deprive any one organization, including the state, of the means to exercise coercive power (Hayek, 1960). Echoes of his reasoning can be found in contemporary economists such as Sachs, and policy-makers such as Klaus in the Czech Republic.

The neo-Austrians tended not to offer prescriptions for techniques of privatization. As well as attacking its supposed enemies, their work describes an idealized capitalist economic system, which has provided some inspiration for writers about change in EITs.

The apologias offered for privatization in Western countries such as France and Britain from the 1980s were discussed in an earlier chapter. Implicit in the varied programmes that they implemented were several economic propositions which have subsequently been applied, sometimes inappropriately, in EITs. These propositions include the following:

1. The form of ownership of an asset, and the identity of the owner, affect the economic performance of it.
2. It is possible to make a clear distinction between 'public' ownership and 'private' ownership.
3. The economic power of the state will be reduced as a result of transferring ownership of assets from public to private hands.
4. Privately controlled enterprises are likely to be more economically efficient than public ones, because private owners will be more likely than the state to display profit maximizing behaviour.
5. The value of privatized assets will be greater in the hands of their new owners than in those of the state.
6. Increasing the proportion of private ownership of productive assets in the economy will encourage greater competition.
7. Therefore, in general, economic welfare will be maximized through private rather than public ownership.

The privatization programmes implemented in Western Europe, furthermore, rested on a number of practical assumptions:

1. The legal system was capable of enforcing private property rights.
2. These same property rights were clearly defined in law or custom.
3. There were persons capable of acquiring ownership and making efficient use of it.
4. The identity of the seller, and their right to sell, were clearly established.
5. The value of assets and of outputs could be defined with reference to prices determined by markets rather than administrators.

Both the economic principles and the practical prerequisites of the privatization measures were integral to the nature of most commonly accepted definitions of a capitalist economy. By no means all of the principles have identical application in EITs, nor have the practical prerequisites often been present. This point will be explored further below.

Post-Communist

The ideas and experiences so far described were the main raw materials available to students and practitioners when it became clear that major economic change was to be contemplated in the EITs after 1989/1990. In effect these consisted of the basic principles of market economics, the works of opponents of socialist statism, and such principles as could be abridged from the practice of Western privatization. Ready-made prescriptions did not exist. The unique circumstances of Central and Eastern Europe after 1990 then rapidly inspired economists of various persuasions to apply other bodies of theory, such as those relating to property rights, questions of principal and agent, pricing, and market structures.

Broadly speaking the justifications advanced for privatization in EITs may be divided into the political and economic. Political arguments are of three principal kinds - the encouragement of pluralist systems, the reduction of bureaucratic influence, and gathering popular support through widespread asset ownership ('popular capitalism'). Economic arguments also have several forms - aiding structural change, promoting efficiency, fostering innovation, imposing financial discipline and improving motivation.

The three main political points mentioned above are all linked together by one overarching reason for privatizing: that it will secure the irreversibility of the reform process. Estrin (1994) mentions this, and Baldassarri and Paganetto (1993, p. 4) claim that it is the 'principal objective'. Indeed it is a point which is widely made. This may have seemed reasonable early in the reform period, when the outcome was very uncertain, but it appears far from obvious now. The existence of a large private sector did not impede the consolidation of the power of the communist party in Hungary or Czechoslovakia in the late 1940s, and the return to power in Poland and Hungary of ex-communists in the mid-1990s has not appreciably slowed the reform process started by their non-communist predecessors. Privatization may help to entrench reform, though whether it would render it irreversible is not clear.

Some observers have argued that the economic case for privatization is unconvincing in itself and that only reinforcement with the political clinches the issue. Stiglitz (1993, p. 187) quotes the Czechoslovakian Minister of Privatization of the day as taking this view. This position may be rather extreme, yet has the virtue of questioning the prevalent assumption in the literature that privatization will be economically beneficial. It takes a political scientist to recognize that, far from being separable spheres, economics and politics were fused in the communist system (Batt, in Estrin, 1994). The Party's ownership of almost all productive assets, and its control of labour markets and prices, underpinned its political position. Any attempt to reform, or analyze, the communist system therefore becomes a study in political economy.

The most sweeping economic justification advanced for privatization is that it is the sine qua non of the entire venture of economic restructuring. Blanchard states this opinion (1991) and it is a theme of the work of Jeffrey Sachs (Lipton and Sachs, 1990). The rationale for this is that the state in general, and individual functionaries in particular, would have no interest in forwarding important reforms, such as market pricing, hard budget constraints, insistence on full market rates of return, or the effective exercise of private property rights, because it would not directly benefit them to do so. Only if significant sections of industry were privatized would such changes occur.

A practical, rather than conceptual, objection to this may be that if economic agents, especially managers of enterprises, have a realistic *expectation* of being subject to market constraints they may adjust their

266

behaviour in anticipation. It may then be possible to conduct other reforms without an immediate change in ownership. Kornai hints at this when he observes that an increase in the proportion of the private sector can only be achieved through an 'organic process of development and social change' (Kornai, 1990a). Moreover, empirical studies quoted by Estrin (1994) of events in Poland, the former Czechoslovakia and Hungary, show that restructuring has taken place in a number of enterprises without privatization. Galbraith, in characteristically contrary fashion, is more robust still, believing that as long as managers of large enterprises are given freedom from bureaucratic control then the location of ownership is not important (Kennet and Lieberman, 1992, ch.11).

Other possible objections to the notion of privatization as sine qua non would come from the 'Market Socialism' school. Academic analysis and historical experience have not been kind to the idea that ownership of productive capital could remain with the state while market mechanisms would be employed to allocate resources efficiently - the 'third way'. The debate has continued since early in this century and a comprehensive survey of the literature and arguments may be found in the more recent study by Lavoie (1985). A market socialist would maintain that if free pricing for all goods and services is enforced it is not only unnecessary to put ownership into private hands but harmful because it will lead to unacceptable levels of personal inequality. This approach has been attacked by many economists on various grounds. The main charge has been that the state will be by definition incapable of imposing market disciplines on part of itself and the result will be 'state failure', the counterpart to the 'market failure' of neo-classical economics (McAuley, 1992). In brief, market socialism is a contradiction in terms. The experience of recent economic history may also be adduced as evidence. It requires a great deal of starry-eyed optimism to interpret the market socialist experiments in Hungary or Poland in the 1970s and 1980s as successful. As Kornai (1990a) has put it, 'market socialism simply fizzled out'. It is precisely for this reason that the transformation debates are now being conducted.

Apart from the central justification discussed above, that privatization is theoretically essential for a fully market-based system, a number of subsidiary reasons have been put forward.

1. The enhancement of government revenues or foreign currency receipts (Estrin, 1994).
2. The encouragement of competition amongst different enterprises (Major, 1993).
3. The familiarization of relevant parties with the possession and exercise of property rights in general and of corporate governance in particular (Baldassarri, *et al.*, 1993).
4. The facilitation of industrial restructuring, internal reorganization and de-concentration.
5. The imposition of more effective financial discipline.
6. The improvement of managerial motivation and entrepreneurial innovation (a neo-Austrian might list these as separate points) (Kornai, 1990a).
7. The facilitation of de novo private business development, assuming that privatization is not defined so widely that de novo business is itself deemed to be part of the process (Estrin, 1994).

The list represents an amalgam of justifications distilled from the literature. Each of these will be briefly assessed in terms of its appropriateness for EITs.

Raising public revenues

It may be thought that in a world of scarce resources there are few governments which will ever relinquish the opportunity to enhance their own revenues. This is especially true in EITs, where the previous fiscal structures of command economies exposed state budgets to the special risk of deficit because of sharply falling revenues from state company profits and increased spending on social benefits. The need for revenue-raising is not therefore in doubt. In practice, however, it has proved a poor justification for privatization. To make a substantial contribution to the state budget it would have been necessary for an EIT to sell assets for a cash sum equivalent to a tangible proportion of GDP. Many of the technical and legal requirements for undertaking such a project were lacking. The financial system was not geared up to the distribution of shares to large numbers of people, as might have occurred in Britain or France, there was no habit or culture of investing in ordinary shares, and in some countries the savings balances were lacking. The existing private business sector was much too small to be able to raise the resources required for purchasing substantial assets. This left the foreign sector. External investment has brought some revenues to the governments of one or two countries, notably Hungary, but only after some delays. The Hungarian State Property Agency announced its first privatization programme to be effected through market sales, including twenty large and apparently profit-making concerns in September 1990, yet by the end of 1992 only three companies had been fully privatized (Canning and Hare, 1994). The Hungarians were still accused by some of rushing, prompting the response from Marton Tardos, the leader of the Free Democratic Party, that if Hungarian privatization were to proceed at the rate it had done under the Thatcher government in Britain, it would take 100 years to privatize the economy (Kennet and Lieberman, 1992).

Many barriers to such sales still exist in EITs, amongst them domestic public unease with sales to 'foreigners' and currency and profit repatriation worries on the part of companies. Besides, privatization for revenue-raising is an argument of practical expediency rather than of economic principle. Even then, governments such as those of the Czech Republic and Poland would be unlikely to be enthusiastic about giving away state concerns through voucher schemes if substantial revenues could instead be raised.

Encouraging competition

A frequent criticism of privatization in the West has been that it was not a sufficient condition for increased competition. An equally insistent criticism of the former command systems of EITs has been that public ownership was organically connected to the exclusion of market competition, and that privatization is therefore a necessary, though clearly not a sufficient, condition for competition (Major, 1993, ch.4). The practical effect of privatization on competition depends on the nature of the assets entering the private sector and on many aspects of the industrial environment. Most EITs have carried out 'small privatization' programmes, in which small businesses such as restaurants, shops and taxi firms have been sold or leased to their operators. The Czech Republic for instance, before its 'velvet divorce' from Slovakia, had already disposed of over 25,000 small businesses in this way (Frydman *et al.*, 1993a). This type of privatization is likely to have increased competition by simultaneously diversifying ownership, encouraging entrepreneurship, and liberalizing industries with low levels of concentration, low entry costs and multiple participants. If the Czech government, on the other hand, had privatized CKD, the giant Prague-based tramway manufacturer, it is difficult to see how this would have increased competition, though it is possible that it would have improved efficiency - that, however, is a separate issue. It was the monopoly producer of trams and associated equipment not just for the Czech Republic but for the whole of the former CMEA[2] area. In this case privatization would not have been enough in itself to increase competition. Very large and monopolistic organizations of this kind were common in the command economies because of the nature of economic planning. So this justification for privatization in EITs has only partial validity, and needs to be considered in conjunction with foreign competition and regulation.

Property rights and corporate governance

These are considered together since they are closely linked, with corporate governance ultimately being concerned with the exercise of property rights. Broadly speaking, there are two main points here. First it is said that people must learn to be owners, there will be no owners without privatization, therefore there must be privatization. Second, this will encourage good governance - that is, the mechanisms for ensuring that assets are exploited for the optimal advantage of their owners rather than for the benefit of their agents or managers.

Mises' belief in the central importance of ownership seems to be more widely favoured in the literature than Galbraith's more sceptical view. Yet, paradoxically, replication in EITs of the intricate web of legal and conventional relationships which make up the institution of property is one of the most difficult aspects of economic reform. Moreover, the institution of property, and the exercise of the rights attaching to it, are themselves subject to evolution in economies where private property appears deeply embedded. What is being replicated in an EIT? Which country, at what point in history, is the model? The problems are numerous. Private property American-style can no more be manufactured instantly than an oak tree can grow overnight.

Changing the nominal ownership of a productive asset from public to private may give it the superficial appearance of having been privatized, and it may be so described in official statistics or in the press, but unless the requisite conditions exist its economic behaviour will bear little resemblance to that of an outwardly similar unit in Germany or Britain. A narrow definition of privatization, therefore, may allow the impression that widespread change in nominal ownership can bolster the institution of private property. A wider definition, which presupposes autonomous profit-maximizing owners with the means to enforce their clearly stated rights, would preclude much current EIT ownership transfer from being described as privatization.

Russian government statistics claim that at the end of 1994, 15,779 medium and large enterprises had been privatized and that the private sector accounted for about 62 per cent of GDP.[3] Nevertheless, there is only a passing similarity between the Russian private sector and the private sector in a Western European country. Just a few of the more salient differences help to illustrate the point: it is difficult to prove ownership of shares in a Russian company because share registration procedures are so rudimentary, anti-monopoly supervision is virtually non-existent, many companies are still responsible for housing and medical services, and there is no consistent enforcement of accounting standards. Many industrial concerns are controlled or managed by former state officials who are more familiar with bureaucratic administration than with commercial business management. So the state may have relinquished control but it cannot be said that privatization has strongly furthered the exercise of property rights as traditionally understood, nor do conditions especially favour the development of good corporate governance. The experience of other countries varies and conditions in some EITs would give more convincing support for this justification for privatization - Poland, where private ownership of agriculture persisted under Communism, or the Czech Republic, where there is evidence of a strong cultural attachment to the idea of private property (Frydman et al., 1993a).

Again, it can be observed that privatization is the necessary, but not sufficient, condition for familiarizing citizens with the holding and exercise of property rights. The question of corporate governance is complicated by the claim that the exercise of ownership and control rights by governments may equally be designated 'governance'. This may be true, but unless the state behaves as a profit-maximizing proprietor towards a commercialized entity, the kind of governance achieved will not be of the type which advocates of privatization have in mind.

Despite the evidence noted earlier that some restructuring of enterprises has taken place without or before privatization, many writers have expressed the opinion that post-privatization is either more likely or more desirable, in some cases because they were writing towards the beginning of the reform period before empirical evidence was available. Others have favoured a more cautious approach.

In an article published soon after the Communist fall from power Alan Walters (1994) argued strongly that restructuring should precede privatization, on the grounds that experience elsewhere was favourable, that too much experimentation should be avoided, and that companies would be less difficult to value after reorganization. A point not mentioned by him, but by many others, is that the privatization of highly concentrated and monopolistic monoliths builds a very poor foundation for a competitive capitalist economy and they should be split up first.

The alternative view is well summarized by Wijnbergen (1993). He argues that uncertainty about ownership is itself a barrier to necessary restructuring, with ill-defined control rights permitting excessive wage claims and poor management practices. In addition, he suggests that private owners, especially strong, re-capitalized banks, will be more competent agents of industrial change than the government itself.

The practice of privatization in EITs has tended to vindicate the Wijnbergen view. Governments have been understandably averse to associating themselves directly with unpopular business decisions. Restructuring is frequently a euphemism for workforce reductions - unemployment from a voter's standpoint. The Czech government much preferred to allow Volkswagen to take responsibility for putting people out of jobs at the Skoda works and the Russian government has found it convenient to be a minority shareholder in the giant Uralmash engineering company as it reduced its payroll from 45,000 to 19,000.[4] In most countries, the impetus for industrial change has come from external advisers, foreign pressure, the threat of privatization or privatization itself. A sceptic might counter that many large privatized companies have inherited excessive market power as they were not broken into smaller parts before disposal. Unwittingly, though, the authorities may have better equipped such companies to cope with the increased external competition which inevitably ensues after gradual trade liberalization with OECD countries.

The links between privatization and deconcentration are more confused. In all the EITs the pre-reform industrial concentration ratios were very high by Western standards, because the planned economic system aspired to eliminate 'waste' by achieving economies of scale. On the face of it, any privatization accompanied by de-monopolization should have reduced industrial concentration. This has not, however, been the case. Countries such as Albania and Romania, which observed autarchical economic policies, maintained industrial units which were locally monopolistic under the previous regime, but which are not of viable size on an international basis, and must either increase in size or disappear. Other industries were concentrated in the sense that they were controlled from a central location, the government ministry in Warsaw or Moscow, and highly dispersed in terms of plant size. The highly fragmented Russian rubber glove industry is a case in point: after privatization there were eighty companies in early 1995, many of which were expected to go out of business.[5]

More effective financial discipline

A recurrent theme in the privatization literature is the persistence of soft budget constraints in the state sector of industry. Kornai (1990b, p. 21) has made special studies of this phenomenon, which he describes as a situation where:

> the strict relationship between expenditure and earnings has been relaxed, because excess expenditure over earnings will be paid by some other institution, typically the state...

and where:

> the decision-maker expects such external financial assistance with high probability and this high probability is firmly built into his behaviour.

Kornai adduced empirical evidence from Hungary, Yugoslavia, and China to support his contention. Other economists have used the soft budget constraint as an explanation of chronic budget deficits in some of the EITs, notably Ukraine, Russia, and Poland, and, through monetization of short term government debt, of inflation. It was estimated in 1993 that 25 per cent of the 8,000 remaining larger Polish enterprises were unable to service their debts to the state (Wijnbergen, 1993). A distinct manifestation of the same primary problem is the widespread accumulation of inter-enterprise credit.

The question at issue here is whether privatizing such businesses hardens their budget constraints. It need not do so, if political or social pressures on government are irresistible. Private businesses have at times secured substantial subsidies in OECD countries where unemployment or social disintegration has threatened. Such problems in EITs tend to be even greater. Subsidies are still in 1995 being paid by government to privatized businesses even in EITs where privatization has in principle been extensive - Russia, Poland, the Czech Republic. On the other hand hardening of budget constraints on companies is more probable if they are distanced from the state, for several reasons. First, accounting procedures in companies with private shareholders are more likely than extensions of government departments to be attuned to profit-making. Second, civil servants who grant subsidies, and industrial managers who ask for them, are not part of the same political structure and do not share a career path. Third, the grant of subsidies is more likely to be transparent. Fourth, Parliamentary or press scrutiny, is likely to be more rigorous where payments are made to private interests.

Economic policy also matters: budget hardening will be credible if the state refuses, through a strict monetary policy, to validate money creation by the commercial banks in support of insolvent industrial clients. The enforcement of bankruptcy laws will prevent unwarranted corporate survival through inter-company credit.

While experiences have varied widely, evidence so far from EITs generally supports the view that privatization assists financial discipline. At first, there were no bankruptcy laws. When these had been introduced, ministries were loath to invoke them in the public sector. In the Czech Republic, the government waited to give effect to bankruptcy laws until April 1993, after the first major voucher privatization wave was well under way (Estrin, 1994). In Romania privatization and the enforcement of bankruptcy have both been slow. An apparent exception is Hungary. Here, a new bankruptcy law was promulgated in 1991 and a number of state-owned companies were quite soon bankrupted. Hungarian circumstances were perhaps unusual, since a bankruptcy law of sorts had existed under Communism, there was a widespread expectation of privatization in 1991, and bankruptcy was to some extent used as an alternative to the normal process of privatization (Frydman *et al.*, 1993a).

Managerial motivation and entrepreneurial innovation

By their nature these are hard to measure and their presence can only be surmised from the performance of economic units. Thinkers of the Classical and Austrian schools have been undaunted by this, placing personal motivation at the heart of their advocacy of capitalist economic systems. These ideas were reviewed briefly above. Other schools of thought have been less enthusiastic about individual effort, preferring to stress collective or cooperative endeavour, their views often overshadowed in the clamour of the reform debate.

Some writers have sought to show that privatization, far from sharpening incentives, will cause a deterioration. Witztum (1994), for instance, constructs a theoretical model showing how a change from an economic system in which all income is earned from effort at work to one in which a part of income is derived from capital, may lead to a second best economic result. The model assumes that popular perceptions of economic ideology would lag behind events and that individuals will judge and react in terms of previous beliefs, probably favourable towards the social messages of socialism.

It is not necessary to concur with such a model to concede that it was possible to motivate managers adequately in the Communist system. It is true that in recent years productivity of labour and capital was inferior to that in capitalist countries. Yet post-war command economies enjoyed relatively fast economic growth for some years and some enterprises were well run. If pay structures and differentials are carefully set it need not matter to salaried managers whether they are employed by a public or by a private body. Very substantial numbers of people work in public sector bodies in successful OECD economies. Efficiency, however, may be another matter. A given amount of effort may be applied in a productive, profit-enhancing fashion, or alternatively, in a wasteful and fruitless way.

As a result of being privatized businesses may be managed in ways which are more productive because they are more closely focused on profit-making. Furthermore, if the level of long-term economic confidence amongst managers is raised as a result of the implementation of a large-scale privatization programme, then overall performance may increase.

Privatization is widely regarded as a means of fostering entrepreneurial innovation. Even former market socialists, such as Brus and Laski (1989), appear to have concluded that the lack of entrepreneurial activity is where the weakness of non-private enterprise is most evident. As Berliner (1992) has observed, innovation is essential for the success of a modern economy. Entrepreneurship seeks innovation because it increases expected future earnings, which are then reflected in the present value of the business. In his words: 'It is that prospect of a large increase in private wealth that energizes the innovational activity of capitalism'. Entrepreneurship will thrive most vigorously in privatized businesses.

Major (1993) has remarked that in some EITs the role of entrepreneurs has been invested with more ambitious purposes. They have been seen by some political groups in Hungary, Poland and elsewhere as the core of a middle class which will sustain the new capitalist order. Privatization thus gains a wider social aim in which wealth-holding becomes as important as wealth-creation, and entrepreneurs become rentiers as well as innovators.

De novo business development

Without careful definition of terms, discussion of this topic is liable to become circular. The creation of entirely new businesses, as opposed to the disposal of state enterprises, is a major contributor to the privatization of economies - privatization in its widest sense - so anything which furthers it may be regarded as desirable. The question to be assessed here, though, is whether transferring companies from the public to the private sector will be beneficial for new business formation and can be justified partly on those grounds.

The two main ways in which it might be so are in the release of people and assets from the former state sector, as a result of either liquidation of state firms or restructuring of privatized firms. Since the state in the command economy was the monopoly employer, de novo businesses in EITs will by definition employ members of the workforce who were previously state employees. Allowing for the fact that parallel employment is widespread in Central and Eastern Europe and that some people will remain employed by the state whilst founding their own businesses, a spirited origination of new businesses is much more likely from people

276

with time and energy available because of unemployment. Similarly, the unwanted physical assets of state industries may find a more profitable use in new private businesses. Privatization may also give rise to demand for sub-contracted supplies from new businesses and cause a strengthening of the legal framework in which they operate.

The growth of private business registrations has been luxuriant. These are a reasonable proxy for private business starts, even though it is not easy to discern how many of them were transformed state businesses rather than entirely new creations. The large numbers involved suggest, however, that very many were de novo businesses. In Hungary, the number of private sector companies rose from 6,607 at 1st January 1989 to 36,549 at 1st October 1991, a nearly six-fold increase (Riecke and Antal, 1993). In the former Czechoslovakia the number of 'registered privately-owned units' rose from 488,361 at the end of 1990 to 1,338,353 only one year later (Frydman et al., 1993a). There has also been rapid growth in Russia. Detailed analytical research needs to be done in this area. In the absence of it at this stage, there appears to be no close statistical correlation between the number of new businesses registered and the pace of privatization, and any causal relationship must remain supposititious.

Privatization models

Privatization justifications tend to be associated with more general models. In principle the proposition that a market economy must be founded on a broad extent of private ownership is sound on theoretical and practical grounds. Given that the state owned everything in EITs at the start, as was virtually the case in Russia or Czechoslovakia (though not in Poland), privatization will therefore have to take place - it is the theoretical sine qua non. This unremarkable conclusion, though, reveals nothing about the timing or manner of the privatization: it does not establish that privatization must happen before other changes, nor is it self-evident that it must take any one course. Most difficult of all, it does not reveal the ultimate destination.

In metaphorical terms many EITs have embraced privatization as a highly visible way of travelling as quickly as possible away from where they do not wish to be; almost anywhere would be better than where they were,

277

and yet where they are going is not certain. Most of the imagined destinations have been modelled on the USA or, to a lesser extent, one or more of the Western European states. This may arise because of the USA's position as hegemon of the capitalist world and because more advisers emanate from that country than from any other. It may also be connected with the reluctance of the intellectuals of viable alternative capitalist models, such as Japan or France, to engage in ideological imperialism.

Robin Marris has pointed out (Marris, 1992) how disagreements in the field of economics can often be explained by the implicit use of different definitions, and the above may be a case in point. He identifies five stereotypes of economic systems: Nineteenth Century Capitalism, Neoclassical Capitalism, Democratic Socialism, Twentieth Century 'managerial' Capitalism and Communism. He claims that only the last two have ever existed in the twentieth century, that the only realistic objective in EITs is managerial capitalism and that this should be the practical objective of EITs, *faute de mieux*.

This author would argue that Marris glosses too lightly over the differences that exist between the economies described as capitalist and that some of them may be illuminating in the privatization debate.

There are really two kinds of relevant model - those concerned with the process of privatization and those concerned with the desired ends of privatization. Means and ends are obviously linked but conceptually distinct. This chapter will continue by briefly examining the applicability to EITs of models drawn from OECD countries, and then describe some of the home-grown solutions.

Historical or non-EIT models

The British model. Walters (1991) advanced a clear prescription for EITs: 'I have no alternative save the Thatcher model - with perhaps a souped-up engine. We know that works. That is a lot.' This model involved restructuring first, selling state industries over a decade or more, and aiming for a very small state sector in the end. Perhaps it is unfair now to challenge Walters with hindsight. The last few years have shown that many of the prerequisites mentioned above for the implementation of a Thatcher model in EITs were lacking and that it has not been seriously attempted.

278

The French model. There appear to have been several factors which contributed to the ability of the French government to privatize in fourteen months assets equivalent in value and extent to those which in Britain it took Mrs Thatcher's government six years to privatize. Amongst these were: underpricing, a carefully devised cocktail of shareholders, the securitization of savings, decreasing inflation and a government programme to restore profitability to public sector companies before privatization.

Andreff (1992) made recommendations for the governments of EITs based on an analysis of these French conditions. They are more realistic than the application of the Thatcher model would have been and include sale rather than free distribution of shares; the establishment of stable core shareholders, if necessary from amongst the former *nomenclature*; and the willingness to sell to foreigners, perhaps through debt-equity swaps. But he also recommends creating a favourable economic background, scarcely a useful suggestion, and predicts that any government following the recommendations may not win the next democratic elections, which though possible is hardly encouraging.

Echoes of French practice can be found in Hungarian sales to foreigners and in the core shareholders of the Polish Mass Privatization Programme.

The Japanese model. Although the Japanese government has privatized a number of companies, the Japanese example is less useful for the example of its privatization process than for pointing to interesting alternative destinations. The process has been described as 'very similar' to that in the UK (Uno, 1990) but the structure of the economic system in which it took place was very different. Acs and Fitzroy (1994), among others, see Japan as a relevant model for EITs.

EIT models

For all the protestations by some commentators (e.g., Galbraith, Nove) that the privatization models favoured for EITs are alien or inappropriate, some of the processes used have been highly innovative and the results so far quite diverse - the act of emulation may also be an act of creation. Even from the incomplete and unreliable data which is so far available on the practical outcome of privatization one feature of it is very clear: that is diversity - of time-scale, of methods used and of the shape of the resulting private sector. The outcomes are as diverse as the justifications

279

elaborated inside and outside EITs for privatizating at all. Some of the prescriptions made originally may need to be revised in the light of this experience.

It is much too early to make firm observations about the final structure of the future privatized EITs. Two aspects of the privatization process, however, are new and may in time be seen as having wider relevance: spontaneous or 'wild' privatization, and voucher privatization.

Spontaneous privatization. A broad definition of this is the acquisition by managers, workers or officials of enterprises with which they are connected in ways which are not fully regulated. It can range from the illegal defraudation of the state at one extreme to a properly agreed management buy-out at the other. It is rarely viewed favourably in the literature, often being seen as an alliance of workers and managers to preserve the status quo, rather than as an over-enthusiastic pursuit of entrepreneurial instincts. It is impossible to quantify accurately the extent of this type of privatization, since much of it appears to have been semi-covert. Examples are given in several recent sources from Bulgaria, Estonia, Hungary, Poland and Russia (see Frydman *et al.*, 1993a, 1993b; Major, 1993; Estrin, 1994) and the phenomenon is believed to have occurred in most EITs.

There can be many objections to spontaneous privatization: it benefits the old guard, it causes popular resentment, it delays necessary reforms, and it fails to uphold nascent property rights. It will require careful empirical research to decide the issue. It seems highly unlikely that spontaneous privatization will ever be a recommendable model, but the devil's advocate might argue that it could in principle have some advantages. It achieves a rapid transfer of assets from the public sector, admittedly genuine in effect only if the state pursues tight budgetary control; it helps to build the nucleus of a property-owning middle class; the new owners would be thoroughly acquainted with their asset and would potentially stand to lose their job as well as their newly acquired capital if they were to fail. Time will tell whether these arguments will be lent any more support by history than by the current governments of EITs.

Voucher/mass distribution privatization. The EIT voucher privatization programmes are audacious and historically unique. They are novel approaches to unusual problems and may yet be found to have some

280

applicability elsewhere. They represent the first clearly original model for economic action to have emerged from the Central and Eastern European reform process.

The Czech Republic, Slovakia and Russia are the prime examples of countries which have implemented radical voucher schemes, with Poland, Lithuania and Romania attempting less ambitious variants. The task here is not to describe the technical details of the programmes but to draw attention to the salient features. These are:

1. free, or virtually free, distribution of privatized assets,
2. very widespread dispersion of assets amongst the population,
3. substantial proportion of state assets privatized,
4. creation of intermediary institutions to exercise rights on behalf of individual shareholders,
5. a relatively high degree of transparency in the disposal process.

There is one main difference between the Czech and Russian schemes on the one hand and the Polish on the other. The former allow voucher holders either to bid directly for shares in companies or to trade in vouchers for participation in a fund which acts on their behalf. The latter requires participating citizens to receive shares in privatization mutual funds, which in turn directly own company shares.

Advantages attach to all of the above features and disadvantages to some of them. The putatively positive aspects are that the programme does not need to call on a pool of savings, it achieves rapid results, it is perceived as fair and open by the populace, and it gives rise to institutions which have a useful governance role. The potentially negative are that it fails to raise revenues for the state, it risks excessive dispersal of ownership leading to weak control, and it catapults companies prematurely into the cold water of the private sector.

If they turn out to be more than superficially successful they may give rise to some interesting consequences. These could include a numerically large share-owning class, even after an expected gradual concentration of ownership, and a new form of capitalist corporate governance based on equity-owning investment companies rather than banks. Clearly taxation, national culture and the accidents of politics and economics will bear heavily on the outcome. At present all that can be said with certainty is that voucher or mass distribution schemes have been associated with the

281

most rapid and widespread change in nominal ownership from public to private. In that limited sense they are the most successful of all the schemes attempted.

Conclusion

In summary, this chapter has noted the wide range of meanings ascribed to privatization. The conceptions derived from the experience of state asset disposals in OECD countries such as the UK or France have been found narrow or inappropriate when applied in Central and Eastern European reforming economies. Some of the advice offered by Western commentators has turned out to be unhelpful. Perhaps this should not be surprising: the situations in Western and Eastern Europe were very different. Moreover, an accident of history brought the collapse of Communism in Russia and Eastern Europe at a time when privatization and the use of markets were favoured by intellectual fashion and practised by governments. What advice would have been offered by Western consultants to EITs if university economics had still been dominated by Keynesianism and governments had still been keen advocates of nationalization? Would they, indeed, have been called *economies* in transition or *polities* in transition?

Privatization needs to be widely construed to have useful meaning in an EIT context, and has to take account of unique circumstances. Many of the theoretical and practical preconditions for the implementation of privatization in Britain or France were found on analysis above to be lacking in EITs. This does not invalidate the attempt to privatize in EITs but it does require that any attempted measures should be well suited to local conditions and it calls for a touch of humility on the part of those outsiders offering prescriptions.

Examination of the justifications for privatization found that the widespread belief in privatization as a theoretical prerequisite for other reforms is largely well-founded but that many problems and weaknesses are associated with implementation and that changing nominal ownership is certainly not a sufficient basis for creating a market economy. Privatization is likely to be economically beneficial only when accompanied by many other changes. It is likely to take several years for the effects of many of these reforms to be measurable.

282

Finally, a variety of models for the process and for the outcome of privatization were analyzed. It was observed that new, perhaps transferable, models of process have emerged in Central and Eastern Europe. The process which has led to the greatest transfer of assets from the public to the private sector, the voucher scheme, had never before been tried in human history. Here, the home-developed solution produced the most remarkable immediate results.

Russia confounded the doubters with a series of voucher auctions conducted in conditions akin at times to the robber capitalism of the American Wild West. The Czech Republic, in calmer fashion, transformed most of the adult population into the nominal, and perhaps temporary, owners of equities in a bold stroke of which Margaret Thatcher might be proud.

As for outcomes, Anglo-American market-based models of corporate governance have been over-emphasized, at the expense of models inspired by Japanese or Continental European experience. In any case EITs have been developing their own pragmatic solutions even when the ultimate destination may have been unclear. In effect new designs of corporate ownership and control are being created. Because of the peculiar historical conditions these are likely to differ significantly from the models which originally inspired them and to involve the invention of new variants of capitalism itself. Whether these resemble Frankenstein's monster or the perfect forms of a Renaissance sculpture only time will tell.

Notes

1.   There are notable academic exceptions, such as the late Alec Nove.
2.   Council for Mutual Economic Assistance, or Comecon, the defunct Soviet-bloc trading organization.
3.   *Economist*, 8 - 14 April 1995, p. 3 of Russian Survey.
4.   *Economist, op.cit.*, p. 9.
5.   *Economist, op.cit.*, p. 10.

References

Acs, Zoltan and Fitzroy, Felix (1994), 'A constitution for privatizing large Eastern enterprises', *Economics of Transition*, vol. 2, no. 1, pp. 83-94.

Andreff, Wladimir (1992), 'French privatization techniques and experience: a model for Central-Eastern Europe?', in Baldassarri, M., Paganetto, L. and Phelps, S (eds), *Privatization Processes in Eastern Europe*, Macmillan, Basingstoke

Baldassarri, M. and Paganetto, L. (1993), 'Introduction', in Baldassarri, M., Paganetto, L. and Phelps, S. (eds), *Privatization Processes in Eastern Europe*, Macmillan, Basingstoke.

Baldassarri, M., Paganetto, L. and Phelps, S. (eds) (1993), *Privatization Processes in Eastern Europe*, Macmillan, Basingstoke.

Batt, Judy (1994), Political Dimensions of Privatization in Eastern Europe', in Estrin, Sail (ed.), *Privatization in Eastern Europe*, Longman, Harlow.

Berliner, Joseph S. (1992), 'Privatization in the USSR', in Keren, M. and Ofer, G. (eds), *Trials of Transition*, Westview Press, Boulder and Oxford.

Blanchard, O. (1991), *Reform in Eastern Europe*, MIT Press, Cambridge, Mass.

Brus, Wlodzimierz and Laski, Kazimierz (1989), *From Marx to Markets: Socialism in Search of an Economic System*, Clarendon Press, Oxford.

Canning, A. and Hare, P. (1994) 'The privatization process - economic and political aspects of the Hungarian approach' in Estrin, S. (ed.), *Privatization in Central and Eastern Europe*, Longman, Harlow.

Estrin, Saul (ed.) (1994), *Privatization in Central and Eastern Europe*, Longman, Harlow.

Frydman, R., Rapaczynski, A., Earle, J.S., *et al.* (1993a), *The Privatization Process in Central Europe*, Central European University Press, London.

Frydman, R., Rapaczysnski, A., Earle, J.S., *et al.* (1993b), *The Privatization Process in Russia, Ukraine, and the Baltic States*, Central European University Press, London.

Frydman, R., and Rapaczynski, A. (1994), *Privatization in Eastern Europe: is the State withering away?*, Central European University Press, London.

Galbraith, John (1992), 'The Rush to Capitalism', in Kennett, D and Lieberman, M. (eds), *The Road to Capitalism*, Granny Dryden Press, Fort Worth.

Hayek, Friedrich von (1960), *The Constitution of Liberty*, Routledge & Kegan Paul, London.

Keren, Michael, and Ofer, Guy (1992), *Trials of Transition*, Westview Press, Boulder and Oxford.

Kennet, David, and Lieberman, Marc (eds) (1992), *The Road to Capitalism*, Granny Dryden Press, Fort Worth.

Kornai, Janos (1990a), *The Road to a Free Economy - Shifting from a Socialist System: The Example of Hungary*, W.W.Norton, New York.

Kornai, Janos (1990b), *Vision and Reality, Market and State*, Harvester Wheatsheaf, Hemel Hempstead.

Lavoie, D. (1985), *Rivalry and Central Planning: The Socialist Calculation Debate Reconsidered*, Cambridge University Press, Cambridge.

Lipton, David and Sachs, Jeffrey (1990), 'Privatization in Eastern Europe: The Case of Poland,' *Brookings Papers on Economic Activity: 2*, pp. 293-341.

Major, Ivan (1993), *Privatization in Eastern Europe*, Edward Elgar, Aldershot.

Marris, Robin (1992), 'Privatization, Markets and Managers', in Targetti, F. (ed.), *Privatization in Europe*, Dartmouth, Aldershot.

McAuley, Alastair (1992), 'Market failure versus state failure: the scope for privatization in a planned economy', in Targetti, F. (ed.) *Privatization in Europe*, Dartmouth, Aldershot.

Mises, Ludwig von (1951), *Socialism - an economic and sociological analysis*, English edition, Jonathan Cape, London.

Peck, Merton J. and Richardson, Thomas J. (eds) (1991), *What is to be done? Proposals for the Soviet Transition to the Market*, Yale University Press, New Haven and London.

Portes, Richard (ed.) (1993), *Economic Transformation in Central Europe*, Centre for Economic Policy Research, London.

Riecke, Werner, and Antal, Laszlo (1993), 'Hungary: sound money, fiscal problems', in Portes, R. (ed.), *Economic Transformation in Central Europe*, Centre for Economic Policy Research, London.

Stiglitz, G. (1993), 'Some Theoretical Aspects of Privatization: Applications to Eastern Europe' in Baldassari, M., Paganetto, L. and

Phelps, S. (eds), *Privatization Processes in Eastern Europe*, Macmillan, Basingstoke.

Targetti, Ferdinando (ed.) (1992), *Privatization in Europe*, Dartmouth, Aldershot.

Uno, Kimio (1990), 'Privatization and the Creation of a Commercial Banking System', in *Peck and Richardson*, 1991.

Vickers, J. and Yarrow, G. (1988) *Privatization: An Economic Analysis*, MIT Press, Boston Mass.

Walters, Alan (1991), 'Misapprehensions on Privatization', *International Economic Insights*, January/February, vol. II, no. 1.

Winiecki, Jan (1993), *Post-Soviet-Type Economies in Transition*, Avebury, Aldershot.

Wijnbergen, Sweder van (1993), 'Enterprise reform in Eastern Europe', *Economics of Transition*, vol. 1(1), pp. 21-38.

Witztum, Amos (1994), 'Privatization, distribution and economic justice: efficiency in transition', in Estrin, S. 1994.

12 An Inter-Disciplinary Approach to the Analysis of Privatization and Marketization

DEBORAH FOSTER AND DEREK BRADDON

Introduction

In this concluding chapter we will put forward our case for advocating the analysis of privatization and marketization within an interdisciplinary social science framework. We will do so by reference to themes in chapters presented in the book, though we are not principally concerned to provide a summary of these chapters; rather, we aim to develop a contextual framework within which issues arising from debates on privatization and marketization can be located. The purpose of this is to explore some of the broader issues of political, economic and sociological importance in relation to some current academic debates in contemporary society. By doing so, we are attempting to forge links between different areas of discussion on privatization, which are often characterized by what might be described as a 'localized' approach, whereby changes in specific areas of public service provision are analyzed in relation to isolated policy developments and within disciplinary boundaries. Whilst we acknowledge the merits of such an approach, which has provided valuable detailed evidence of changes in public services, we also believe that there is a broader picture which needs to be addressed. This would benefit from a synthesis of more 'localized' debates on the impact of market policies in the public sector and would identify key areas which interrelate with wider processes of change. Such a project would necessarily be inter-disciplinary in its approach and analysis.

Privatization and marketization : The case for an interdisciplinary approach

Chapters previously presented in this book cover a broad range of themes and issues commonly united by their evaluation of the impact of policies of privatization and marketization. The breadth of issues explored demonstrates the degree of interest within the social sciences in such policies and the variety of approaches that can be taken in analysing their outcomes. Contributors concentrating on their own areas of specialism, in both a disciplinary and subject-specific sense, have provided a multi-disciplinary perspective on issues of privatization and marketization. The apparent disciplinary intention of the book is however deceptive, for whilst the book does provide contrasting approaches of disciplinary relevance, it also reveals the extent to which debates that have emerged from privatization and marketization naturally transcend these boundaries. We argue, therefore, that the politics of privatization cannot be divorced from economic and sociological debate and cannot be claimed as the preserve of any one social science discipline. Indeed, if we attempt to separate out issues into subject discipline frameworks it becomes evident that many disciplinary distinctions are false, and that policies of privatization encapsulate aspects of the political, economic and social when actively applied to an analysis of the policy process and its subsequent outcomes. So whilst it may be prudent to acknowledge that the political scientist might focus on a specific aspect of privatization (e.g., the neo-liberal ideology underpinning it, particularly in the UK and US); and that the economist may adopt a different focus (e.g., the impact and character of new markets) to the sociologist, it is our contention that benefits can be gained from a fusion of these different approaches.

A truly interdisciplinary social science perspective needs to include significant aspects of the impact of policies of privatization on the political, economic and social spheres. Given that these are difficult to separate out when addressing a range of policies which characteristically challenge many established norms and values in each of these areas, we will proceed by identifying a number of key themes or debates of relevance across each discipline, around which further discussion can be organized. This approach fulfils two objectives. First, the identification of issues which are central to current debates across the social sciences provides a broader analytical framework for the investigation of the impact of privatization and marketization. Second, such an inter-disciplinary approach can bring together social scientists from different disciplines, to develop new ways of looking at problems in contemporary society, which may go beyond, but interrelate with, privatization debates. This is certainly worthwhile in terms of advancing academic debate, though could be subject to the criticism that the themes selected will be value-laden, given the politically controversial nature of this investigation. It is therefore necessary to stress that our list of topics is not exclusive and is flexible enough to be added to, as our understanding of the subject is enlarged. It will also be necessary to take account of *context* and *change* - relevant factors when addressing current and future post-national developments in the European Union and Eastern Europe.

From our evaluation of themes raised within this text we have identified six key areas around which further discussion can be organized and developed. These are:

1.   the role of the state;
2.   the role and nature of markets;
3.   the concept and definition of welfare (including the concept of public service);
4.   factors associated with post-industrial and social structural change;
5.   post-nationalism and globalization;
6.   social citizenship.

Whilst we acknowledge that each of these areas individually forms the basis of substantial contemporary debate, not all of this debate has explicitly sought to address issues of privatization and marketization. This is true, for example, of recent discussions of the concept of citizenship, which have amongst other things, been concerned with aspects of welfare rights (and duties) and developments in relation to the European Union, but have not featured strongly in mainstream literature on privatization, despite the fact that the outcomes of such policies have a direct bearing on social citizenship (see Buttle, Chapter 2). An evaluation of the UK government's interpretation and utilization of the concept of citizenship in the public sector, represented by 'Citizens Charters' is one point of reference for further analysis on this subject, although we intend to extend debate beyond these somewhat limited parameters. To return to the six areas of

289

interest identified above, we will show in the rest of this chapter how each relates to aspects of the privatization debate and demonstrate their relevant inclusion in an inter-disciplinary approach to the subject. Practical limitations of space of course prevent us from exploring each area in great depth and therefore our main objective is to establish a framework for further development.

Privatization : The broader context

An appropriate starting point in any analysis of the significance of policies of privatization and marketization is to examine the role of the state. Such evaluations in the realm of political science have often been concerned with investigating the development and content of ideologies that have sought to popularize policies of privatization and marketization. This has been particularly important in the UK, given the predominance of market based policies in the public sector, and the subsequent impact of neo-liberal ideology on the culture of public service. The promotion of policies by the New Right, incorporating a vision of minimal state responsibility in the provision of public services, has contested dominant post-war paradigms around welfare (see Buttle, Chapter 2). In turn, this has disrupted old value and belief systems relating to the role that the state should play in directly providing welfare and services to the public, emphasizing instead the role of the market and, somewhat paradoxically, state management of that market. Moreover, in the provision of basic services to its population, for example gas, water, electricity and transport, the state has disengaged from assumptions that planning and responsibility lies with the nation state, preferring to adopt a competitive, consumerist, model of service provision, which has subsequently resulted in the involvement of a number of international players.

The extent to which the role of the state has been reduced in the area of public service provision, as a consequence of policies of privatization and marketization, is open to debate. Undoubtedly its role has changed, though in many instances overt state intervention has simply been replaced with covert intervention. In the UK we have witnessed an increase in regulatory activity (often beyond democratic control, e.g. quangos), and the introduction of legislation by central government into public service areas in an effort to create, sustain and - significantly - control new

290

markets. Essentially what we have seen is the application of a radical political ideology aimed at de-politicizing public services via the imposition of policies of a political/ideological nature. In many instances this has created a new phenomenon which could be termed 'state regulated market bureaucracies', whereby the introduction of market principles into public service areas, which by their nature must be seen to be fair and equitable in their provision, require regulation by the state through bureaucratic means and greater centralized control. Decisions about the distribution of limited resources within the public service sector are by their very nature political, and claims to the contrary are therefore, in essence, misleading. Furthermore, in relation to the privatized utilities, in the absence of real competition the continued role of the state is necessary to regulate their activities in the public interest; this again amounts to political intervention. What this, therefore, serves to demonstrate is that the state finds it difficult to withdraw from areas of the public sphere that directly bear on the welfare of its citizens (a point to which we will return when addressing the concepts of welfare and social citizenship).

If we now examine some of the economic objectives of privatization in relation to the state, we can see similar problems arising. The economic rationale for the privatization of public sector utilities in the UK, according to Helm *et al* (1992 p.11):

> has been to remove the constraints of public sector ownership and....to give incentives to private sector management to improve efficiency and to expose managers to the disciplines of the capital market.

The drive for enhanced efficiency lies at the core of the economic case for privatization. Economists define the term carefully as 'Pareto efficiency'; i.e., a point achieved from which it is impossible to improve the economic conditions affecting one person without making another worse off. However, as is often the case with real world examples of privatization, if the competitive system that emerges from that process is imperfect, or if other forms of market failure arise, Pareto efficiency cannot be achieved.

Economic efficiency takes two principal forms: allocative and technical. Allocative efficiency implies that it is impossible to rearrange the amount, composition and quality of outputs without making one consumer better off at the expense of another. Technical efficiency focuses upon production inputs and implies that it is impossible to rearrange inputs in the production process of an economy to obtain more of one good without sacrificing part of another. As Jackson and Price (1994 p. 9) contend, 'the popular literature on privatization has tended to focus upon technical efficiency and ignore allocative efficiency'.

In the UK, many planned privatizations have been accompanied by a prior period during which the performance of the organization to be offered to the market is targeted for improvement. The drive for efficiency gains prior to privatization, therefore, both makes the organization more attractive to potential purchasers but also questions the extent to which further efficiency gains can be delivered by actual privatization. Where this has happened, the justification for privatization moves from the economic arena and is located more clearly within that of political ideology (for a fuller discussion, see Ott and Hartley, 1991).

Other economic objectives underpinning the drive towards privatization have included the reduction of state spending on public services through the introduction of competitive mechanisms and the creation of new markets, with an emphasis on greater efficiency and value for money. In turn, the desire to reduce state spending on services is frequently driven by the urgent need to address a nation's deteriorating fiscal position. Privatization is seen as the most effective means to both reduce state spending and to enforce market discipline in the provision of key services, thereby securing a more efficient allocation and use of resources. Critics contend, however, that privatization alone is insufficient to meet the desired goal. More important, the entire sector or industry being privatized needs to be completely restructured to ensure competitiveness if real gains in efficiency are to materialize. Particularly for natural monopolies, it is essential to implement regulation and supervision mechanisms to prevent private monopolies acquiring excessive profits, measures which may, in turn, reduce actual efficiency gains. Improvements in efficiency, then, do not follow privatization per se but may flow instead from the associated industrial restructuring that accompanies the move towards the competitive provision of a service.

Privatization without gains in efficiency through industrial restructuring will have little beneficial impact upon a nation's fiscal stance. Where state-owned enterprises are sold at a realistic market price, the sales value will approximate the net present value of future after-tax earnings. Privatization provides the state with initial sales proceeds but denies it the flow of future earnings. Essentially, all that happens is a trade-off between current and future net proceeds with minimal consequences for the fiscal position. Evidence from Eastern Europe (Schwartz and Lopes, 1993, p. 14) suggests that enhanced allocation and use of resources that may be derived from the privatization process may only be achieved at the expense of privatization proceeds, thereby eliminating any positive impact on fiscal stance.

Underpinning the economic rationale for privatization is the contentious issue of the appropriate range of services that the public sector should continue to provide or, alternatively, the exact range of publicly-provided services which a citizen may reasonably expect to be offered by the state. Orthodox economics would restrict (or, perhaps, extend) such provision to include a range of public goods which cannot: 'even in principle be provided by the invisible hand of market forces' (Alt and Chrystal, 1983, p. 176). Public goods are usually defined by their particular characteristics. The consumption of the public good by one individual does not adversely affect consumption by others. Similarly, once a public good is provided to a community, no member of that community can be excluded from enjoying the consequent benefits.

Having identified which goods are 'public' in nature, the state needs to decide how much of each to supply. Economic theory provides a relatively simple answer: supply up to the point at which the marginal rates of substitution and transformation are equal. However, in reality, there is no mechanism available (other than the ballot box) by which individuals can make clear their valuation of the benefits derived from public goods. Furthermore, the possibility of 'free rider' problems may encourage some individuals to understate the benefits they derive from public good provision. What is particularly striking about the recent experience of privatization in the UK is the degree to which even those areas of the public sector that, traditionally, would have been considered to be providers of the most basic and genuine public goods (e.g. the defence sector - see Braddon et al, Chapter 5) have been exposed to the dynamics of market forces.

The economic objectives of privatization have been pursued through either the wholesale privatization of previously state-owned industries or the introduction/imposition of devices aimed at creating competition. Yet the nature and role of these new markets are highly controversial, for they have required state intervention to create or sustain them (i.e. political intervention) and have often resulted in little more than the substitution of public for private sector monopolies (a feature most evident in privatized utilities). The result has been a somewhat confusing situation whereby public policy is driven by a dogmatic assumption that markets are always good, whilst the distinctive and enduring basis of public service values stresses, amongst other things, equity, responsiveness to need and social justice, which are objectives not wholly compatible with market approaches. This incompatibility might be illustrated by the simple example that whilst in the private sector price acts as the regulator between supply and demand: in the public sector this is inappropriate given that supply and therefore effective demand is often controlled by rationed budgets, which necessarily require the application of political judgement to regulate and evaluate entitlements and priorities, rather than what can be sold (see Flynn, 1993, for further discussion). In addition, those services now outside the public sector (water, electricity, etc.) are providing essential services to a captive market whose only means of taking their business elsewhere is to move to a different area. Comparisons between the public and private sector markets and the newly created monopolistic private service markets are therefore both economically and politically problematic.

The role and character of newly created public service markets have also been the focus of attention within the disciplines of sociology and public administration. Some debates, particularly within areas concerned with the sociology of organizations and the impact of public policy on organizational culture within the public services, have drawn on emerging literature relating to what has been termed, 'New Public Management' (NPM) (see Pollitt, 1993). This literature is of interest because it attempts to assess how private sector practices, introduced through market mechanisms, co-exist with public sector aims and values and how managerial practices have changed as a consequence.

Pollitt (1993) investigates the ways in which changes in managerial ideology have had concrete effects on organizational practices and culture. The construction of new discourses within public service organizations (see Foster, Chapter 3), to accommodate the new competitive culture, has brought about identifiable changes in the ways services are run, although how far these effectively integrate with public service values, or merely act as 'window-dressing' to provide evidence of 'conversion' to market-based principles, is questionable. Underlying many of the ideas which constitute NPM is the belief that the public services are moving away from a highly standardized, bureaucratic, unresponsive mode of service delivery, towards a more flexible, responsive approach more in character with the expectations of people in the 1980s and 1990s. However, if we examine the Thatcher administrations' approach to the public sector, as Pollitt (1993, p. 188) rightly argues, it opted for 'narrow and mechanistic' solutions, concentrating on detailed measurement of effort and activity in its emphasis on efficiency, rather than quality and flexibility. This is evident in, for example, legislation regulating compulsory competitive tendering (CCT), where efficiency is measured in terms of savings made on contracts awarded in the CCT process, regardless of quality; and where contracts are regulated by stringent, inflexible specifications which incur punitive sanctions if not met. Such an approach is described by Pollitt (1993) as neo-Taylorist, given the way practices advocated resemble those put forward by the school of Scientific Management:

> The chief features of both classic Taylorism and its 1980s descendant were that they were above all concerned with *control* and that this control was to be achieved through an essentially *administrative* approach - the fixing of effort levels that were to be expressed in quantitative terms' (*ibid.*, p. 188, italics in original (Pollitt, 1993).

This approach, whilst aimed at measuring and controlling the activities of public service organizations, was simultaneously dependent on the deregulation or relinquishing of state control over employment relationships. The latter strategy aimed to de-standardize nationally negotiated terms and conditions of employment, thus allowing local labour market factors to influence their determination, while also giving greater power to local managers. This could only be achieved, however, if internal resistance to change from the traditionally powerful public service trade unions was weakened and industrial relations were de-politicized. Policies of privatization and marketization aimed to achieve these objectives, either by removing large groups of public service employees from the public sector per se, or by forcing them through competitive mechanisms to compete for their own jobs, often on worse terms and conditions of employment (Foster, 1993). Changes that have occurred in the public service labour market are significant and will be related to later discussions on post-industrialism and social structural change.

The argument that control has been paramount in transforming the public services is consistent with both the interventionist stance of the UK government in transforming the public sector and with early, purely quantitative, emphases on efficiency and value-for-money. Lack of concern for quality, nevertheless, sat somewhat uneasily with both the perceived benefits of market-based provision and the development of a new language within the public services, which included the re-conceptualization of users of services as consumers or customers; inconsistencies which the Major administration in 1990 attempted to address. Subsequent reforms included the introduction of highly managed quasi-markets (for example, in the NHS and education), alongside a new emphasis on quality and greater attention on the 'consumer' (Pollitt, 1993, p. 180). These became influential in shaping the philosophies inherent in New Public Management and the government itself gave clear guidance on the 'role of public sector managers in buying services on behalf of citizens' (Treasury 1991, p. ii) in its 1991 White Paper, *Competing for Quality*. This was accompanied by a campaign led by the Prime Minister himself to promote the idea of 'Citizens Charters' as a means of making public services appear more responsive. But in his assessment of this new equation of NPM and Citizens Charters Pollitt (1993) argues:

> The role accorded to citizens… is mainly one of feeding back, via questionnaires and other market research, their (dis)satisfaction levels with what managements have designed and delivered. NPM, in other words, is not so much a charter for citizen empowerment as managerialism with a human face'(Pollitt, 1993, p. 187).

Moreover, Citizens Charters, whilst outlining what the new public service 'customer' should expect from the service provider and offering channels for complaint, has done nothing to extend their legal rights.

A central problem with the new conception of the public service user as customer is the way in which it individualizes the user rather than addresses the collective needs of all. Whilst comparisons of the private and public sector market are being popularly invoked by some, the reality is that the customer/consumer in the public sector market-place is constrained by both their entitlement to services and their choice of services, which is often exercised on their behalf by the public agency concerned. Moreover, even when evidence of consumer choice does exist, it is open to question whether choice is always of primary concern in the delivery of public services. Barnes and Prior (1995) whilst acknowledging the value of choice in certain services, for example those which meet very personal needs (e.g. therapy), also provide evidence through research that choice is sometimes inappropriate and can generate confusion and uncertainty, which may actually result in disempowering the user. They argue therefore that in some circumstances (especially when the user is vulnerable (e.g. elderly or sick), that:

> at the point of consumption, values such as confidence, security and trust may be more appreciated by users than the opportunity for choice' (Barnes and Prior, 1995, p. 58).

Moreover they add:

> Choice is invoked as a mantra replacing analysis of the circumstances and ways in which people use services and whether choosing has real meaning in such circumstances' (Barnes and Prior, 1995, p. 54).

The actual meaning and relevance of choice within the public sector market does appear to be confusing. One reason for this is the way in which choice as promoted by the New Right is invoked as an individual rather than a collective right. Whilst a consensus seems to exist across the political spectrum, from right to left, that public services have in the past been unresponsive to public needs, the solutions proposed in addressing this problem differ. Alternatives to the current consumerist model have tended to stress public participation, accountability and empowerment of the users through their collective involvement in service provision. Such alternatives have been espoused by opposition parties and trade unions and have been in evidence within local government. During the mid-1980s what was termed the 'public-service orientation' (PSO) became increasingly popular in local government circles (Stewart and Clarke, 1987) and its advocates distinguished it from current approaches because it stressed 'concern for the citizen as well as the customer... For this reason issues such as participation and public accountability are raised' (Stewart and Clarke, 1987, p. 170). Recent interest in work in the United States by

Osborne and Gaebler (1993) on 're-inventing government' has focused attention on devising a radically different way of doing business in the public sector. The evolution of 'entrepreneurial government' requires public sector organizations to seek new ways to maximize the productivity, efficiency and effectiveness of government-managed enterprise. Osborne and Gaebler contend that privatization is simply the wrong starting point for a discussion of the role of government. The key issue is not the 'ownership' of a particular good or service but the process by which a market or public institution produces and supplies it. The issues that matter most relate to incentives that operate within the process of service provision, whether this is in the hands of public or private institutions. Motivation, accountability, the capacity for flexible response, the incorporation of quality/reward stimuli and so on are the hallmarks of the effective, responsive organization and are not necessarily attributes of a privatized service which, all too often, may degenerate into a private monopoly where higher costs and inefficiency can result.

Whilst this final chapter is too brief to explore the PSO and other approaches in detail (see Stewart and Clarke, 1987; Stewart and Ranson, 1988; Pollitt, 1993), it does illustrate conflicts between current approaches within the public sector and alternatives or critiques which tend to emphasize decentralization and participation, rather than what is currently being experienced - centralization. Moreover, this aspect of our debate has yet again highlighted the need incorporate collectivist concepts of social citizenship into public service provision.

Questions about the role and nature of markets in public service provision and the role and responsibilities of the state naturally lead us to consider further how the state through the use of markets has sought to re-define the concept and definition of welfare, and how the concept of a public sector interrelates with this. Prior (1993) argues that increasingly the concept of the public sector and public services is becoming confused:

> The increasingly popular view that the public services now display characteristics of a new politico-economic form called 'quasi-markets' (or social markets) is helpful in understanding the processes of change that have occurred, but does not in itself clear up the confusion over the definition of public services' (Prior, 1993, p. 458)

298

This confusion has arisen because of the way in which different public services have changed in different respects to accommodate new market requirements and practices. Perhaps as Prior (1993, p. 460) points out, the only thing that sustains the 'public sector' as a coherent concept is a specific set of values or a public service ethos, although he even casts doubt on whether these can be coherently articulated any longer. This raises a broader concern of relevance, for we need to note that already in this discussion the terms 'welfare', 'public service' and 'public sector' are being used interchangeably, which we argue is analytically problematic. This is important, since many debates about public services or the welfare state that relate to privatization and marketization are definitionally imprecise and yet it is these very policies which are fundamental to this confusion.

To begin with, if we insist on talking about a public sector or public sector provision of services what are we actually referring to? Given that policies of privatization and marketization have radically altered the way in which public services are organized and their relationships with public and private sector organizations, as well as the public at large, is there any merit in referring to a 'public sector' as if it is a universal, self-evident, concept. Prior (1993) elaborates this point when he says:

> It is arguable that the fundamental change that has occurred in the public sector is not the replacement of one broadly uniform set of arrangements (in which ownership, financing and operational responsibility rested with the state) with another uniform set, but the fracturing of the public sector into a plethora of different sets of arrangements with few common features. It is then questionable whether the term 'public sector' is any longer useful as a generic analytical concept' (Prior, 1993, p. 459).

What this suggests is that we need to acknowledge the distinctive features of public sector organizations as a consequence of reforms and changes in their character.

Whilst arguments about the 'public sector' highlight conceptual problems, further difficulties arise when referring to the concept of the 'welfare state' particularly in relation to the concept of 'public service' generally. For example, the question could be posed: is it sufficient when talking about public services to restrict this meaning to traditional welfare state services

299

e.g. health, social services, education? Or should we acknowledge that a wide range of services are indeed public services but are not necessarily associated with traditional notions of welfare? These include, on the one hand, services such as street cleaning, refuse collection, environmental health (associated with local government), or defence and security services (associated with the Ministry of Defence and police); they also include services to the public which were once, but are no longer, provided by publicly owned utilities. The fact that water, electricity, gas and telecommunications now reside outside the public sector (and have never been deemed welfare services), does not automatically mean they are no longer providers of essential public services. What this debate therefore serves to illustrate is that as a consequence of policies of privatization and marketization the concept of the 'public sector' cannot be sustained in relation to the concept of 'public service' and, moreover, to equate public services with 'welfare' serves only to confuse the issue further. Yet a survey of a wide range of literature in the social sciences reveals how in particular the concepts of welfare and public service are used either interchangeably or without recourse to definitional criteria.

In order to capture a sense of the environment of change in relation to public service provision we advocate the use of the term 'public service' to refer to service functions traditionally, but no longer exclusively, performed within the public sector or by the welfare state. By doing so we aim to avoid the trap of assimilation into, and acceptance of, a neo-liberal agenda which has sought to reconceptualize certain essential public services (e.g. water) as mere commodities (see the chapter by Taylor in this volume). Moreover, given that the concept of the 'welfare state' is problematic in its traditional usage, being commonly employed to refer to a limited number of services, we advocate its replacement with a broader concept of 'welfare'. This concept of 'welfare' embraces a range of areas in which the state is directly or indirectly involved that 'objectively bear on citizens' welfare, above and beyond those officially and narrowly designated as welfare' (Roche, 1992, p. 23). Such a concept can accommodate traditionally defined areas such as education, health, housing, etc., but will also include less traditionally associated areas such as the environment, consumer policies and employment policies. This description of 'welfare' recognizes the interrelationship of social policy and broader social problems in society; it recognizes that state policy in what might be designated non-welfare areas, such as economic policy, can impact directly on welfare concerns. Furthermore, it acknowledges the role of 'civil society' and non-state areas in contributing to welfare (e.g. voluntary organizations and the family) and ways in which state policy seeks to influence such areas (this has been particularly evident in the Conservative Party's espousal of 'family values').

Concepts of welfare have been intrinsically bound up with concepts of citizenship, which in the UK have emphasized social rights and the need for state welfare institutions to service these rights. However, the post-war political ideologies which helped to establish this framework of rights and duties have been in decline, and challenges to what Roche (1992) has described as the 'dominant paradigm' of social citizenship have come from a number of sources. These have included hitherto discussed ideological challenges from the New Right in the UK (and US), from new social movements (e.g. feminism and ecology) and from social structural change in society. In relation to policies of privatization and marketization social structural change has been important in a number of respects. Such policies can be intrinsically linked to responses to crises of the welfare state, state overload, or legitimacy crises (see, for example, O'Connor, 1973, 1984, 1987; Habermas, 1975; Offe, 1984, 1985) brought about by the increasing financial burden of state provision identified during the 1970s. Additionally, they may be seen as a response to new pressures on state-provided public services derived from changes in the economies of western societies and, in particular, processes associated with post-industrial change.

The way in which post-industrial change has impacted on employment, particularly in relation to the decline of traditional labour-intensive industries, has increased the potential for long-term unemployment, which in turn affects the generation of income that will contribute to public expenditure. The use of policies of privatization and marketization as vehicles for addressing problems associated with post-industrialism, should however, be evaluated in relation to their role in generating the very labour market practices (e.g. employment insecurity, flexible working practices etc.) which have contributed to the additional pressures on public services, a point which we shall return to. For the moment, however, if these factors are assessed in the context of other changes in society, such as demographic change and broader cultural processes (e.g. attitudes towards the family and the impact of the women's movement; new social movements) what emerges is a highly complex picture of social and

301

economic change that is being met with a response guided by an ideological position that has not only failed to acknowlege the realities of the situation but, from evidence during the 1980s, has also failed to reduce public expenditure on service provision (Roche, 1992; on the UK see Brindle, 1990; on the US Pierson, 1991).

Some of the problems associated with social structural change and public service provision during the 1980s and 1990s are addressed by contributors to this book. In the chapters on housing (Plumridge), pensions (Sullivan) and the NHS (Ahmad), for example, we see instances of how the state is increasingly facing new circumstances and demands. In general, however, a theme underlying many of the contributions is a questioning of whether policies of privatization and marketization, particularly in the UK, have offered effective long-term solutions to the problems they seek to address. To return to the issue of employment as an example: whilst public services are coming under increasing pressure to support a larger number of unemployed and unemployable people, who because of their situation may generate multiple demands on welfare services, the government's own policies in the public sector have served to add to this problem. As Roche (1992) says:

> The shift towards flexibilized labour uses and markets is structurally based and capable of being steered in various political directions. But the insecurity problems associated with it have been greatly accentuated by the social and economic policies of Right governments in the West during the 1980s' (Roche, 1992, p.166).

In the UK, government intervention in the public sector aimed at de-regulating hitherto 'sheltered' labour markets has served only to mimic employment insecurities in the private sector. This has been driven by the assumption that the effective functioning of the national labour market is fundamentally linked to the public sector and its problems, which are characteristically presented as over-powerful trade unions, interfering professionals and a 'nanny state' encouraging reliance on state finances. However, an assault on these areas has produced problems of a different kind. The 'more for less' ethos that has guided such policies relies on crude market mechanisms to provide the same services at a lower cost, which is being paid for in terms of job losses, lower wages and increased

302

job insecurity amongst public service employees. The long-term implication of such a strategy is that higher demand for welfare and public service provision will be created. Today's savings may therefore be tomorrow's costs. This analysis applies not only to areas of public service provision remaining within the state sector, but also to areas now outside, where privatization has resulted in massive job losses and in some cases (e.g. mining) will result in the dimunition of whole communities - an important source of informal welfare.

Problems associated with social structural change in the UK, it may be argued, cannot be divorced from a consideration of the wider post-national context, particularly given the 'accelerating development of contemporary capitalism towards a global economy inhabited and organized by multi-national corporations and globalized capital and currency markets' (Roche 1992, p. 46). In this global economy, unprecedented international corporate restructuring is transforming established economic, social and political relationships and is creating a flexible but intensely volatile environment worldwide. At the corporate level, revolutionary changes have been implemented: decentralizing management, reducing and flattening hierarchies, targeting quality, working closely with consumers, establishing 'networks' and 'partnerships' and so forth. Society's needs have also changed and the provision of public services to meet these needs must also change, becoming as responsive and efficiently managed as is the rest of the global system.

With regard to privatization and marketization the post-national context is significant in three respects. First, the ability of governments to plan their economies and subsequent social policy within a national context is becoming more difficult. Second, in relation to public service provision in the UK, the development of new markets has seen a number of international participants entering the arena (e.g. the recent take-over of South Western Electricity by an American company and the participation of international players in CCT in local government). Third, there has been a serious challenge to traditional conceptions of social citizenship and associated rights, including welfare rights, in the UK, because of membership of the European Union (EU). Whilst the first two issues are important, particularly in relation to a new framework for understanding the role of the nation state in the provision of essential services, it is the latter issue - the European dimension - which we wish to address in further detail.

The post-national context in relation to welfare, public service provision and social citizenship must incorporate a European dimension, given the important potential role of the EU in the future development of social policy and citizenship rights. Considering Europe as a whole, whilst there is evidence that Eastern European countries are attempting to re-assert their national identities, the predominant trend in Western Europe is a move towards accommodating nationalism within the EU. Cooperation between nation-states does tend to fit with a more general trend towards globalization in capitalist economies, which would suggest that, in the future, Eastern European countries will seek to form alliances with other nation states, or apply for membership of the EU (Roche, 1992). Such a prospect was elucidated in the famous Bruges speech given by Margaret Thatcher in 1988, in which she outlined the possibility of a European Union which might include parts of Eastern Europe (and the US!) (Thatcher, 1988). Considering for the moment the present EU membership, it is important to note that the idea that member-state citizens could also be 'citizens of the Union' was for the first time formally acknowledged in the 1991 Maastricht Treaty (Lambert, 1991), an event greeted with less enthusiasm from Margaret Thatcher and the British Conservative Party.

The potential for the development of a European citizenship has been the subject of extensive recent debate (see, for example, Meehan, 1993; Twine, 1994; Roche, 1992). These debates, whilst addressing general issues of welfare and social rights, have not been explicitly linked to debates about privatization and marketization, although they have considered the role of the UK and New Right ideology in relation (or as an obstacle) to, the development of citizenship in Europe. Yet, in many respects, issues previously discussed in this chapter relating to policies of marketization have a direct bearing on debates about social citizenship both in the UK and Europe, because what these debates have in common is a concern for social rights and the welfare of people as citizens. Roche (1992) nevertheless points to important differences between classical theories of citizenship in the British context, outlined in particular by T.H. Marshall, (Marshall, 1963) and the development of citizenship in the European context:

> T.H. Marshall's schema for the emergence of citizenship (based on British history but implicitly generalizable) saw the

achievement of social rights as the coping stone completing a movement which had begun from civil rights and had then added political rights. The EC looks set to disrupt this schema by begining with civil rights... by going on to develop social rights in the early mid-1990's, but only promising the development of political citizenship through some as yet unclear enhancement of the powers of the EC Parliament beginning later in the 1990's' (Roche, 1992, pp. 201-202).

Successive British governments' reluctance to participate in economic and political union, and continued nationalism within the Conservative Party, undermine such developments in the UK. The negative perception of social rights adopted by the Thatcher administrations which de-emphasized social rights in favour of social duties (e.g. in relation to the family), was also accompanied by shifts from social rights to 'means testing' in areas of social policy (e.g. unemployment benefits).

This drift away from social rights has since been accompanied by the Major government's emphasis on individualized consumer rights, as opposed to collective social rights, articulated through market relationships in the public service sector. Policies of privatization and marketization have been central to this process, for as Esping-Anderson (1990, cited in Twine, 1994, p. 102) argues:

> the outstanding criterion of social rights must be the degree to which they *permit people to make their living standards independent of pure market forces.'* (italics in Twine).

Given the role and impact of market forces in the UK on areas associated with social rights, it is relevant to ask how Britain's membership of the EU might affect this? Much debate in this area has focused on the 'Social Charter' and its potential for establishing basic social rights across member-state countries. Nonetheless, it must be remembered that provisions within it mainly relate to workers' rights, not citizens' rights, and have characteristically met with strong resistance from the UK government.

If the concept of citizenship within the EU is bound up with the status of citizens as workers, a number of problems emerge. A focus on workers' rights most obviously excludes the unemployed, the impoverished 'underclass', and a significant proportion of women (see Meehan, 1993, Chapter 6, for a good discussion). There is also a related problem that the concept of 'the worker' is itself based on a traditional model of male full-time employment throughout one's working life (Meehan, 1993). This is unrealistic because on the one hand it actively excludes large numbers of women who work part-time, and is nevertheless incompatible with trends in employment generally. Twine (1994) thus argues that:

> a social right of citizenship that recognizes interdependence [between paid and unpaid labour] is required if both women and men are to be equal citizens' (Twine, 1994, pp. 160-161).

Moreover, we must recognize that womens' position in the labour market and the family often excludes them from certain welfare entitlements which are seen as basic to citizenship rights. This is particularly relevant in the case of pension provision and is explored by Walby (1994) in her consideration of whether citizenship is a gendered concept. The fact that women often lose out in the labour market because of their position in the family and that the family plays a role in supporting or supplementing welfare services highlights a major injustice, seriously undermining any notion of citizenship exclusively based on a 'workers charter'.

Throughout this chapter the concept of social citizenship has been intertwined with different areas of discussion either implicitly or explicitly. Renewed interest in this area amongst social scientists can in part be explained by developments in Europe, where issues of both nationalism and post-nationalism have thrown up new questions and dilemmas. In the UK we have witnessed the erosion of basic social rights and an ideological assualt on public services and areas of welfare, which has sharpened the debate about social citizenship. In a country which lacks even a Bill of Rights, perhaps it is not surprising that the role of the European Union is being emphasized by those in opposition to neo-liberal policies, such as trade unions and the Labour Party.

In this respect the European Court of Human Rights has played an important role as a court of appeal at the post-national level, and has served to influence areas of employment policy. In relation to market policies introduced into the public sector, it has become the new battle-ground for many public service trade unions opposing the negative impact of policies on employment. Cases involving equal opportunities, equal pay for work of equal value, and the transfer of public service employees to private contractors on less preferential terms and conditions (TUPE) as a consequence of CCT in different areas of the public sector, have been pursued through the European Court. Trade unions, in their weakened bargaining role and excluded from consultation, have had some success in countering the detrimental impact of policies in the public sector, but this juridification of industrial relations is only piecemeal and strips them of the wider role that unions play in the rest of Europe with a liberal corporatist tradition. The future role of the EU is unclear and, moreover, its actual ability to develop a Community-wide concept of citizenship has been questioned (Meehan, 1993).

In this concluding chapter, we have aimed to draw together the analytical tools of the disciplines of sociology, economics and politics and explored the relevance and value of an inter-disciplinary approach in evaluating the process of privatization and its associated variants. Our contention is that such an inter-disciplinary approach would yield a deeper understanding of the privatization process and would call into question the justification for such a strategy. However, the development of such a social science approach to the analysis of privatization is very much in its infancy and we have only been able to hint here at the potential for such an approach.

In a sense we are proposing in this chapter a research agenda for the future. Such an agenda would necessarily encompass the key issues which feature in the above discussion. Precisely what should citizens of a community expect to be provided by their governments? What are their entitlements and how best can they be empowered to achieve their desired goals? What is the most effective framework within which governments or private sector agencies can best deliver the services required? How can and should the relative performance of private and public sector institutions be compared and with what consequences? What incentive mechanisms can be devised to ensure maximum efficiency in the delivery of services to consumers while enabling broader goals of equity and social welfare to be protected? and so forth.

The research agenda is both extensive and challenging; it is our contention that adequate answers to the above key questions that surround the privatization debate can only be effectively addressed by pooling the analytical techniques and approaches of the main social science disciplines. In this book, we have sought to establish and highlight links between the concerns of different social scientists regarding privatization and have

307

attempted to provide signposts for future analysis and debate to be undertaken from a more distinct but integrated social science perspective.

References

Alt, J.E. and Chrystal, K.A. (1983), *Political Economics*, Wheatsheaf Books, London.

Barnes, M. and Prior, D. (1995), 'Spoilt for Choice? How Consumerism can Disempower Public Service Users.' *Public Money and Management*, vol. 15, no. 3, July-September.

Brindle, D. (1990), 'Thatcher years failed to roll back the welfare state', *The Guardian*, 13 December.

Flynn, N. (1993), *Public Sector Management*. (2nd Edition), Harvester Wheatsheaf, Hemel Hempstead.

Foster, C.D. (1992), *Privatization, Public Ownership and Regulation of Natural Monopoly*, Blackwell, Oxford.

Foster, D. (1993), 'Industrial Relations in Local Government: The Impact of Privatization', *The Political Quarterly*, vol. 64, no. 1. January-March.

Habermas, J. (1975), *Legitimacy Crisis*, Beacon Press, Boston.

Helm, D., Aveline, M. and Lawrence, R. (1992), *Acquisitions and Diversification: The Record of Public Utilities*. Oxford Research Associates, Oxford.

Her Majesty's Treasury (1991), *Competing for quality: buying public services*, Cmnd. 1730, HMSO, London.

Jackson, P.M. and Price, C.M. (1994), *Privatization and Regulation: A Review of the Issues*, Longman, London.

Lambert, S. (1991), 'Beyond the little red passport to Euro-citizenship', *The Independent*, 22 November.

Marshall, T.H. (1963), *Citizenship and Social Class*. (Original 1950 in Sociology at the Crossroads), Heinemann, London.

Meehan, E. (1993), *Citizenship and the European Community*. Sage Publications Ltd.

O'Connor, J. (1973), *The Fiscal Crisis of the State*. St. Martin's Press, New York.

O'Connor, J. (1984), *Accumulation Crisis*, Blackwell, Oxford.

O'Connor, J. (1987), *The Meaning of Crisis*, Blackwell, Oxford.

Offe, C. (1984), *Contradiction of the Welfare State*, Hutchinson, London.

Offe, C. (1985), *Disorganised Capitalism*, Polity Press, Cambridge.

Osborne, D. and Gaebler, T. (1993), *Reinventing Government: How the Entrepreneurial Spirit is Transforming the Public Sector*, Plume, New York.

Ott, A.F. and Hartley, K. (1991), *Privatization and Economic Efficiency*, Edward Elgar, London.

Pierson, C. (1991), *Beyond the Welfare State. The New Political Economy of Welfare*, Polity Press, Cambridge.

Pollitt, C. (1993), *Managerialism and the Public Services* (2nd Edition), Blackwell, Oxford.

Prior, D. (1993), 'In Search of the New Public Management', Review Article, *Local Government Studies*, vol. 19, no. 3, Autumn, pp. 447-460.

Roche, M. (1992), *Rethinking Citizenship : Welfare, Ideology and Change in Modern Society*, Polity Press in association with Blackwell, Oxford.

Schwartz, G. and Lopes, P.S. (1993), 'Privatization Expectations, Trade-Offs, and Results', *Finance and Development*, June.

Stewart, J. and Clarke, M. (1987), 'The Public Service Orientation: Issues and Dilemmas', *Public Administration*, vol. 65, no. 2, Summer, pp. 161-78.

Stewart, J. and Ranson, S. (1988), 'Management in the Public Domain', *Public Money and Management*, 8(2) Spring-Summer, pp. 13-19.

Thatcher, M. (1988), 'Heirs to Europe : the Bruges Speech'. *The Guardian*, 21 September.

Twine, F. (1994), *Citizenship and Social Rights (The interdependence of self and society)*, Sage Publications Ltd.

Walby, S. (1994), 'Is Citizenship gendered?', *Sociology*, vol. 28, no. 2, May, pp. 379-395.

Index

314